PRAISE FOR

"In a welcoming volume on self-care approached via practical and magical means . . . Scelsa sensitively emphasizes inclusion and curating affirming spaces for audiences across myriad identities. It's a useful starting point for those looking for a wider awareness of the possibilities of magic and magical thinking—one that encourages self-understanding, self-confidence, curiosity, and compassion." —*Publishers Weekly*

"This book is a combination of personal history, explorations of occult practices, interviews, self-help, hands-on how-tos, reassurances, and affirmations. The result is a useful guide that should help magic-minded teens get their lives together, or at least feel better about themselves. . . . This respectful, in-depth guide will make a handsome addition to collections that support a spiritual-minded clientele." —*Booklist*

"From spells to mindfulness, this work offers some methods to help boost holistic health. . . . [W]hether readers are seasoned practitioners or baby witches—or just open-minded people interested in expanding their self-care toolboxes—this is a fantastic resource for getting a new perspective on *why* these practices are potentially valuable and how they interrelate to one's physical, mental, and metaphysical well-being. A valuable resource filled with productive possibilities." —*Kirkus Reviews*

An imprint of Simon & Schuster Children's Publishing Division
1230 Avenue of the Americas, New York, New York 10020

Illustrations of tarot cards on pages 30–36 by miki-pearly/iStock
Illustrations of tarot cards on page 39 (also used as frames throughout) by Maria Leonova/iStock
Illustrations of zodiac symbols on pages 63–66 by ProVectors/iStock
Illustration of starry pattern on exercise pages by LisaAlisa_ill/iStock

Also available in a SIMON & SCHUSTER BFYR hardcover edition
Interior design by Lizzy Bromley • The text for this book was set in Bell. • Manufactured in China
First SIMON & SCHUSTER BFYR paperback edition September 2023
2 4 6 8 10 9 7 5 3 1
The Library of Congress has cataloged the hardcover edition as follows:
Names: Scelsa, Kate, author.
Title: Luminary : a magical guide to self-care / Kate Scelsa.
Description: First Edition. | New York : Simon & Schuster Books for Young Readers, 2022. |
Audience: Ages 12 up | Audience: Grades 7–9 | Summary: "Self-care is not only necessary, it's magical! Your road to self-care can be a mystical journey that leaves you feeling more confident, determined and ready to accomplish all those bucket-list items and dreams you have scribbled in your journal. So why not start that journey now? Within Luminary you will find both mystical and practical tools to help deal with stress, depression, and other challenges. Gorgeously illustrated and highly designed, this guide offers different creative ways of living a heart-centered, mindful, and magical life through concrete tools for self-care and advice from a diverse group of practitioners in areas like tarot, astrology, energy work, and much more. Luminary is a book of practical magic that will empower you to pursue mental wellness with curiosity and confidence. But it's also a book of possibility that pushes the boundaries of what self-help can be"
—Provided by publisher.
Identifiers: LCCN 2022002385 | ISBN 9781665902342 (paper-over-board) |
ISBN 9781665902359 (paperback) | ISBN 9781665902366 (ebook)
Subjects: LCSH: Emotions in children—Juvenile literature. | Mindfulness (Psychology)—Juvenile literature. |
Magic—Juvenile literature. | Self-acceptance—Juvenile literature.
Classification: LCC BF723.E6 S34 2022 | DDC 155.4/124—dc23/eng/20220715
LC record available at https://lccn.loc.gov/2022002385

LUMINARY

A *Magical* Guide to Self-Care

KATE SCELSA

SIMON & SCHUSTER BFYR

New York London Toronto Sydney New Delhi

Contents

FOR
ALL
THE
witches

Introduction

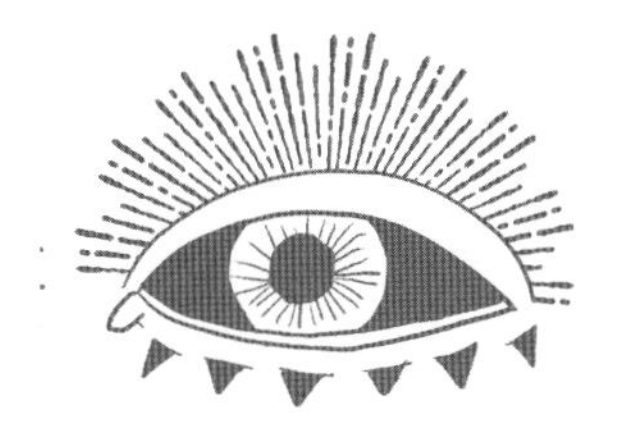

A CAVE PERSON AND A SABER-TOOTHED TIGER WALK INTO OUR BRAINS

I formed my first coven when I was seven years old by passing a note to three girls in my second-grade class. My proposal was that we would learn to cast spells, communicate with animals, and eventually be able to fly. I still have a tiny note written on a ripped piece of notebook paper in which one of my friends agreed to join me. The coven only met a few times, our potions were improvised collections of liquids from the kitchen cabinet, and our animal familiars were stuffed cat dolls, but at seven years old I knew without a doubt that the magic was real.

Fifteen years later I found myself standing in a new age store in suburban New Jersey, having recently graduated from college and suffering from a particularly persistent bout of anxiety and depression. The store was filled with old-school new age décor—lots of fairy figurines, capes, and crystals—all things I had loved without judgment as a kid, and now regarded as deeply cheesy.

It was not my idea to go into this store. I was there to use a gift certificate for an astrological reading that my aunt had given me as a birthday present. She was into all things witchy—there was a tiny cauldron on the shelf in her home, she wore a pentagram around her neck, and she regularly attended drum circles and spirit guide meditations. I loved talking to her about all her mystical practices, but I saw myself as just a curious observer. Even if I was intrigued by my aunt's commitment to it, at the end of the day any sincere belief in magic was pure silliness. This was the attitude that I used to protect myself for a very long time.

Starting in middle school I had been dubbed too loud, too emotional, too nerdy. I cared about school too much, spending hours each night on my homework until I decided that I had done it "perfectly." The things I liked to do for fun were often deemed "weird" or "immature" by other kids. If I was invited to a sleepover party, I would inevitably spend most of it alone, too scared to watch whatever horror movie was on. My feelings were easily hurt, my laugh was too loud, and I cried at the drop of a hat. I just couldn't bring myself to be that weird witch girl on top of all that, no matter how much I might have loved the magical and mystical when I was younger.

So my only reaction to standing in this cheesy new age store waiting to use a gift certificate for an astrological reading was to write it all off as slightly embarrassing. I certainly didn't *like* this kind of stuff or *believe* in this kind of thing.

I was called into a back office by a man who looked like a cleaned-up version of Comic Book Guy from *The Simpsons.* An elderly terrier followed us into a room that was decorated with tapestries and crystal balls. I sat down in a chair at a small round table that had a stack of papers on it, a color-coded circular chart on the top page. This was my natal chart, the astrologer explained to me, the position of the planets relative to me at the moment that I was born.

He pressed record on an old-fashioned tape recorder.

"You're going to want to listen to this again later," he said, as the little dog curled up at our feet.

He then proceeded to change my entire life.

When Comic Book Guy started the tape recorder, I imagined playing the tape for people later as a joke. I assumed that the recording would be full of vague movie-style fortune-teller predictions about money and love. Sixty minutes later I was just grateful that I had a record of the most transformative hour of my life.

As the astrologer broke down my chart for me, it was as if someone was telling me my own life story, explaining parts of myself that I had never been able to explain, that I didn't know could be explained. They were the parts that activated the big neon sign in my brain that flashed the word "FLAW" over and over. Suddenly all this mystical astrology stuff started to feel a lot less funny. How could he not only know these things about me and be able to explain them to me in specific detail, but also talk about them as if they weren't flaws at all, but simply parts of who I am?

As I sat in that chair and listened, the astrologer's dog curled up at my feet, I felt something in me start to relax for the first time in a long time. I realized that I didn't even fully understand how unhappy I had been feeling. I knew that I had been suffering from anxiety in my post-college life, but I couldn't put my finger on what was wrong. Now a picture was beginning to form—I was exhausted all the time no matter how much sleep I got. Not having accomplished anything yet in my life depressed me. I had finished the mandated sixteen years of education. I had worked hard, gotten good grades, followed the rules set out in front of me. I was twenty-two—wasn't I supposed to have everything figured out by now? Shouldn't I feel happy and fulfilled, with a clear direction in my life and constant outside assurance that all my hard work was paying off? If none of that was happening, then it must mean that I was doing something wrong. And if I was doing something wrong, it must mean that there was something wrong with me.

And here was an astrologer casually implying that there was nothing wrong with me at all, and that everything that was happening to me was right on time when it came to astrological alignment.

I started asking questions. I needed details.

"I'm totally anxious living in the city all the time," I said. "Why can't I calm down and just deal with it the way everyone one else seems to?"

"Of course you're overly sensitive to your environment," he told me. "Your chart has tons of water in it. You're an emotional person. Just look at your moon placement."

I'm an emotional person????? That's it? I was just allowed to say that and point to a place on this chart that explained it? Not presenting it as an excuse, but as a part of me that needed extra attention, that I might even learn how to work with rather than fight against?

If this chart was able to explain things to me about myself that I had never even been able to articulate, was it really possible that there wasn't anything wrong with me at all? Could it be true that it wasn't my job to change in order to conform to my perception of what other people expected of me, but just that I needed to figure out how to work with these elements of my personality, and, heaven forbid, even celebrate them????

I believe this is what they call an aha moment.

By this point in my life, I had already seen multiple traditional therapists, gone to wellness retreats, and sat through tons of visits to doctors to try to raise my energy level and make me feel like a "normal" person. And in every single one of those situations my takeaway had been, "There is something wrong with me, and if I can't fix it, then I am a lazy, pathetic failure."

No one had ever suggested that there was nothing wrong with me at all, or wrong with anyone. That, in fact, everyone is different for a very good reason—because we are not all here to do the same work. That we are each actually meant to learn to work with our different strengths and weaknesses. And that there is no such thing as "normal."

Here was my natal chart, depicting the energetic makeup of the time and place where I was born, not only pinning me to that unique moment but also setting down my relationship to the energy of the universe in this lifetime. Here was the setup for a lifelong conversation in which the universe and I were going to work together to figure out how all the pieces of this mysterious puzzle fit together. Here was a map for meaning that every person in the world has, which means that every single person is engaged in a deeply mysterious and beautiful conversation with the most magical forces imaginable at all times. And it all fit in a manila envelope.

Mind. Blown.

Over the next eighteen years I slowly moved from curious spectator to participant in almost every mystical practice you can think of. Health problems had me seeking out energy healers along with traditional doctors. Tarot helped my feelings of anxiety and disconnection along with therapy. Guided meditations, connection to spirit guides, witchy ceremonies, holistic creativity, mindfulness—all of it was leading me right back to the person I was at seven years old, that happy little witch who so deeply believed in magic as a path to personal empowerment and as something to be shared with others. I couldn't believe I had ever let it go.

In witch culture, there is something called a Book of Shadows, which is a personal account of helpful spells, rituals, and experiences that a witch records to pass on to the next generation of practitioners. This passing along of information is seen as a sacred magical act, essential to helping us better develop as individuals and as a collective. This book is my Book of Shadows for you—a guide to mystical and practical tools that empower us to better navigate our mental, physical, and even metaphysical health.

As teenagers we are presented with an especially difficult proposition—how can we start to figure out who we are, what we care about, and how to live a fulfilling and interesting life without basing those things solely on the expectations of the people and the systems around us? At a time in our lives when achievement is often being pushed on us, we inevitably start to put more value on external factors than on our own intuition. Anxiety and depression are natural reactions to this level of pressure, but not only do they make us sick and miserable, they also take away our agency and keep us from doing the real work that we are here on this planet to do.

CHANGING THE STORIES

Just as I had decided at twenty-two that there was something irreparably wrong with me, most of us are very good at making up stories about what is wrong with us, and the more creative and sensitive we are, the more elaborate those stories become. Making up stories about ourselves might be okay if we created nice, happy, positive narratives where we show ourselves a lot of compassion and approach our own struggles with patience. Instead, our brains seem to be programmed to revel in the worst possible scenarios. There's a good reason for this, though, and once we fully understand it, we can start to use the tools presented in the book to work with our busy minds, rather than letting them work against us.

The problem is that we are still attached to our very earliest animal/cave person programming of fight or flight. This means that our brains are hardwired to be on the lookout for an attack at any time, and to be ready to assess if the threat can be fought off, or if it would be better to just run. This hair-trigger instinct definitely served us as an evolving species. Cave people who were wise enough to understand danger lived to pass on their genes. They remembered which berries made them sick and which animals would chase them, and it was these hearty people who became our ancestors. We can try all day to tell those ancestors that daily life is comparatively safer now, but they will never release us completely from the grip of their survivalist worldviews.

The truth is that we wouldn't want to completely abandon our ability to tell safety from danger. We want to be able to remember situations that hurt us so that we can try to avoid that hurt again in the future. This is an important skill, and it is possibly our first relationship to storytelling with a beginning, middle, and an end.

"I picked this red berry. I ate this red berry. I was very sick."

It's not exactly a great American novel, but it's the kind of story our brain likes, because it is unambiguous.

Now here's the problem with this holdover cave person brain—because cave person brain's only priority is to stay alive at all costs, even over the idea of staying alive to live a happy life, it tends to focus on the negative. If the priority is survival, then a list of poisonous berries is going to be a more important thing to hold on to than a list of pretty lakes where you like to go swimming and relax. The irony is that going swimming and relaxing would actually make that cave person's life longer and healthier. But cave person has one thing on its mind: making it to tomorrow. That's it.

Understanding that our brains are hardwired to catalog dangers and hurts is the first step toward easing the grip that cave person brain has on us. We must remember that, with all respect to our ancestors, cave person brain had no ability to understand complexity. Something was either labeled "death" or "no death." "Good" or "bad." And most of the situations that we encounter in our everyday lives are not quite that simple. So we need to start to sort through our stories and decide which information is actually helpful, and which is just cave person instinct kicking in to proclaim a judgment.

How might cave person brain show up in your everyday life? Let's say you didn't study enough for a test, and then you got a bad grade. It feels pretty safe to draw the conclusion from this series of events that if you want to do well on tests in the future, you should study more. The bad thing that happened (being eaten by a saber-toothed tiger) was doing badly on the test. The reason that happened (you walked into the saber-toothed tiger's cave) was that you didn't study enough. From this simple story we can learn that not studying enough causes something unpleasant to happen.

But there are the objective events of our lives, and then there are the stories that we tell ourselves about those events, and these are often two very different things. So what is the objective truth of the narrative of the failed test? You didn't study enough, and you got a bad grade. That's it. That's what happened. But because you are very clever, you are going to ask your brain for some more information about what led to this situation that your brain can categorize as "bad" in order to better protect you.

Why didn't you study enough? Will your brain invent a story that it is because you are lazy? Because you are bad at school? Because you hate this subject? Because you are A BAD PERSON?!?

As soon as humans got a tiny little bit of time on their hands, they invented self-loathing. Your cave person brain has evolved enough to understand not only that the saber-toothed tiger cave is a bad place to go, but also that YOU are the one who decided to go in there in the first place, which may cause your brain to create a story that YOU are BAD. Maybe it will now come up with an entire list of the ways in which YOU are BAD and file them away forever! Hold on to them for your entire lifetime!

If we search ourselves and can't find the thing to blame, then we might invent a story about someone else, hoping to pin the BADNESS on them. Trying to find the BADNESS in a situation that involves other people is very fertile ground for cave person brain. You might start trying to guess what the other person is thinking and feeling, and ascribe all kinds of motivations to them with no guarantee that any of it is true. The more creative and sensitive you are, the more elaborate these narratives will become. We are so desperate to figure out what went wrong in the hopes of avoiding something painful in the future that we can't help ourselves. And we end up spending the life that our cave person ancestors worked so hard to give us cataloging miseries. Cave people didn't pass on their hard-won genes to us just for us to be so unhappy!

Part of the solution is remembering that sometimes discomfort is okay. The feeling of doing badly on a test isn't great, but you can certainly survive it, and even come to know that there are things to be learned from that experience of failure without your brain setting off a very loud BADNESS panic alarm. Can we turn the BADNESS alarm down on experiences that are not particularly comfortable, knowing that they have their place in our lives?

What are the more complicated possible explanations for why you didn't study enough for the test? Explanations that can't be labeled GOOD or BAD. NO DEATH or DEATH. Did you have a fight with a family member that distracted you? Were you working at your job and weren't able to budget your time correctly? Do you need help with studying and find it too challenging to do on your own? Even the worst-case scenario—you had plenty of time and headspace to study and you just didn't do it—might simply mean you had a bad night and made a mistake. But your brain isn't interested in coming up with these nuanced narratives on its own. All it is interested in is YOU ARE THE WORST.

This was exactly my frame of mind when I walked into that new age store all those years ago. Sure, the world can be a tough place, but if I was overly affected by it all the time, then

I must be at fault. I was obviously too sensitive, too emotional, too easily bothered by things that didn't seem to bother other people. So in trying to make sense of my depression, I was creating a false story about myself and what I was doing wrong, setting off the BADNESS alarm every time I exhibited any of that "too sensitive" behavior. *There you go again, ruining things by not being tougher!*

In some schools of mysticism there is an idea that we are each constantly unconsciously creating a false scale of good and bad for ourselves based on all those stories that our brain has concocted, continuously moving the marker depending on the arbitrary standards by which we measure our successes and failures on any given day. If we believe we are measuring up on that scale of standards, we feel amazing, but when things aren't going well, we think there must be something wrong with us, with our lives, and with an unjust world that would put us so far down on that arbitrary scale that we have invented in our minds.

What we want to do is step off this scale completely by tuning into the truth of the present moment, empowering us to take care of ourselves and figure out what we really need. We want to be able to step into an unshakable understanding that we are each complicated, magical beings here to do some very important work. We actually don't have time to waste with all that self-measurement. We are meant to spend our time being curious about ourselves and how we fit into the crazy tapestry of this planet, not judging ourselves.

OUR TOOLS

Giving ourselves a break from that relentless score keeping isn't easy, but this is where our tools come in. In each chapter in this book, I am going to present you with a different set of tools that can help you engage with the energy of the present moment and interrupt the false narratives of that good/bad binary scale. We'll look at tarot, astrology, witchcraft, energy work, mindfulness, creating a creative practice, and working with spirit guides, along with talking about our relationships to our bodies and exploring more traditional therapy techniques. In each chapter I also have conversations with some of my favorite practitioners and all-around wise humans, who will explain to us how they use these tools to tap into the truth and potential of the present moment.

When we use the tools in this book as paths toward self-understanding, we interrupt those false narratives that we create in our cave person brains. Every tool presented here is designed to connect to the energy of the present moment to give you a new perspective on the ways in which you may be falsely limiting your own sense of self. The magic lies in that truth of the present moment, in getting curious about who we really are and what we want this lifetime to look like.

ENERGY

I'm going to talk a lot about energy in this book, and you should feel free to decide for yourself what that word means to you. To me, "magic" is energy, and when I talk about magic, I am talking about the generative, energetic possibility that creates and sustains everything. It is you, it is all around you, and it is the substance of all life.

Energy goes by a lot of different names in different cultures and traditions—chi, prana, ki. Some people who talk about God or gods or Goddess or Source are using those names to simply describe generative, creative energy. Some people use the word "Spirit" to encompass both generative energy and actual spirits or ancestors. Some people might see energy by the way it manifests in nature.

If spirituality is a part of your understanding of energy, that's great, but having spiritual beliefs or a spiritual practice is not a requirement in order to be able to use and appreciate the tools in this book. If you are someone who was raised with a very traditional idea of a God or gods that exist separate from humanity, judging people while looking down on them from a throne on a cloud, I would gently urge you to start to think about those forces in a less binary way, less about two opposite sides, God and human, heaven and earth, and more as different manifestations of one, unifying energy. A lot of mystical practices see God energy and the energy of humans, animals, objects, nature, and the earth as the same thing. If everything around you is an expression of this energy, you start to see some exciting possibilities in the present moment that did not exist when you just thought of yourself as a separate, completely autonomous being.

The fact that people have a lot of different ways of looking at and experiencing spirituality and having a relationship to energy is a bonus, not a flaw. We are each meant to have our own private, individual relationship to these things, one that we might not even be able to completely explain to other people. But again, that is a good thing! We are forming something that we will have our entire lives—our relationship to ourselves and to the world around us.

There's a story I love that has been retold in many cultures, but that seems to originally date back to either early Buddhism or Jainism (another ancient Indian religion), about a group of blind men who come across an elephant and attempt to figure out what it is by each feeling a different part of its body. One man gets ahold of the animal's ear and declares, "It's a big leaf!" One grabs onto a leg and says, "It's a tree." Another finds its tail and yells, "We found a rope!"

I think about this story a lot when I am using these different tools. Each of the tools presents just a small piece of a bigger truth. That's the beauty of them, and why we must always look at them as tools, and not as end truths in themselves. No matter what, we are only ever looking at one piece of an unknowable whole.

I find that unknowable part thrilling. It excites me that we can only comprehend a part of the elephant at a time, because it also means that no one system is better than another. No one has authority over anyone else about how to take care of ourselves, and how to connect to deeper truths about who we are and what is important to us in this life.

Imagine what kind of world we would live in if we all acknowledged that we are just fumbling around on this elephant, doing our best! If we understood that we all have access to only parts of an unknowable truth, and that our version of that might look very different from that of the person sitting next to us! Imagine if we each had boundless patience for ourselves on this journey, and were then able to have boundless patience with each other! I believe that such a world is possible, and if you're reading this right now, I have a feeling that you do too.

THE HERO IS YOU

One of our favorite kinds of stories as humans is something that the mythologist Joseph Campbell called the "hero's journey." This is where a chosen person must fight evil and face down many obstacles to save themselves and usually a planet or two. It's a story that we keep telling ourselves over and over again in different forms because it's a good metaphor for how each of us feels about our own lifetime and struggles. We are each the protagonists of our own life stories, and part of our responsibility is to take ownership of our story, and to recognize it as an incredible gift.

Like any of the heroes in your favorite stories, you need to learn about your powers in order to face down the obstacles that will come your way. You need to receive your magic wand, train in the Force, and figure out what kind of mutant you are. Parts of you that you had seen as weaknesses will become strengths. Things that you have kept in the shadows will be ready to see the light. This is the business of your life—the point of your narrative!

As with the narrative of the heroes in those stories, the path is never easy, and it often will not look like what you expected it to look like. But once our heroes realize what is at stake, they are determined to learn how to live fully in the truth of who they are.

The stakes are pretty high for us, too. Our mental and physical health, our ability to care for those around us, to be a kind friend, a loving member of a family and a community, to stand up for what we know is right, to find activities and work that we care about, to engage our hearts and minds—I believe that all these things are just as important as saving the planet. And here is the big, very important secret of this book—those things actually will save the planet. Once we realize the power we each contain as energetic puzzle pieces of this universe, we realize that we can begin to live in flow with our own energy and with the energy of those around us. Imagine if everyone in the world took the responsibility of managing their own plot of energy as a service not only to themselves, but also to each other! The entire world would change for the better. The stakes are that high.

This book is meant to be a kind of map, with different detours that you can take, and different paths to explore. The tools presented here are simply a means to the end of working with and better understanding our relationship to energy, so that we may better manage stress, depression, fight those false narratives, step off that good/bad scale, and foster a deep and sustaining relationship with ourselves. There is no one way of working with energy that makes sense for everyone, and part of the fun is figuring out what tools you enjoy and what sparks excitement for you.

Know that as you dive deeper into the potential of each of these tools that not everyone is willing to do the work to ask these important questions and to question the structure of outside validation. Unfortunately, it's sort of easier to just be angry or stressed or frustrated much of the time because it requires very little self-examination. Looking directly at the parts of ourselves that we have been taught are unworthy is a hard task for most people, and you must give yourself a lot of credit for being willing to do this work. Even beginning to explore the sense of wonder and possibility in your life is an exciting and honorable undertaking, as you learn to cultivate skills that will help you throughout your life.

Oh, and by the way, this stuff can also be really fun! Did you know that you're actually allowed to enjoy yourself while you're figuring out how to manage stress, balance your energy, and connect with deeper mystical truths? Why not allow play, joy, and creativity to become a part of how we take care of ourselves?

My understanding of these tools (and of myself) evolves every single day, and I am writing this book for myself as much as for you. We never stop learning about ourselves, and the process of self-understanding and growth is never linear. There may be no place to arrive where we will have solved our problems, where we will have figured it all out and everything is simply easy breezy from now on, but the point of working with all these tools is to learn to appreciate the complexities of the ongoing process of life.

The challenges in our lives are not there to tear us down. They are part of the system of energy, asking us to tune out the unnecessary noise, and tune in to what really matters to us. Every moment, every part of our mental, emotional, and physical makeup has something to teach us. These tools will help us learn how to listen.

Now let's go make some magic.

CHAPTER ONE:
Tarot

I am basically the poster child for seasonal affective disorder (SAD). Traditionally my mental health takes a nosedive somewhere around the middle of January and usually stays missing in action until the end of May. So deep in the winter of 2015, when my friend Bakara told me that she was going to be coteaching a four-month-long weekly class on tarot in a yoga studio in Brooklyn, I decided to sign up. I figured it would be something to at least keep my mind busy until it got warm again.

I had gotten tarot readings over the years, mostly from friends, but I had never picked up a deck myself. I went to the first meeting of the Brooklyn Fools expecting to remain an appreciative spectator, but it quickly became clear that I wasn't going to get away with that.

Every week of the Fools we focused on a different card in the Major Arcana, the archetypal cards of tarot. Some weeks we were encouraged to dress in a way that was inspired by the card of the week. For the indulgent Empress I wore a flowery blue caftan, and a ton of jewelry, and tied my dyed-pink hair up in a scarf. For the week of the Devil we dressed up as our shadow selves. For the Star we created a huge altar made up of hundreds of tea-light candles. In class we would talk about personal connections that we felt to the card of that week. There was music, and food, and poetry. And somewhere in the middle of all this I realized that my SAD had lifted for the first time in years.

There was something here that was worth paying attention to.

The further along that we got in the class, the more I found that the part of my brain that had formed in middle school as a way to seemingly protect myself against ridicule (good old judgy cave person brain declaring a part of me BAD because it made me vulnerable) was getting very quiet. The more I worked with the cards and saw how they helped me and others, the less I cared about logic, or looking silly, or what it would mean to go all in on my belief in magic.

A couple of years after this, when I had finally committed to stop standing on the sidelines of having a magical life and had started working as a tarot reader, I was reminded of that judgy voice and how the assumed risk of ridicule was almost enough to stop me from embracing a tool that has helped me in more ways than I can count. I was reading tarot for a group of high school seniors at the birthday party of a friend's daughter. One by one the daughter's friends came to me with the same questions I had at their age. *What should I do about school, summer camp, friends, family?* Kids who had been laughing and goofing around in the other room suddenly became deeply serious in the face of the guidance that the cards provided.

Then there was JVP. I will call him that for short, because I believe that his full name was Judgy Voice Personified. JVP came over to the table where I was giving his friend a reading. He just wanted to watch, he said. (I usually discourage this, since a reading often becomes way more personal than the person who is receiving the reading expected it to, but I figured I would make an exception since this was a party.) As JVP watched his friend get a reading, he had on the face that all JVPs have worn since the beginning of time—a permanent smirk punctuated by some eye rolls and a couple of disbelieving snorts.

JVP also kept interrupting the reading with questions.

"Is this real?"

"Do you actually believe all of this?"

And best of all, "Yeah, but how does it work?" which revealed the ultimate sentiment behind any judgy question: *"How can you justify this thing to me in terms of the rules about the world that I have been conditioned to follow?"*

In response to JVP's question, I said something like: "Well, the cards read the energy of the moment and the energy of the querent, the person asking the question, and then they present a new perspective on the situation by laying out a narrative that the reader is able to interpret."

(I'm pretty sure he zoned out about halfway through this monologue.)

What do I wish I had said?

"Relax, kid. It's magic."

To my surprise, when I was done reading for his friend, JVP declared that he wanted a reading. I assumed that he was just looking for more ammunition to make snarky comments. But I had learned enough at this point not to prejudge the people I read for, even Judgy himself. If JVP said he wanted a reading, I would give him a reading.

I shuffled the deck and handed it to him.

"Hold the deck and think about your question," I said.

He took it. *Smirk.*

"Now cut the deck in whatever way feels good to you."

JVP suddenly got nervous.

"Like, just cut it? In how many piles?"

"Whatever feels right to you," I offered.

JVP seemed uncomfortable with this answer, but he did it.

He wants to make sure he gets it right, I realized. It would immediately become clear that this was at the heart of many of JVP's problems.

For the next twenty minutes (a short reading, since it was a party), I was able to see JVP's judgments of others for what they really were, judgments of himself that stemmed from deep fears about his own life. What goes on between a reader and a querent in a reading should always stay confidential, but I will tell you that JVP was deeply uncomfortable with uncertainty in pretty much all areas of his life. He wanted concrete answers, and the fact that he was not getting them was making him miserable.

There is a misconception that tarot is a tool of simple fortune-telling. Ask a question, get an answer. *Will I meet the love of my life? Will I ace that test? Will that person forgive me?* In my experience, the deck rarely responds well to a request for such concrete answers. In fact, it tends to rebel against them. I have seen people ask questions only to have the cards go off on a tangent about a family member, or basically spell out to the reader, "Not only are you doing the wrong thing, you're not even asking the right question!" This is no Magic 8 Ball. The tarot wants to show you a new perspective on the situation so that you can make your own decisions. It's like a close friend who tells you the (sometimes harsh) truth, but in the end knows that you have to work this out on your own.

I ask my friend, the genius tarot teacher Lindsay Mack, about this. "The tarot is happiest when it's being used as a tool for clarity about this moment," she tells me, "because it is in this moment that we are really free not only to show up, but also to make choices and to change our lives, because the future is not fixed. And very often we're fumbling through life through the lens of our egos and our personas, and we think that we're clear about what's going on in our lives, and we're not. So the tarot can be this beautiful tuning of the Technicolor of life."

I realized halfway through JVP's reading that what he was being asked to pay attention to was not these questions about uncertainty in his own life, but his attitude toward uncertainty itself. The reading itself was the lesson! Unpredictable magic was attempting to tell him, "Your attitude toward unpredictable magic is the problem! Your entire life is going to be made up of unpredictable magic that you will not be able to explain! And this is exactly what will make it amazing! Get used to it, kid!"

It also became clear during the reading that JVP was being incredibly (and unfairly) hard on himself. He thought the fact that he could not find certainty in his life meant that there was something wrong with him. The particular set of rules that had been established in his mind told him that uncertainty left the door open for failure, and that failure was unacceptable.

By the end of the reading, JVP had transformed into a completely different person. He was worried, and vulnerable, and no longer hiding behind smirks. He no longer cared about how the cards worked, or why. His mocking questions had vanished in the face of the beautiful generosity that the cards give us simply by offering up a new perspective.

EMPOWER WITH THE TAROT

Tarot doesn't just read the energy of a moment; it actually has the power to change the energy. Every single person I have read for has seemed lighter and happier after a reading, even if there was some difficult wisdom imparted. I think that relief comes from the fact that the burden of certainty has been taken off their shoulders. The whole point of tarot is to show you that there is no one fixed answer, and there's not supposed to be.

What a comfort! To be reassured that you're not missing out on some secret map that everyone else in the world has been given!

"This is a free-will universe, baby!" Lindsay declares. "We're not supposed to know everything."

Because I'm not a fan of being told that I need to follow a lot of arbitrary rules and restrictions, one of the things that I love so much about tarot is the way that it personally empowers us. It puts a tool in our hands and says, "Figure out what works for you about it." I know people who will pull out decks for a

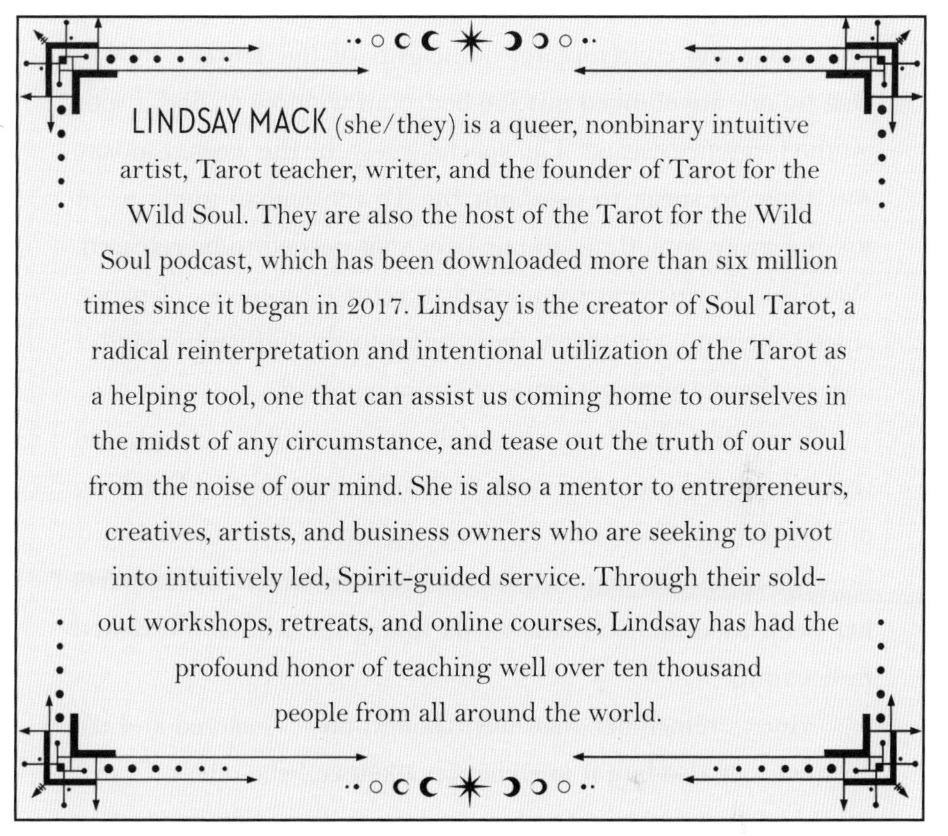

LINDSAY MACK (she/they) is a queer, nonbinary intuitive artist, Tarot teacher, writer, and the founder of Tarot for the Wild Soul. They are also the host of the Tarot for the Wild Soul podcast, which has been downloaded more than six million times since it began in 2017. Lindsay is the creator of Soul Tarot, a radical reinterpretation and intentional utilization of the Tarot as a helping tool, one that can assist us coming home to ourselves in the midst of any circumstance, and tease out the truth of our soul from the noise of our mind. She is also a mentor to entrepreneurs, creatives, artists, and business owners who are seeking to pivot into intuitively led, Spirit-guided service. Through their sold-out workshops, retreats, and online courses, Lindsay has had the profound honor of teaching well over ten thousand people from all around the world.

quick reading on a park bench or a subway platform. I also know people who enjoy the ceremony of lighting a candle before a reading, unwrapping their deck from a silk scarf, maybe doing a smoke cleansing of the room with an herb bundle.

"Anytime I had a get-together, sleepover, saw a movie, my deck was always in my bag and I would whip it out and do a reading for somebody," Lindsay tells me about her early years as a teen reader.

I first met Lindsay through the Brooklyn Fools. We were studying the Tower card that week, and the class was meeting at someone's apartment so we could sit up high on a fifth-floor fire escape and contemplate the heights of the Tower's hubris. One by one we climbed out the bedroom window to find a spot on the large fire escape. The special guest for the week, Lindsay was there to speak to us about the Tower, and to guide us in tossing away something in our lives that needed to be released. We wrote down what we needed to release on pieces of paper, ripped them up, and threw them out into the nighttime wind. I believe there was also a game of Jenga involved.

Since then Lindsay has built an incredible educational resource for those who want to learn about tarot. Teaching online tarot courses and hosting a podcast downloaded millions of times are just two of the ways in which she imparts her deep wisdom about the cards to anyone who is interested in learning.

"Always remember that even though tarot is sacred and it's holy, we can also buy it at a chain bookstore," she offers. "Tarot would lie on a table for one hundred years if we didn't pick it up and breathe life into it. We are the magic. It holds all this medicine, but it's us. We're bringing the heat."

GETTING A DECK

I bought my first deck for myself online. And my second, third, fourth, and tenth decks (yes, I have a problem). There is an old and sadly enduring myth that a new reader needs to have a deck gifted to them in order for it to be "legitimate." Wow, that sounds like a very arbitrary rule, and as I have already established, I AM VERY NOT INTO ARBITRARY RULES.

There are so many decks out there to choose from. Find one that speaks to you. If you can imagine a kind of tarot deck, it probably exists (and if it doesn't, please make it yourself so that we can all enjoy your vision!). There are even decks that detour completely away from tarot symbolism, usually called oracle decks, which you can use alone or in conjunction with a tarot deck to add an extra element to your readings.

The most well-known deck, the one that gets pulled out by fortune-tellers in movies to foreshadow something terrible happening, is called the Rider Waite Smith. The illustrator of this deck, Pamela Colman Smith, was a British occultist who hung out with Bram Stoker (of *Dracula* fame), published her own magazine, had a neurological condition called synesthesia (where sounds made her see images), fought for women's right to vote, and went by the nickname Pixie. It is unfortunately not surprising that such a cool-sounding woman was erased from the history of her own work for many years. There are versions of her deck published to this day that include only the "author" Waite and the name Rider, the publisher of the original deck.

"Tarot has always been a representation of human consciousness," Lindsay tells me. "As human consciousness shifts, it shifts too."

Beyond the traditional meanings for the cards, the real point is for them to come to mean something to you. What has come before should just be a starting point for your own participation in the evolution of tarot as a tool.

A tarot deck is divided into four suits, almost like a regular deck of playing cards—cups, pentacles, swords, and wands. There are fourteen cards in each suit, including the court cards, in most traditional decks called the page, knight, queen, and king, in some other decks called the princess, prince, queen, and king, or the daughter, son, mother, and father.

Keep in mind that references to gender in the deck are not meant to necessarily indicate actual biological gender, but are dealing with the archetypes of masculine and feminine energies that all people possess in different amounts. If assigning gendered words to your cards doesn't feel right for you, by all means seek out a deck that uses less gendered imagery and terms.

Then there is the Major Arcana—twenty-two cards that represent larger archetypes and life themes, stringing together a narrative of a life's journey. The Major Arcana bring together the big themes of tarot. After spending a week with each of them in the Fools, I feel quite close to them all. Let me introduce you:

THE FOOL: The Fool is the beginning of everything. He doesn't know exactly what he is jumping into, but he is jumping in with full gusto! Embrace the potential of the future! You don't know yet what all the complications will be, so enjoy this optimistic energy.

THE MAGICIAN: He straddles the place between heaven and earth, transforming divine knowledge into something that other humans can connect with and understand. He knows how to put on a show, how to play the game, and although there might be a lot of flash and fireworks, the magic is real.

THE HIGH PRIESTESS: She is our connection to our highest receptive, feminine wisdom. She is the wise goddess, informing us of eternal truths.

THE EMPRESS: She is the sensual goddess, lounging in a caftan, being fed peeled grapes by an adoring crowd. She is the connection to a generous, extravagant divine that asks us to embrace our truest, most fabulous selves.

THE EMPEROR: On the most superficial level, he is the king, imposing structure on kingdoms and systems, but he is also authority and strength in general. He can wield his power with a just, gentle hand, or he can wrongly prioritize rules over the needs of the heart.

THE HIEROPHANT: He is channeling psychic, eternal wisdom, but unlike the Magician's song and dance, or the High Priestess and her secret wisdoms, he is meant to teach what he knows. The world needs to hear his lessons.

THE LOVERS: Romance, sure, but also union, partnership, and the joining of opposite energies even within yourself. Balance, but in a different way from justice. This isn't about rules, it's about complementary energies working together.

THE CHARIOT: Full steam ahead! The Chariot is barreling toward the future. Ride this energy, just don't burn out or forget to check in with the details.

STRENGTH: Strength of character, of mind, of body. You are capable. You've got this. Call on your reserves of perseverance. You can be there for yourself and others. Fierce and powerful.

THE HERMIT: Time to take some time for yourself—offline, private, and contemplative. Hermit time is not for show. It's for restoration, for figuring things out, for getting comfortable with self. The Hermit can get a lot of work done in his isolation, and will emerge from solitude with some important lessons learned and some new information to share with the world.

THE WHEEL OF FORTUNE: Facing challenges that keep coming back around again. Every time we encounter the same problem, we find ourselves wiser, able to make it further in the work of untangling this particular karmic knot. Be patient with the idea of time as a spiral. Recognize old patterns when they come up again. It's not a failure; it's an opportunity to learn more.

JUSTICE: What is fair? What is right? What is just? Weigh the pros and cons. Consider the moral implications. Make your decision based on facts, not emotions.

THE HANGED MAN: Not ready to be here or there, he's biding his time in the middle for now. Be patient: the right time will come. It may feel awkward and uncomfortable right now, but that's okay. Decisive times will return.

DEATH: The time for an ending. Completion. Time for rest. Time to let it go. An ending that might be more peaceful than the Tower, which will end something through some possibly tough destruction. Death is a winding down, a natural conclusion. Its time has come.

TEMPERANCE: Balance in service of moderation. There's been too much of something. Smooth down fiery, unmanageable emotions. They won't get you anywhere right now. Pull back, reassess, prioritize yourself and what balance means for you.

THE DEVIL: Vice, sure, but also false ideas of self and of others. Behavior that you know doesn't serve you, or perhaps another person who doesn't seem to have your best interests in mind. You're getting dragged down by the wrong priorities. Raise yourself up.

THE TOWER: One of the most powerful cards in my experience, a sign that some structure, some way of being, needs to go, so that it might be replaced by a brand-new way of life. Like a forest fire, the woods must burn down completely so that new trees can take root. Not an easy card, but one that is closely linked to our individual evolution.

THE STAR: Not the all-encompassing heat of the sun, but a nighttime companion to the Moon. Follow your instincts toward that pinprick of light. You'll find a connection to your true self waiting there for you, stripped down to its essence after the destruction of the Tower. Soon it will be time for your star to shine.

THE MOON: Riding the tides of our deepest emotions. Like the Wheel of Fortune, we want to learn to accept the ongoing phases of life, to be patient with them, but the Moon also asks us to dig into the intuition of our bodies and feelings. We are the werewolf wandering in the woods. If we learn to conquer our fear of the dark, we will finally come to understand that we are safe here.

THE SUN: The source of light, heat, life! Turn your face to the light and soak it in! Radiate positivity! Let yourself shine brightly!

JUDGMENT: Looking at the content of your life and the potential that it holds. Don't shy away from your talents and skills; they are magical gifts. In this instance, consider the idea that you might be the cleverest person in the room. Own it.

THE WORLD: The World is yours. If you open your heart to all the complexities of this big, crazy planet and your existence on it, you will find a beautiful abundance at your disposal. Don't shrink. You have so much. This world needs you.

STARTING TO READ

"Material and teachers and literature are there for you to have until you're ready to throw it away," Lindsay says when I ask how she feels about using tarot guidebooks to help us interpret the cards, especially as beginners. "It's a stepping-stone for you to get to your knowing."

We can talk about intuition all we want, but one of the things I appreciate about the cards is that they start you off with something concrete to work with when it comes to accessing our magical intuition. There's a narrative to jump off from if you need it. And guidebooks can help establish that framework, which then creates a container in which our intuition can begin to flourish. (I have listed some of my favorites in the "recommended reading" in the back of this book.) When it comes to working with mystical tools, it can be difficult to learn to trust your own intuition, and I find that the structure of the cards and working with their traditional meanings can almost trick us into accessing our own inner wisdom.

Reading for yourself and reading for someone else are not that different in practice. As I said, some people will enjoy creating a small ritual around the beginning of a reading, while others might think nothing of pulling out their deck on a park bench. The important thing is bringing your energy and intention to the deck.

If you are reading for yourself, shuffle your deck while thinking about the particular question or area in which you are looking for guidance.

"You can just start with the question: What am I being invited to pay attention to in this moment?" Lindsay offers.

When you are done shuffling, you might want to close your eyes and hold your deck in your hands. Think about your inquiry and take some calming deep breaths to ground yourself fully in the present moment. Then put the deck down and cut it in whatever way feels good to you. Some people cut with the left hand, believing it to be the more spiritually receptive hand. Some like to cut the deck into three piles and then put it back together. Do whatever feels right to you.

If you are reading for someone else, shuffle the deck while asking them to tell you as much as they feel comfortable sharing about their query. The deck responds well to specificity, so if they feel comfortable asking a question (knowing that they won't necessarily receive a definitive yes or no answer about something), then have them do that now. When you feel that you have shuffled enough (and really let yourself feel into your intuition on this), hand the deck to them, and have them hold it and think about their question. When they feel ready, they should put the deck down and cut it.

The kind of card pull or spread that you do is up to you, and will depend on the type of question being asked. Some people like to pick one card (usually from the top of the deck) every day in the morning to give them some guidance for that day. A simple three-card spread would involve putting down one card for the past, one for the present, and one for guidance about the future. There are many different kinds of spreads out there, and you should feel free to create your own, but below I will outline one of my favorites in order to get you started.

The Celtic cross is one of the most classic tarot spreads. I like it because it provides many different perspectives on a situation. Together the cards in a Celtic cross spread paint a picture of all the different factors at play in your query. To me, reading a Celtic cross feels like piecing together the chapters of a book.

The Celtic Cross Tarot Spread

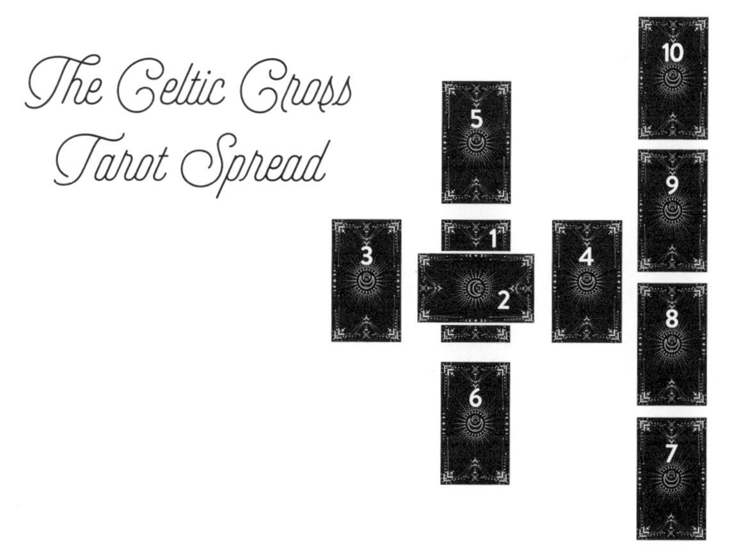

After the deck has been shuffled and cut, pick the cards from the top of the deck and lay them down in the following order, each position corresponding to a particular aspect of the question at hand:

1. The present situation.
   What you're dealing with.

2. The challenge to the present situation.

3. The recent past.

4. The near future.

5. The public face you are currently presenting to the world.

6. The private face, how you are processing things right now.

7. Advice. A path forward.

8. Outside influences. What is going on around you right now?

9. Your hopes and/or fears.

10. Probable outcome if you follow the advice mentioned here.

If you read further about tarot, you will find that there are many interpretations even of the positions in such a classic spread. Don't be afraid to experiment with different versions and find the one that works for you.

When it comes to interpreting the cards, I usually begin with the present situation and then move around the cross in order, but sometimes certain cards might confuse you at first, and it's okay to skip them and come back as the bigger picture of the reading starts to come into focus. The nice thing about the Celtic cross is that there is a lot on the table to work with, so you shouldn't get hung up on any single card.

As you move through a spread, look carefully at the story that the cards are telling together. Maybe you're doing a past, present, future three-card spread and the Tower comes up in the past, Temperance in the present, and the Empress in the future.

This might indicate that the person has just been through a moment of upheaval or reassessment that was emotionally difficult, and now they are being called to find balance and reassess. Soon it will be time for them to step into their own goddess power and find new ways to experience joy and pamper themselves.

There are some pretty big and sometimes intense themes that show up in the tarot, especially in the Major Arcana, and a lot of people freak out when they see a card like the Tower or Death in a reading, thinking that this must be a bad omen.

"It's a journey to undo our conditioning about what's scary and what's not scary in the tarot," Lindsay suggests when I ask her about how we should approach the "scary" cards. "All the cards bring medicine."

In these moments, try to think beyond the literal and move into the metaphorical. A hero's journey may contain many different kinds of death—death of the ego, of false expectations, of something that was ready to go away.

It also helps to remember that reading tarot is like checking the energetic weather. If you know it is likely to rain, then you will be prepared with an umbrella, and be able to avoid getting soaked in a torrential downpour. Getting wet is not inevitable; you just have to have all the information in order to be prepared.

The important thing here is not to worry too much about "making sense" when you're reading tarot and instead to tune in to what comes up for you when you look at the spread in front of you. What story is taking shape? If you had to tell someone the story of this spread, could you do it? Is it possible not to worry too much about whether you are "making something up" (which would make it "not real") and instead start to pay attention to what resonates?

If you are doing a reading for someone else, you definitely want to pay close attention to what is resonating for them. In that situation, you are providing a service, acting as a conduit for the conversation between them and the universe. I often finish a reading for someone else not really understanding the significance of half of what I told them, but the truth is that it's not completely my business. We have to trust what the cards want to communicate to the person seeking their wisdom, and let the full possibility of their narrative sink in.

The only way to truly begin to develop your skills as a reader, and to understand how to trust your intuition when it comes to the cards, is to start reading! As with all our tools, there is no way to prove to you that they work other than having you see their effectiveness with your own eyes. That's the beauty of such personal magic. It exists for you to have an individual relationship with it, not just for someone else to tell you about it and for you to blindly believe them.

And remember that if you pull cards or try a reading and not everything that comes up speaks to you, that's okay too!

"If you don't understand part of the wisdom that came through your hands, if your brain cannot yet compute what an invisible part of you knows, it'll find another way," Lindsay says when I ask her what do to with a particularly inscrutable spread. "It's always okay to say that you don't understand it. That is how you learn. So if you don't know how to interpret a card, that's an opportunity for you to say, 'I don't know.' And how exciting!"

Imagine feeling free to simply say, "I don't know!" What if our old friend Judgy Voice Personified knew that such a thing was an option? What if all JVPs everywhere felt that they were allowed to admit this? Tarot shows us that this not-knowing, this ongoing examination of the complexities of life, is something to be embraced. Once we stop thinking of the present moment as something to be fixed in a specific way, we can open up to the possibilities of what is actually in front of us. And tarot is there to support us in this practice of glorious not-knowing!

HOLDING SPACE FOR THE SPIRAL

More often than not I find that a reading speaks to me as much as it does to the person I am reading for. There is a beautiful kind of communion in this, an erasing of hierarchy. Suddenly we are unified in this task of peering into the possibilities and challenges of this moment.

The truth is that even when I was at that birthday party reading for JVP, attempting to convince him to let go of the need for certainty and control, I was also talking to myself. He was mirroring back to me something that was difficult for me to admit about my own need for control in my life. So in this way, that reading was a huge gift to me, allowing me to look objectively at a challenging part of my own psyche, even as I attempted to help JVP consider alternate ways of thinking about his problems.

A big part of this is the concept of "holding space" in a reading. This is when we act as a safe witness to someone else's fears and emotions. When a friend is having a hard time, often our instinct is to rush in and try to fix everything, or even to offer up our own story of discomfort. This can certainly be helpful sometimes, especially if someone has asked for our guidance or assistance. But holding space asks us to just exist in the present moment of someone's feelings without trying to alter them.

"Rather than trying to fix or advise and make everything clean and pretty, it's giving the permission to let the storm come in and to be a safe harbor for them," Lindsay explains.

And we can even do this for ourselves.

"When we are sad, it is part of our instinct to run away from that sadness," Lindsay says, "not to engage with things that feel uncomfortable. Sometimes grief and sadness might even be covered over by anger and fear. So holding space for ourselves might look like essentially opening the door and feeling all the tough feelings, letting ourselves cry or just feel sad, and not needing to adjust or change."

For me, the tarot itself has a way of holding space for us, and it was just that magic that allowed me to relinquish my title of Queen of Seasonal Affective Disorder all those years ago. It was not just the feeling of access to a kind of empowering magic that could fit in my pocket that helped relieve my SAD, but also the sense that at any moment I had access to this energetic conversation with the universe, which seemed very eager to engage me in a compassionate conversation about things that I had never had the vocabulary to talk about before. It was only through the archetypes of the tarot that I could suddenly see myself clearly and without judgment. Some days I was the Fool, some days the Empress, and some days I felt thrown around by the Wheel of Fortune. It was all valid. It was all information.

This is where I find the most serenity with tarot. Just as there are no bad cards, only cards that sometimes bring difficult truths, there are no bad feelings. And if we allow ourselves to get curious about all of our feelings rather than try to reject them, we can become compassionate observers of our own lives. The tarot provides a model for how to do that. Just as all feelings pass, we will pull a different card tomorrow. Tarot will change as we change, and we are supposed to live in the flow of this change, and to examine it and embrace it the best that we can.

"We are living in one of the great revolutions and evolutions of how tarot is interpreted," Lindsay says. "When I was a teenager it was very black-and-white, very patriarchal, very hierarchical, not soulful, not spiralic."

We will go into this more in our chapters on astrology and therapy, but we often assume that the narratives of our lives should be linear, existing in a straight line with a comprehendible beginning, middle, and end. Based on what we have been taught about achievement, we seem to believe that we should always be improving at things until we arrive at some high-status destination that we have earned. We are often even receiving this kind of messaging when it comes to self-help or self-improvement. We may be able to acknowledge that there are things that we need to work on healing about ourselves, parts of ourselves that may need extra patience or guidance, but we often mistakenly expect this healing to happen in a linear way, a straight shot to "better." This is our old friend capitalism as work (more on him soon!), and this mindset brings a harmful self-judgment to our own process of learning about ourselves, by falsely expecting our narrative to look like someone else's story or adhere to some arbitrary rules. So no wonder my yearly SAD felt so discouraging. I believed that I was *supposed to* get better, not find myself back around again in the same old challenging place every winter.

In this way, the Wheel of Fortune card really sums up so much about the revolutionary framework that the tarot provides for us. As Lindsay describes it, the tarot allows us to take a "spiralic" view of healing, understanding that sometimes we need to revisit something that we thought was long gone, while knowing that this time we are wiser and can bring new information to the table. The Wheel reminds us that you can pick another card next week, tomorrow, even a few minutes from now, and be engaging in a completely new conversation with the energy of the moment. That sense of change is a feature, not a flaw, and the tarot is the best tool we have to teach us how to flow with that energetic change and allow ourselves not only to make peace with it, but maybe even to enjoy it sometimes.

Also, giving a tarot reading makes you feel awesome—like someone with mystical connections to the secrets of the universe.

Which—SPOILER ALERT—is exactly what you are.

Exercises

SINGLE-CARD PULL

Commit to a week of pulling a single card in the morning and spending a few minutes meditating on what that card means to you, and what kind of guidance it might bring to your day. At the end of the day, take fifteen minutes to journal about that card and the lessons it brought to your day.

CELTIC CROSS

For a longer exercise, lay down a Celtic cross spread for yourself. On a blank piece of paper or in a journal, write down which cards showed up in each position, and see if you can begin to form a narrative between the different cards. How does the recent past lead to the present, and then take us to the future? What is the relationship between advice and outcome? If nothing is coming to you through your intuition, simply write the traditional card meanings down and see if having the definitions in front of you brings you some new insights. When you feel ready, offer a reading to a willing friend.

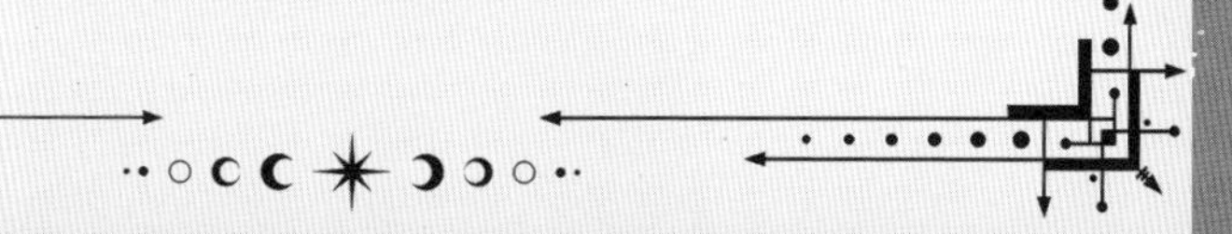

CHAPTER TWO:
Astrology

Although I find tarot to be the most accessible of the mystical tools that we will cover in this book, astrology is the tool that has had the biggest impact on how I look at my life and my mental health. I think a lot about the person that I was when I first walked into that cheesy new age store at twenty-two, clutching a gift certificate, not quite prepared to have my entire existence handed to me on some sheets of printer paper in a manila folder. Maybe that person would have found her way back to understanding and accepting herself through magic eventually, but without that reading I'm sure it would have taken me a lot longer to get there.

I never went through an astrology phase as a teenager. I knew "my sign," I had read goofy one-paragraph horoscopes for fun, and I had a vague understanding that being a Cancer meant I was moody and mothering. I didn't really feel like I needed a horoscope to tell me those things, but thanks, Universe.

What was not being explained to me, and what the universe was not offering up through horoscopes in the back of magazines, was an explanation for the things that I found frustrating about myself.

My parents' gentle term for my temperament as a kid was "sensitive."

"You're very sensitive," my mom would say when we needed to leave a movie theater because something upsetting was happening on the screen and I couldn't handle it. Or when I would call her and my dad to come pick me up from a sleepover party because the other girls were playing "light as a feather, stiff as a board." (My sensitivities often involved me leaving places before I was supposed to.) This was the explanation given when I would get overly upset when someone would say something that hurt my feelings, when something sad happened to someone around me, and especially when I was afraid of the dark.

When my mom would say, "You're very sensitive," to explain my behavior, she didn't mean this as a bad thing. It was simply a fact of life, and she never made me feel like it was something I needed to change.

But then my fear of the dark kicked in big-time. From the ages of about six to twelve I went through extended periods where I was so terrified of being alone at night that I had to employ various stages of darkness intervention in order to even think about falling asleep. I started with a night-light, then moved on to keeping a regular light on, then having my dog sleep in the room with me to keep me company. And finally, at its worst, I could not calm down unless one of my parents sat with me until I was mostly asleep. (Please pity my poor parents here—this was before the age of smartphones and tablets, which might have helped to distract them during those long hours. One of them would sit in the half darkness, silently begging me to doze off, usually falling asleep themselves.)

My parents were probably more frustrated with me than they let on, but again they never made me feel bad about my fears. I, however, was embarrassed and worried that I was not simply going to "grow out of" this problem. If it wasn't going away on its own, I obviously needed to do something to move things along. So I asked my parents if I could talk to a psychologist. They agreed to take me to see someone.

I remember very little about this visit to a psychologist. I do remember making lighthearted conversation with them, prattling on about school and friends and things I was interested in. I was good at talking to adults, sometimes better at it than talking to people my own age, and I know that I turned on the charm, believing that this was what was expected of me. I'm sure we touched on the "afraid of the dark" problem, but I'm also sure that I described it to them in casual terms, not wanting to overstate a problem that seemed pretty silly in the grand scheme of things.

The one thing that I remember clearly is that after the session, they took me out to the waiting room to meet my dad and said to both of us, "There's nothing wrong with her. She seems like a very well-adjusted kid."

Two things happened inside me in that moment. The first

was that I felt relieved, having been given an official non-diagnosis. Could I relax now after being reassured that I was "normal"? But a much deeper part of me felt betrayed. Here I was coming to a professional saying, "I need help dealing with this problem. I feel scared and I don't know why, because I have a very harmonious and happy home and no reason to be freaking out every night." And their response was to turn me away. That night, when I would inevitably have yet another panic attack in the dark, should I just inform myself that I was "very well-adjusted" and snap out of it? Hearing that my problem didn't sound like a big deal to this person still left me without any tools to cope with something that was disrupting my life.

I also had a vague understanding of the fact that my preternatural chattering, which had charmed this adult, was the result of a tactic that I had carefully constructed to please, while I somehow expected this person to see through my agreeable nature to the secret dark heart of my problem.

As much as I felt betrayed by this psychologist in this moment, I had no way to contextualize a very profound truth—that it was possible both that there was "nothing wrong" with me and also that I was struggling with something. But all I knew was that I did not feel at all "normal," and that I was tired of being so "sensitive."

It wasn't until ten years later, when I finally had my natal chart read, that I was able to fully understand what this all meant.

FINDING THE MAP

Just as there are no good or bad cards in tarot, in astrology there is no binary judgment of "good" or "bad" in our natal charts. There is simply information. When we delve into astrology beyond the one-paragraph horoscope of our sun sign, we find a combination of elements that is like a recipe for what makes up each of us. To say that any ingredient in a recipe is "bad" would make no sense. Pepper can't be bad. Flour can't be bad. You might not like cilantro, but it's not inherently "bad." These ingredients simply "are," and in the right combination they make up a delicious meal!

Yes, I am calling each of us a delicious meal. Because recipes are all about balance and how we work with our ingredients. And sometimes they are difficult and they require practice. And sometimes we are difficult, and we require practice.

So what exactly is this magical list of ingredients that can explain you to you? Your natal chart is a map of where the planets were in the sky at the moment that you were born. You are at the center of the chart, with the planets in formation around you based on your location at birth. Even someone born in the same minute as you would have a different chart based on their location. Twins might even have slightly different charts if something shifted in the few minutes between their births.

So in order to create a natal chart, you need your birth date, time, and place. The planets are then categorized into signs and houses based on their relationship to different constellations and to Earth in that moment.

But how do these placements affect us, exactly? Some

people believe that the planets influence us the way the moon influences the tides, creating a complicated energetic push and pull that changes depending on their relationship to you. But I think you know me well enough by now to know I'm happy to simply say, "It's magic."

Here's a particularly poetic description of the natal chart from one of my favorite astrology books, *Astrology: The Only Introduction You'll Ever Need*, quoting nuclear physicist Will Keepin: "It is almost as if the chart is an index for the creative process of cosmic evolution. And when one is born with a particular chart, one becomes an ambassador of sorts to the rest of the cosmos, representing a unique moment in the cosmic space-time to the rest of the cosmos as it continues to unfold."

An ambassador of a unique moment in time and space! Isn't it lovely to think that you were born into this world with your own unique set of questions, strengths, and information to communicate to the rest of us? That your job while you're here is to help nurture those parts of yourself, so that you may come to share with us all that you learn about your unique moment in the universe's conversation with itself?

Although there is currently a resurgence of interest in astrology in popular culture, people have been working with these systems of organizing the sky for a very long time. The practice of astrology can be traced back to at least 1800 BC. Ancient Mesopotamians believed that the planets could communicate omens from the gods, and might indicate if a god was displeased with humanity. From there, astrological practices spread to Egypt, then Greece, then Rome. By the ninth century AD, astrology was showing up in Arabic texts that were then translated into Latin, becoming popular in medieval Europe. Meanwhile similar systems were being used in India, China, and Mesoamerica.

Here is evidence of our mystical elephant even within one way of working with a tool—almost every culture in the world developed their own system to read and try to understand the movement of the planets. No one system has more authority than another, and in the end they are all attempting to do the same thing—create a harmonious understanding between humanity, Earth, and the ever-evolving energetic forces of the universe.

You might want to do some research and see if your ancestors had a system of astrology and how they used it (or continue to use it—in India you can hire a matchmaker who will set you up with someone based on your natal charts). Even with modern-day Western astrology there are different systems and ways of organizing astrological information, so once you have the basics down, there is always more to discover.

SUN, MOON, RISING

When I received my first natal chart reading, I learned about two aspects of my chart that explained so much about that childhood interaction with the psychologist to me. The first was that I learned about my rising sign—Libra—which dictates the way that I interact with the world. When people first meet me, they meet the Libra version of me, which is much more social and outgoing than my moody Cancer sun, the part of me that wants to crawl into bed and stay there, preferably with a few blankets and pets piled on top of me.

This relationship between the sun sign and the rising sign is the reason why many people seem different once you get to know them a little better. Having a public face that's different from your private one doesn't necessarily mean that the public face is insincere, just that you may have a different set of strategies with which you deal with daily, public life than you do when you are relaxed and around people you feel comfortable with. Your rising sign provides the lens through which you see the world, and the terms on which you are meeting it.

So for that hour that I spent in that psychologist's office, they were only meeting my Libra self—chatty, observant, interested in making everyone comfortable and keeping the peace. Of course I seemed well-adjusted! My rising sign default behaviors knew exactly how to protect my sensitive sun and moon.

And about that moon . . .

The rising, sun, and moon signs are like the human version of a Russian nesting doll. You may need to get to know someone before you move beyond the rising sign persona and meet the true essential "sun" version of them, but you need to know them very well before you meet their moon self. And as far as I'm concerned, the moon is where all the good stuff happens.

The placement of our moon tells us about our deepest emotional selves—our fears, desires, dreams, and creativity. The moon is, quite simply, how we feel, and how we manage our feelings.

I, dear reader, have my moon in Scorpio. That's right—Scorpio. The most witchy, deep, dark, secretive, angsty, mystical waters that you can swim in when it comes to the zodiac. Scorpio energy digs deep into hidden truths and refuses to ignore them, even when they are dark or scary. And it is deeply empathic, just as all water signs are, but poor Scorpio often holds on to the dark and difficult feelings of others.

So it was only at the age of twenty-two that I was finally being saved from the binary of bad or good—the idea of there either being something "BAD and wrong" with me, or that I was "GOOD and normal." I was simply a sensitive little witch, often affected deeply by the energy around me in ways that might not be obvious to others, and in need of some strong emotional and energetic boundaries to protect that very intense emotional part of me.

For the first time, I started to realize that I actually cherished this "too sensitive" part of myself, and that it was often a positive force in my life. My Scorpio moon drove my budding interest in spirituality and magic, and the more I was learning, the more I started to see that my fear of the dark (both literal and figurative) had been related to a lack of understanding about the energies that I was picking up on.

I also found that my writing felt deeply centered in my moon self. When people told me that they connected emotionally to something that I wrote, I knew that they were seeing my moon at work, and I was grateful for that connection.

Suddenly there was an easing up around any shame that I had experienced about being the kid who had to leave the scary movie, or bail on the sleepover. Even if others couldn't understand this part of me, their judgment didn't matter, because I had discovered the gift behind the challenge.

I understand why some people don't "believe" in astrology. But every time I encounter a skeptic, I find that they are someone who only knows their sun sign, has read only those one-paragraph horoscopes, and doesn't understand what all the fuss is about. Maybe they've seen some silly memes that reduce each of us to funny clichés about our sun sign, or they've had someone make a judgment about them based on their sign that they didn't relate to. Of course I understand—I was once one of these people. But forming an impression of astrology based on only sun signs and memes would be like going to an amusement park, never leaving the parking lot, and declaring the experience boring. You never even made it through the front gate!

It is because astrology can be such a powerful tool of self-acceptance that I feel so passionately about it. If tarot allows for a magical relationship to the narrative of the current moment, astrology provides that kind of relationship to your entire lifetime.

"Astrology has given me permission to be watery, and to be emotional," my friend Jeff tells me, proving to me that I'm not alone in feeling that a better understanding of my chart gave me access to allowing for the more emotional parts of myself. "It's shown me that it's okay, especially as someone who was born male and was not really given permission to be emotional, or permission to lean into any of my psychic gifts."

It's New Year's Eve, and Jeff and I are talking over video chat. He has informed me that the moon has just moved from Cancer into Leo a few minutes before our conversation began, which is good timing, since we both admit that the Cancer moon has had us both exhausted for days.

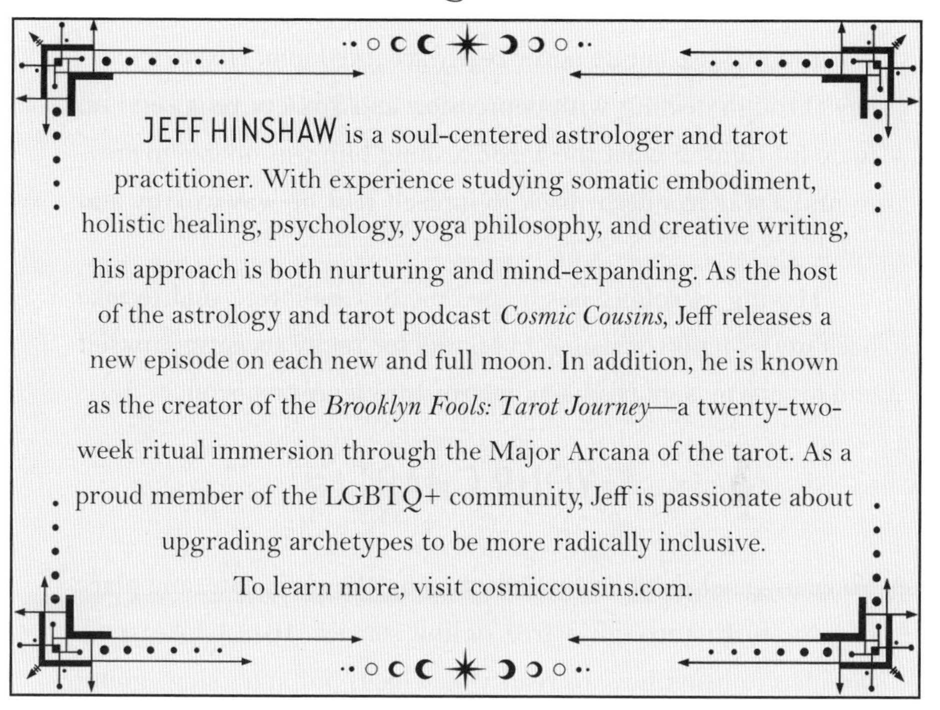

JEFF HINSHAW is a soul-centered astrologer and tarot practitioner. With experience studying somatic embodiment, holistic healing, psychology, yoga philosophy, and creative writing, his approach is both nurturing and mind-expanding. As the host of the astrology and tarot podcast *Cosmic Cousins*, Jeff releases a new episode on each new and full moon. In addition, he is known as the creator of the *Brooklyn Fools: Tarot Journey*—a twenty-two-week ritual immersion through the Major Arcana of the tarot. As a proud member of the LGBTQ+ community, Jeff is passionate about upgrading archetypes to be more radically inclusive.

To learn more, visit cosmiccousins.com.

Jeff Hinshaw was one of the founders of the Brooklyn Fools, the tarot course that brought me further into my witchy self, and his watchful and attentive Aquarius demeanor helped to set the tone for our mystical gatherings. Like most of the practitioners I know, Jeff wears many hats—he's a tarot reader, esoteric astrologer, and somatic healer (a therapist who uses an energetic, body-based approach).

"I've always had an interest in human psychology, which is kind of how I have come into these esoteric practices of astrology and tarot," Jeff tells me. "But getting my BA in psychology was like slogging through mud for me. It was missing the magic side of it, and the spiritual side of it too."

Jeff tells me about how he grew up in the South as the outsider queer kid whose family never really accepted him. His own journey through dealing with depression and anxiety required him to do for himself what the world around him was unable to do—to find a way to mirror back to himself that he was worthy and valid.

"Having astrology has helped me to recalibrate, and to take back my own power, using it as a tool for really accepting myself and loving myself. It's like a mirror into your own soul."

YOUR CHART

You can generate your own chart using the time, date, and place of your birth through a free online service. It can take some practice to learn how to read your chart, but start slow, going planet by planet. Your chart is a kind of puzzle, and it helps to identify the different elements that you're working with before you start to try to piece it all together.

Every planet on your chart will be categorized into both a sign and a house. This can be seen as the what, how, and where of astrology. The planet is the what, the sign is the how, and the house is the where.

For example: What are you doing? Maybe you are vacuuming! How are you doing it? Angrily! Where are you doing it? In the living room!

Let's say your chart tells you that you have Venus in Pisces in the first house. So the answer to "What is it?" is: Venus, the planet of love. How is it? In Pisces, so it is engaged in our most watery feelings. And where is it? The first house—the house of self. So we might conclude that this is someone who approaches love with a lot of deep, sensitive emotions, and who sees their relationships as a big part of their sense of self.

Below is an extremely simplified definition of the planets, signs, and houses to get you started in looking at your own chart. This is just the tip of the iceberg, and one way to dive deeper into your chart is to simply search for your placements online ("Venus in Pisces in the first house") and start to piece together your own interpretation of your chart. As with my tarot definitions, keep in mind that this is my personal interpretation of the planets, signs, and houses, taken from my own studying and experience, and you may come to have a very different interpretation of them. As with all these tools, you will learn best by practicing using astrology, and developing your own vocabulary around it.

THE PLANETS

Sun

sense of self—changes signs every month

Moon

emotions, creativity—changes signs every two to three days

Mercury

communication—changes signs every three to four weeks

Venus

love, relationships—changes signs
every four to five weeks

Mars

energy, drive, anger—changes signs
every six to seven weeks

Jupiter

growth, wisdom—changes signs
every twelve to thirteen months

Saturn

discipline, challenges—changes signs
every two to three years

Uranus

change, originality—
changes signs every seven years

Neptune

dreams—changes signs
every ten to twelve years

Pluto

transformation—changes signs
approximately every twelve to fifteen years

THE SIGNS

Aries (fire, the ram): impulsive, fiery, often bringing fresh and unique energy to a room. Perhaps not always thinking through all the consequences of their actions. Aries likes attention and can often seem young and impulsive, as the first sign in the wheel of the zodiac.

Taurus (earth, the bull): Taurus likes comfort—good food, good fun, and overall stability. Stubborn as all get-out, though—watch out for those bull horns!

Gemini (air, the twins): Gemini is all about communication—quick and with a lot of people, with potential social butterfly tendencies. They are clever and they don't mind if you know it. But the sign of the twins brings us two versions of self—you won't know them completely until you see their other side.

Cancer (water, the crab): the sensitive, mothering, deeply protective, moody crustacean of the zodiac. They want a home-cooked meal with loved ones followed by a snuggle under many blankets. But cross them or someone they care about and the crab shell will go up and the claws will come out.

Leo (fire, the lion): Leo shines like the sun and has no problem accepting your attention and adoration. As long as their need to shine bright stays generous and doesn't veer into narcissism, they are true beacons of light.

Virgo (earth, the maiden): Virgo values precision over all else. They need life to be organized according to their system, and you must either appreciate them for their unique ability to create order out of any chaos or simply get out of their way while they reorganize your sock drawer by thread count.

Libra (air, the scales): Libra believes in justice and balance above all else (also, they don't mind looking cute). They are the diplomats of the world, able to take the temperature of a room and act accordingly to make sure they are considering everyone's point of view. But if they put too much stock in everyone else's opinions, they might forget how to make a decision for themselves.

Scorpio (water, the scorpion): the most mystical and secretive of the water signs, Scorpio can't stand anything fake or superficial, and it will dig down deep in the dirt to get to the truth of something, even if it's painful. If they don't get stuck in the darkness, they can provide a powerful service for humanity as empaths and mystics.

Sagittarius (fire, the archer): they care about philosophy, religion, learning, teaching, and travel. They are usually on the lookout for their next adventure (or party), and they can be easily distracted and become bored with everyday life.

Capricorn (earth, sea goat): Capricorns are like louder Virgos with a business plan. They know the best way to do something, and they are usually correct. They like to be in charge but sometimes lack the diplomacy to deal with those who don't have the same kind of work ethic that they do. They believe in paying attention to the details, creating structure and stability, and earning money.

Aquarius (air, water bearer): they are our beautiful benevolent aliens visiting Earth to observe and instruct. They care about the collective, social justice, science, and technology, and they love a conspiracy theory. They are friends of the mystical and the bizarre, and are not easily fazed. As long as they don't feel too alienated from the rest of humanity, they are natural healers and leaders.

Pisces (water, fish): the most deeply empathetic of the water signs, Pisces can become easily overwhelmed by the energy of others. Pisces energy is gentle, loving, loyal, romantic, intuitive, and in need of lots of naps. Pisces needs to create clear boundaries between self and others, or else it will exhaust itself with picking up on energies and sensitivities that are not its own.

THE HOUSES

1st house: self, appearance, identity
2nd house: material possessions, money, resources, work ethic
3rd house: communication, thinking, the mind
4th house: home, roots, family
5th house: creativity, self-expression, play
6th house: the body, health, fitness
7th house: relationships, partnerships
8th house: sex, death (and taxes)
9th house: philosophy, travel, wisdom
10th house: career, public image, fame
11th house: groups of people, friends, social awareness
12th house: healing, spirituality, the subconscious

When you read the descriptions of the signs, you probably see yourself in different elements of many of them. That's because you actually do contain these multitudes. Maybe you are very regimented about your work, but sloppy about organizing your closet. Maybe you are confident on your own, but become shy around others. No one person can be summed up in a single sign, and investigating your unique combination of these elements is the whole point of astrology. Once you start to understand the significance of the planets and houses in relationship to the signs, the whole world of your chart opens up to you.

The best way to become familiar with your chart is to get a reading from a professional astrologer, but by no means is it the only way to learn.

"I didn't receive a reading for years," Jeff tells me. "It was more of my own deep-dive exploration and about getting my hands on everything I could find."

There is pretty much no limit to how deep we can go with astrology. But I find that even a beginner's understanding of our own charts can be a huge help in learning to navigate our sense of self and mental health, providing clues around where we need to work on being self-sufficient and where we might need to ask for help.

THE NORTH AND SOUTH NODES

Astrology is a tool, not a belief system, but it can easily be applied to certain belief systems. Some astrologers believe that our soul chooses its chart before we agree to incarnate (or reincarnate) on this planet, the idea being that we are looking to experience certain karmic lessons this time around based on past life experience. "Karma" is a Sanskrit word that refers to the idea that our actions affect our personal futures, both in this lifetime and in subsequent lifetimes. An important principle in many Indian religions, karma is what we carry with us, for better or worse, based on past deeds. There are parts of our charts that point to this kind of karmic mission, and you should choose to look at these aspects of your chart in whatever way feels comfortable for you. Even taken simply as a metaphor, I find that I appreciate the idea of looking at particular lifetime challenges through the lens of my personal chart.

The places on our charts that particularly speak to our karmic missions are called the north and south nodes. The south node represents where we are coming from, lessons we have already learned, places where we feel strong, confident, and grounded. Across our charts, we find the north node—a kind of mission statement for this lifetime. This is what you are striving toward and possibly struggling with. The north node presents something that is a recurring theme in your life, showing you an area that you hope to master, or at least learn to navigate. If you believe in reincarnation, you might see your north node as the future placement of your south node in the next lifetime, the place of expertise that you learned so much about in your previous life.

Just like with the planets, our nodes are placed in a sign and a house. My south node is in Aquarius in the fifth house. I interpret this as meaning that I am very comfortable being a creative (fifth house) weirdo (Aquarius). And then across the way my north node is in Leo in the eleventh house. For me, the simple interpretation of this is that my challenge in this lifetime is to bring what I make creatively with confidence (Leo) to groups of people (eleventh house). So looking at the rest of my chart to gain an understanding of what kind of tools are at my disposal, I see this as an exciting challenge to become comfortable sharing my weirdo creativity with others.

The thing about your north node challenges in this lifetime is that they may always present you with some level of struggle. The challenges may ease up a little, or manifest in new ways, but the struggle is actually the point. The fact that it doesn't always come easily is what allows for growth. This gets me thinking once again about the Wheel of Fortune card in tarot. When there is an issue in our lives that continues to resurface, sometimes taking different forms with different people or in different places, our first reaction might be to get annoyed.

"THIS again? Why is this always happening to me?"

But to accept that there are certain themes that reoccur throughout our life is to reframe our relationship with these north node issues when they come back around again. It is built into the system that you will revisit some of the same issues over and over again in your life. No one is exempt. So it's helpful to be able to point to the places on your personal map where these issues flare up for you.

Rather than feeling like we have failed in some way, we can look at these returns as opportunities to learn more, and to understand that we have made progress since the last time we dealt with this issue, even if that progress feels painfully slow. We have a whole lifetime to work on this. There's no rush.

I can tell you from experience that the worst thing you can

do is ignore a dynamic that continues to resurface in your life. Many people see this happen in relationships, both romantic and platonic, as they repeat the same dynamics over and over again, and then wonder why the outcome is always the same. "You have to feel it to heal it," is a popular new age saying that asks us to allow ourselves to look directly at hard truths in order to learn from them and grow. If you do not learn to work with these parts of your chart as tools, you are going to continue to manifest very hard lessons that are going to try to force you to do that.

UNDERSTANDING OTHERS

As with all our tools, our purpose in using astrology is to gain a greater self-understanding, so that we then may come to understand, or at least have empathy for, other people. When you realize that we all have very unique strengths and weaknesses, you can come to understand the behavior of others in a way that may not have made sense to you before. No one has a chart that doesn't contain some challenging aspects, and no one is exempt from the push and pull between their personal chart and the astrology of each moment. We may all react and possibly cope with these issues differently, but no one is excused from these challenges.

This makes me think of a popular quote that is often misattributed to Plato: "Be kind, for everyone you meet is fighting a hard battle."

An astrologer might say: "Be kind, because everyone has challenging placements in their natal chart."

"This past year, I received my grandmother's birth certificate," Jeff tells me. "She was an Aquarius sun with a Taurus moon, Scorpio rising. Everything just clicked in. I felt like I could understand what it was like for her to be a woman who grew up in the thirties in the South. And looking at my parents' charts, for instance, has been deeply healing. Even though I can't have a conversation with my parents around psychology or healing or spirituality, I can look at their charts and have a window into their souls and empathize with them."

When I find myself in a conflict with someone, or if a friend or loved one is behaving in a frustrating way, one look at their chart can help me put their behavior in perspective, and help me learn how to take their actions less personally. Someone with a lot of fire in their chart, for example, might have trouble expressing their feelings, but they always bring the excitement and passion to a situation. Someone with a very watery chart (insert hand-raise emoji here) may have no problem with expressing their emotions, and can cry at the drop of a hat, but might have trouble feeling grounded or energized.

Add to this the complication that throughout our lifetimes we are all in the ongoing process of learning how to navigate our charts, and there may be times when someone with a Cancer sun (I'll just keep picking on myself) is leaning into the more dysfunctional side of Cancer energy for a period of time—being needy, possessive, moody, easily hurt. Hopefully, that person will be able to come back around to being the loving, nurturing, fiercely loyal friend-mom that they were always meant to be, but their path to get back there might not be something that you are able to understand from the outside.

We can save ourselves a lot of heartache in life if we can learn that so often other people's behavior has very little to do with us. When a friend or loved one acts in a way that is hard to understand, we are able to have more compassion for them if we remember that they have different kinds of challenges from the ones that we have, and they may not be able to see themselves clearly in this moment. That's not to excuse anyone's bad behavior, but to let you get some distance from feeling responsible for someone else's experience in a way that might be more harmful than helpful, for both them and you.

It is important for you to realize that someone else's internal struggle is their responsibility and it is theirs for life. You can't take it on for them. And they can't take yours on for you. It would be like doing someone else's homework. You can have compassion for them, you can hold space for them, but the work belongs to the individual. We can and must be supportive friends, help those in need, and provide support for each other whenever we can, but the internal conversation with ourselves will always be our own.

So how can we have compassion for others while still allowing ourselves to be sad or disappointed about our incompatibilities with them? You can set a strong boundary with a person, even be angry with them, and still hold on to the perspective that they are struggling with their own difficulties. We'll talk about this more in our chapter on energy, but setting a boundary can be as simple as checking in with yourself and realizing when it's time to end an interaction with someone. In this way, you learn to prioritize your own energy. If you know your chart, you can keep an eye on the places where you are likely to give at the expense of taking care of your own needs, and make sure that you protect those parts of yourself.

Sometimes someone we are having a problem with is actually providing us with a helpful cautionary example. If someone is behaving in a way that is frustrating to you, try to get curious and identify for yourself what is frustrating about it. Do you see any part of yourself in their behavior? Do you feel personally implicated? It is likely that something in their chart is reflected in yours, and they are modeling a kind of fun-house-mirror version of a placement that you recognize from your own chart. If you can have compassion for that person, even in your frustration, then you can start to have compassion for that part of yourself that might have the potential to behave in this way.

This practice of understanding our different challenges can help release us from the expectation that our way of doing something needs to look like anyone else's. Someone with strong Virgo energy can give you the advice that if you would just organize every inch of your desk and keep a detailed schedule, you will feel better, but this is terrible advice for someone with strong Sagittarius energy, who needs to live unfettered by such restrictions. There are certainly times when we can and should listen to advice, to ask for and accept help, but at the end of the day it is up to us to grant ourselves the ultimate authority over our way of doing things. No one knows you better than you. And if you want to know yourself even better, your chart is the place to begin.

"I think it is really helpful to get to know the characteristics of a sign," Jeff offers, "but to also know that there's a story of evolution for each sign too. That moodiness of Scorpio, that depth of emotion, is also Scorpio's greatest gift. So how am I working with this energy to creatively transform, which is what Scorpio wants to do?"

When we go back to this idea of stepping off the good/bad binary, we can start to recognize that the things we find challenging about ourselves are often the flip side of our greatest gifts. You can't have one without the other, and you're not supposed to. So that challenge for us becomes about recognizing when we have moved toward this more difficult side of a placement, and to figure out what we need in order to be able to use this part of ourselves for our own good, rather than as something self-destructive. We are never trying to eliminate something that is inherent within us. That would be an impossible task, and one that we would inevitably "fail" at, which would bring on even more self-loathing. We are simply trying to learn from these parts of ourselves by asking them what they need in order to feel safe and able to function in ways that are in alignment with the rest of our charts.

Remember that a sign or placement is never an excuse. Bad behavior is bad behavior no matter what your sign is, and every sign and placement is capable of kindness and consideration. If your behavior negatively affects others, saying, "But I'm a Gemini, I can't help it," is not the correct response. You have complete free will when it comes to how you use the elements in your chart, and one of our main missions in learning about our charts is to figure out how to responsibly tend to our own energetic landscape. We learn to help ourselves and take care of ourselves, with the result that we are then able to be there for others and share our gifts with the collective.

We also want to be careful when we consider the esoteric belief that our souls choose our natal charts before we were born in a kind of contract with the universe. While this can be an interesting lens through which to view our charts, we never want to use this idea to justify thinking that someone with many challenges in their life has brought those challenges upon themselves. That would be a vastly oversimplified view of how the true magic of astrology works. Remember our great cosmic elephant? Never forget that even as we begin to reveal these exciting truths for ourselves, if we get too literal about things, we are going to start calling the thing in our hand a rope, when it's really the tail of our elephant friend.

It is also important never to discount the difficulty of the challenges in our charts. Just because a challenging placement may have a positive flip side, that doesn't necessarily make the challenge any less difficult to navigate. Hopefully, we can remove judgment and embrace compassion for ourselves in those moments, since that sensation of "I shouldn't be feeling this" can often make us feel even worse than facing the difficulty in the first place.

NONLINEAR HEALING

We are not asking astrology to lead us down a singular path that will arrive in a place where we will be given a medal for "Best at Self-Understanding!" This is a lifelong process. Our life is the process, and the process is our life.

"This patriarchal idea of the world that we live in is so linear," Jeff says when I ask him about this idea of personal evolution throughout our lifetimes. "The idea that you go to a psychologist, and you heal, right now, and it's over, is such a linear way of thinking about mental health, when we know that there are both linear and cyclical ways, both working in tandem with each other."

We tend to want a solution that could fit into an hour-long reality show in which someone has a problem, they fight hard for the solution, and at the end they are all better and that is the way that it will stay! This fits nicely into that Hero's Journey structure that we love, and while the concept behind a hero stepping up into their own gifts is lovely, the actual narrative of the hero is never this clear-cut, and to expect our lives to adhere to a linear narrative is to set ourselves up for disappointment.

Even when it comes to mental health (or health in general)—sometimes we get a little better, then get worse. Sometimes we get much better but it takes a very long time. Sometimes a way of doing something that was working suddenly stops working, and we need to find a new way. Or maybe one of those Wheel of Fortune moments knocks us off track, back into a feeling that we thought we were done with.

The cycles of astrology give us a good context to understand this nonlinear healing. Every moment of every day has a chart, with the planets each moving at their own pace, bringing up different issues and challenges for the collective. No matter what our personal chart looks like, we are all existing in relationship to the chart of this moment. Just as we can pull a tarot card in any moment and gain insight into the shifting energetic tides, we can check in with the current astrology and see what energies are affecting the current moment, and how they may be interacting with our personal charts. You can visualize this interaction as a kind of push and pull, almost like the current sky is tugging at different parts of your chart.

Many people understand this in the case of "Mercury retrograde" entering the popular lexicon. Most people have a vague understanding that when "Mercury is retrograde," things seem more likely to go wrong. Communication is difficult, technology malfunctions, unexpected complications arise. But at any given moment each of the planets is giving off a particular energy like this that influences how we experience the world.

As with using tarot, looking at current and upcoming astrology is similar to checking the weather report. If you know that it's going to rain, you can bring an umbrella so you won't get wet. The rain might be inevitable, but getting wet isn't, if you're prepared. This is the place where fate meets free will. We may not have control over the conditions, but we can always control our way of reacting to them and managing them.

Of course, sometimes you read the weather report and expect a light sprinkle of rain, but it ends up being a tsunami. Or maybe you brought your umbrella with the best of intentions and it turned inside out in the first gust of wind. If a particularly difficult Mercury retrograde sends us reeling, we just take this as information for next time, a reminder to back up our files, do things more slowly and deliberately, and triple-check our work. Rather than feeling at the mercy of the planets, we want to look at them as teachers delivering (sometimes difficult) lessons.

Although the rising sign changes multiple times during a day (it's based on where the sun is rising in that moment in relationship to you), and the moon changes signs every few days, completing a full cycle every twenty-nine and a half days, some planets take decades to complete a cycle. Slow-moving Saturn, for example, our largest planet, takes twenty-nine years to return to the place that it was in when you were born, triggering your Saturn return. This is a moment where you are asked to take stock in issues of structure and responsibility in your life, carefully determining what should and should not come with you into your next twenty-nine-year Saturn cycle.

In this way, astrology gives us a clear framework for understanding nonlinear healing. Just as we are not surprised to move through the course of a single day, starting with the sun rising and ending with it setting, the entire universe exists and functions through cycles.

"Astrology is a practice of cosmic mindfulness," Jeff tells me. "Remembering that we do have a body that we are in and that we are here on this planet right now, and knowing that this is part of those bigger cycles, is super magical."

When I visited Ireland, I didn't go a day without a local cheerfully declaring, "Hate the weather? Wait five minutes!" I think about this often when I am going through a difficult moment. If there are phases and transits that hit my personal chart in a way that is particularly challenging, if I wait a couple of days the cycle will have moved on to something else, and I'll probably feel completely differently.

A little secret is that you can have this attitude even if you aren't filtering it through the lens of astrology. No matter what is happening in the current moment, soon it will change into something else. Problems get solved, other challenges arrive, something that felt hugely important suddenly become less significant, maybe even a lovely surprise happens. Nothing is fixed. Change is built into the system.

If you take nothing else from this book, I ask that you promise me that in a moment when life feels intolerable, you will conjure up your inner Irish person to tell yourself to wait five minutes for the weather to change.

THE AGE OF AQUARIUS

Although the way we each react to the astrology of the current moment is influenced by our personal charts, I do love the idea that everyone on this planet is always experiencing the same astrological phenomenon together. Especially when it comes to big, important astrological movements.

"I think that astrology does give you a sense of understanding that not only are we moving through cycles in our own life, but there are also greater cycles at hand," Jeff offers. "It does give me that energy to wake up and be part of that movement."

One of my favorite astrological concepts is that history moves through different ages, represented by the different signs of the zodiac, in which the energy of a certain sign dominates the direction of humanity and of the earth. Ages last a long time—about

2,160 years—the most recent being the Age of Pisces. We are currently in a moment of transition into the Age of Aquarius, popularized many years ago by a song in the musical *Hair*, which associated the Age of Aquarius with a cliché version of sixties flower children. The reality is far more complicated and interesting than that.

My overly simplified description of the sign of Aquarius is that it represents the amazing weirdo, which is partially true. Aquarius is also the sign of the humanitarian, of concern about justice and the collective, and of science and technology.

"Aquarius is here to upgrade archetypes," Jeff says, "so that we can come together with collective intention, and realize that all the archetypes live within us."

It's not difficult to see the ways in which the world has been influenced by these issues in the past fifty or so years, and the ways in which our Aquarian tendencies have advanced very quickly in the past couple of years.

"It's still kind of up for grabs when the Age of Aquarius exactly starts," Jeff tells me. "A lot of people said the one-hundred-and-sixty-year portal started in 1969. And so for the next seventy years after that, basically until around 2040, we're in this initiation into the Age of Aquarius."

It should be no surprise that a number of the people I interview in this book are Aquarians, Jeff included. They tend to be very comfortable with the mystical world and with looking at the bigger-picture issues affecting humanity. I like to think of them as friendly, wise aliens, who are able to zoom out on their spaceships and see the true and complicated energy of the human collective.

I ask Jeff what he thinks about the ways in which the collective has really felt this accelerated Aquarian energy recently.

"Aquarius is about space," he tells me. "It's about the stars, but it's also about all of us having space from each other, so that we can be in our own unique vibration. Then once we're clear on our own unique vibration, it starts to ripple out.

"Aquarius also rules over the internet," Jeff explains. "It's about asking how we can come together and use all our intellectual power and intuition to continue to expand out so that we can really create the future that we feel inside ourselves. It's through shared differences that we come together to form more of a collective intention. We're starting to see that—how to create a supportive community even though we're not together in person. We don't need to be together if it's about energetics. We're in the baby stages of that."

Pluto, which changes signs every twelve to fifteen years, is another interesting lens through which we can look at different generations and their unique strengths and struggles. We might call people boomers, Gen Xers, millennials, and Gen Z, but you could just as easily group them by their Pluto signs. I love this idea that a generation of people is destined to work through something together, while the next generation is meant to evolve it into something else.

These generational trends are just another way of asking some big questions about what it means to live in the age that we live in. What is being asked of us? What is the lens through which we have to learn to communicate with each other?

As someone who is so often caught up in waves of emotions,

I find it very helpful to be able to zoom out to a bigger picture in this way, where we can start to envision ourselves as part of an exciting moment in human history. When so much challenges us, it helps me to understand a context for the ways in which those hardships continue to push us in these new Aquarian directions.

SPIRITUAL BYPASSING

One way that the idea of this collective Aquarian evolution can get misused is to claim that we will only move forward as a collective if we all think happy, positive thoughts all the time. This is a version of what some people call "spiritual bypassing," which we will come back to a few times in this book. Even though the idea of positive thinking and manifesting has its place, to claim that fear and sadness are not a part of our collective evolution is to discount an entire side of our humanity. I would argue that we must allow ourselves to fully experience these difficult emotions in order to understand our full humanity.

In our chapter on witchcraft we will further discuss the ways in which this balance is so important, but if we have learned nothing else from our charts, we know that no human came to this earth to experience one emotion and stop there. We are built to learn to navigate the vast complications of life on this planet, and the more we allow for these complications, the more we move away from the binary thinking of categorizing thoughts and feelings as good or bad. This is also a deeply bastardized version of Buddhism, which asks for mindfulness in the face of all emotions and thoughts, not for an erasure of "bad vibes."

I get very aggravated when I hear people using astrological or other mystical language to promote a way of thinking in which someone rejects not only difficult emotions, but also science—one of the main tenets of Aquarian evolution!

I tell Jeff about my concerns that some people may be using these tools in a way that claims to care about the collective, when really they are shutting out big truths about our human experience.

"The Fool is one of the tarot cards associated with Aquarius," Jeff explains, "which represents a desire to step off the cliff into the unknown and to go on a journey of exploration. And that doesn't always feel safe to some people. It can be really scary to say yes to yourself, to say yes to expanding beyond the boundaries of what you were taught. Aquarian energy does inspire us to show up as ourselves, and the truth that we feel within ourselves, and it can be really painful to do that. Because sometimes it means you have to leave behind relationships that are no longer supportive of that evolution. So we have to have compassion for people who aren't willing to step off the side of the cliff."

When this idea of evolution, both personal and collective, becomes overwhelming for us, we return to our tools, especially our natal chart. Here in your chart you can find that recipe for your own evolution, and allow yourself to take responsibility for your own energetic space in this world. This does not mean creating a happy, impenetrable bubble around you that attempts to send only "love and light" as the singular response to anything difficult. It means learning about yourself in a way that allows you to respect and honor your own individual needs and challenges.

It is about learning to understand how you fit into these big historical cycles that we are all experiencing together.

EVOLUTION

"There's something about participating in this collective experience on Earth that feels celebratory to me," I tell Jeff. "Asking 'Why are you and I, and everyone we know, here at this moment in time?' What is the significance? We're all in this together."

"I believe that the reason that I chose to incarnate here was to evolve," Jeff tells me when I boldly ask him for his own meaning behind human existence. "And I think that, when looking at our birth chart, it offers us a compass to understand our evolution. It's also knowing that everyone's form of evolution is different. It's not going to look the same for everyone. And that really has helped me understand that evolution isn't something for us to pursue in a very type A, Western culture kind of way."

The fact that everyone's evolution will look different also means that it can be difficult to explain your own form of evolution to other people.

"We so often go through these evolutionary changes alone," I say to Jeff, thinking of times when I have felt big shifts in my own life. "There might be only so much about it that we can explain to somebody else. And where we get lost is when we think that we're so alone in it that no one else can understand it. So for me there is a lot of power in having a way to talk about this evolution and a system to help us understand it."

Our tools give us a vocabulary around this evolution. If

change and dealing with difficult situations feels unmooring, we can look at our chart to see what's going on, or pull a card. Maybe we get the Hermit, and all of a sudden we're grounded back down on earth with the idea of needing some quiet time to be alone and process our feelings.

"Working with astrology and tarot isn't for the faint of heart," Jeff says. "Because it is always going to encourage you to evolve and transform. And evolving can be really painful. You can also not be open to the invitation of growing and learning and evolving. And that's also okay."

So we find ourselves back at a theme that we are going to revisit a lot in this book, which is that it's not supposed to be easy. If you are struggling, it doesn't mean that you are doing it wrong. "It" being life itself. Birth and evolution are a messy business, and it is our job to engage with that messiness, to dig around in it to find some important truths for ourselves.

At the end of our conversation, Jeff reminds me of the strange process of how a caterpillar turns into a butterfly. When a caterpillar is in a cocoon, it isn't transforming into an elegant butterfly in some pretty, picture-perfect way. First it has to turn into a bizarre mass of goo that looks nothing like what it was before or what it will become. The cocoon exists to protect the delicate mass of goo in this vulnerable moment, so that it may continue this complicated process of its own personal evolution in security, knowing it is safe to engage with the full messiness of its own existence.

Can we build that cocoon for ourselves? Can we have compassion for those moments in our lives when we feel like a mass of goo longing to skip ahead to the moment when we can spread our beautiful new butterfly wings? And can we allow each other the space that we each need for those gooier moments? Can we have compassion for other goo, remembering our own goo struggles?

Our personal charts give us a path toward understanding that even in our gooiest moments, we are being witnessed by the universe. We are being provided with an identity beyond what we accomplish in our lives, what we do, where we live, what we have. What if who we really are is way more complicated and interesting than these things?

Astrology is a tool that helps us to get deeply curious about ourselves, and to learn that becoming curious about ourselves means becoming curious about humanity, and even about the universe. Another popular new age expression is, "As above, so below." The patterns that exist in the universe also exist inside us, and vice versa. We have to learn that we are each organisms that are part of this bigger whole and that what we do deeply affects one another.

Meanwhile, we can take a cue from our Aquarius friends, and see ourselves as curious visitors to this planet, trying to learn a language that might take us a bunch of lifetimes to figure out, savoring the opportunity to be a part of this ongoing human conversation.

And remember, if you don't like the weather, wait five minutes!

Exercises

BIG THREE

Using your birth information, look up your natal chart online. Write down your "top three"—rising sign, sun sign, and moon sign. Think about how these parts of you overlap, or possibly even contradict each other. If you feel comfortable, do this exercise with a friend, and offer each other mini readings. Someone who knows you well might have insight into the differences (and similarities) between your public and private selves. Do your charts illuminate anything interesting about how your friendship works?

MERCURY RETROGRADE

Check online to see when the next time Mercury goes retrograde and mark it in your calendar. During that time, and in the week leading up to it and the week after, notice what happens to communication and how people around you react to it. Try to get curious about any misunderstandings and see what kind of lessons you might be able to glean from them. Journal about this!

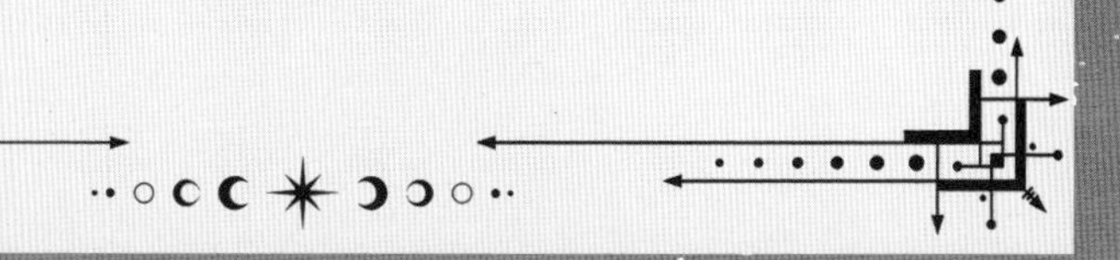

CHAPTER THREE:
Witchcraft

Once you start publicly self-identifying as a "witch," you quickly learn that this word means many different things to different people. For some it's a word that is used by followers of certain cultural and religious traditions. For some it's simply a way of reclaiming an idea about having a relationship to magic and nature. For some it's a political statement—like for the group of activists called W.I.T.C.H. who show up to protests in all black with pointy hats and veils covering their faces. And for some people it's a Halloween costume.

In my opinion, the word "witch" is big enough to contain these multitudes. There is room for all in "witch." Part of why the word is so important to me is that it represents a claiming of personal power, and of self-definition. If you are a witch, you are the one who gets to say what kind of witch you are.

Even within the modern-day witch movement there are many different self-defined witch types—a kitchen witch enjoys a hands-on approach to working with herbs and tinctures. A Wiccan follows the tenants of Wicca, a pagan religion that was developed in the mid–1900s. There are nature witches, water witches, cosmic witches, and many more.

You can adopt any of these titles. Or you can simply be a You Witch.

The history of the cultural representation of witches can be very informative for anyone trying to figure out what this word might mean to them, and if you're drawn to the word, it's probably because of something that you saw in popular culture. Are the witches that you have seen represented always being defined in terms of good and evil? Are the evil ones presented as elderly, traditionally unattractive women, living alone on the edge of town with a bunch of cats, brewing things in a cauldron and possibly luring children to their homes to eat them?

When I was a kid, the very innocent image of the witch that I was peddling in my second-grade class was mostly about possessing supernatural powers. I was pretty sure I couldn't fly, but what if I could? I knew I couldn't move things with my mind, but was there any harm in trying? I was drawn to the title through the promise of being able to engage with magic on a daily basis. I wanted to infuse the everyday with that sense of wonder.

As I got older, there were other parts of the witch mythology that started to become meaningful to me, like the image of the fairy-tale witch who is seen as a threat simply because she exists outside the expectations of her society. If she is categorized as female, she often does not conform to society's expectations of femaleness. Maybe she is draped in black cloaks, with wild hair, warts on her chin, and hair on the warts on her chin. She is uninterested in editing her appearance to fit other people's ideas about her identity. Because of her relationship to nature and to the elements, she is further categorized as wild and evil, even as working against humanity. This image of the witch is so pervasive that it fueled centuries of witch hunts, accusations made against those who did not seem to conform to society's standards.

One of the reasons why the word "witch" and witchy practices have become more popular recently is that some people who identify as members of marginalized groups have found a kinship in this image of the misunderstood female figure. ("Female" here should be understood as available to people of any gender, not a biological categorization. It is important to remember also that there have been many cis male and certainly trans and nonbinary witches throughout history.) For some people, this is a way to reclaim the figure of the outcast, but also of the person who is involved in a private conversation with mystical forces that those living "normal" lives can't possibly understand.

There is a path toward very profound self-acceptance through the idea of the witch. The witch is far too busy with more important things to let herself be distracted by what other people think of her. She therefore has room to define her own ideas about gender and how she presents herself. There is a place for all her hairy warts, both literal and metaphorical. If our true magic lies in our differences, our individual strengths and talents and destinies, then the figure of the witch helps us to celebrate this part of ourselves.

I asked my friend Staci Ivori, one of the most magical practitioners that I know, how she came to use the word "witch" for herself.

"To me it's a form of identity and something that I feel like I just accepted and surrendered to. Not that I became one. It was just something that I was able to embrace."

If you saw Staci walking down the street, even if you didn't know that she is a witch, you would inevitably think, *That person is magic.* I met Staci when we were both asked to be a part of a video shoot for a mutual friend who was making a line of "witch dresses" (yes, I did feel that I had made the correct choices in my life when I was asked to participate in a witch dress video shoot), and I think I probably had cartoon hearts in my eyes the first time I saw Staci. That day she had cascading blue hair with a large blue bow in it, topping off the witch dress with the most voluminous ruffles. Later we sat in my car to warm up from the December cold, and we witches laughed harder than I have ever laughed in my life (there is a reason why witches are accused of cackling).

"The movie *The Craft* sticks out," Staci tells me when I ask about her earliest witchy influences. "That came out when I was thirteen. That was also around the time when *Charmed* came out. But it goes back further than that, when I think about watching *Bewitched* and *I Dream of Jeannie* in my childhood and just really feeling drawn and connected in some sort of way but not really understanding it. Just thinking, 'These are my people.'"

Like me, Staci felt deeply connected to this witchy identity when she was young, but didn't fully embrace the word as an adult until much later.

"I realize now that in having this attraction to creating spells or magic as a kid, there was this desperate need to be saved from

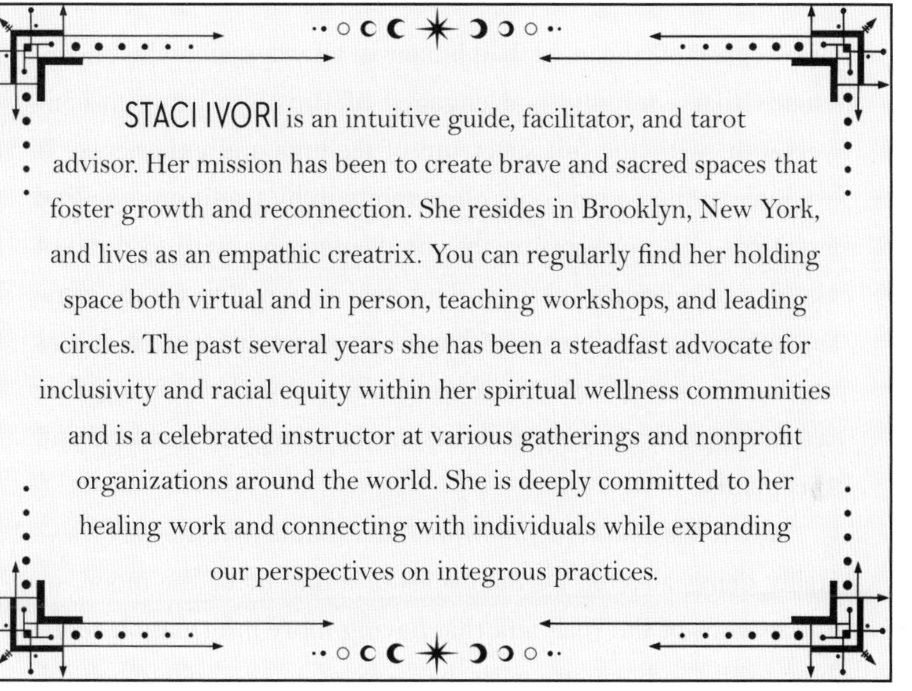

STACI IVORI is an intuitive guide, facilitator, and tarot advisor. Her mission has been to create brave and sacred spaces that foster growth and reconnection. She resides in Brooklyn, New York, and lives as an empathic creatrix. You can regularly find her holding space both virtual and in person, teaching workshops, and leading circles. The past several years she has been a steadfast advocate for inclusivity and racial equity within her spiritual wellness communities and is a celebrated instructor at various gatherings and nonprofit organizations around the world. She is deeply committed to her healing work and connecting with individuals while expanding our perspectives on integrous practices.

the life that I had, dealing with so much trauma and abuse," she says. "I needed something to take it away. Ultimately that became a part of myself that I suppressed for a long time, into my twenties, when I was wanting to believe in something and just feeling disconnected. And then I slowly found my way back to it. I started to unabashedly just identify as a witch and come out of the broom closet."

I ask Staci what kind of reaction she received when she returned to using the word "witch" as an adult.

"I definitely have family members that don't like the word. And there was a little bit of fear with friends, but most people were like, 'Oh, yeah, that sounds about right.'" She laughs.

One of the reasons why "witch" is important to me is that in my definition of the word, "witch" represents someone who has stepped off the good/bad binary in all ways, and who understands that a mindful and engaged life involves being in conversation with the full spectrum of feelings and experience. If we look to the pagan roots of certain witchy traditions, we find practices that were primarily about engaging with cycles—of the day, the year, a lifetime. The goal was not to create some unchanging set existence of happiness and achievement; it was about cocreating with existence itself, and understanding that we, as humans, are inseparable from the energy of this land and this planet.

A witch is also someone who understands that they are inevitably being affected by the cycles of a day, or of the moon, or the seasons of the year, and that having more information about how to live in harmony with these cycles can be hugely helpful. When we suddenly stop expecting ourselves to be active and energized in the middle of winter, for example, when most other animals have gone into hibernation, we are able to release judgment around a lack of productivity. Even if our society is not built to accommodate these cycles (an industrialized capitalist society can't simply decide to just slow down in winter the way a farmer with no fields to plow would), we can find some room to allow ourselves to process these cycles for ourselves.

I believe that witches are the guardians of those things that do not receive enough directed attention in modern culture—the difficult feelings, the cycles of the seasons, the energy of animals and nature. To claim witchiness is to claim an attunement with and responsibility for these things. The true magic comes in the fact that when we pay attention to and honor something that has been neglected by the majority of humanity, it rewards us for this gift of attention. It quickly becomes a symbiotic relationship between you and it.

If you are someone who likes to go foraging for herbs or flowers, the gift of your attention will be rewarded with a kind of abundance that is invisible to someone who simply rushes by the same field to get to a bus stop. This isn't just a "stop and smell the flowers" idea. It's about developing a relationship with the neglected details of our world. Witches know that magic can exist in any moment, and the more of it that you can allow in, the more profound your relationship with it will be.

I have found that the essence of a witchy practice is this kind of directed attention. Spells and ceremonies are simply attention combined with intention, looking at what is here and getting curious about what could be.

CEREMONY

Every culture and religion throughout history has engaged in ceremonies to mark important events or the passage of time, and witchy ceremonies are no different. The idea is to create a container of time and space in which magic can safely flourish and our directed intention can allow for healing and celebration. As with all magic, I believe you can look at the practice of sitting in ceremony literally or metaphorically, or even see it as a mix of both.

What is most important is that a ceremony feels like a safe space for energetic work. This is like our deck of tarot cards waiting to be picked up, or a blank page waiting to be written on. What we are looking for are containers for our feelings so that they can be fully felt and looked at in a way that feels safe.

Usually a ceremony has one or more leaders, who help provide a structure for the group. It can be nerve-wracking to be in charge of a ceremony. I still feel self-conscious sometimes, especially if I am creating a circle for people who have not sat in ceremony with me before. I can get a kind of stage fright, worried that the participants won't be willing to go along with what we're doing. When you are working with energy and magic in this way, you are not only making yourself vulnerable by sharing your energy, but also inevitably becoming hyperaware of the energy of the people around you. There can be a desire to manage their energetic experience in a way that might distract you from the task at hand. Of course you want people to be comfortable, but you shouldn't try to control their experience.

Here's what I can tell you—just as I would often hear months later that an initially skeptical tarot client had later experienced something exactly as I had mentioned in their reading, I have seen deeply skeptical people become enthusiastic participants in ceremony just by letting them get comfortable on their own terms. Something that can help with this is to simply make it fun—is there a dress code? Large flowing muumuus or flower crowns? Maybe you have a friend who is not as much into the magic side as they are the visual elements—why not ask them to make some art objects for your altar?

There are many magical traditions with preset formats for ceremony that you can learn, but for me, I find it best not to worry too much about an idea of legitimacy. Since intention is the main thing that we are working with here, if your intention is to create a safe, magical space, then you have shifted the energy in yourself and in the room simply by focusing on this idea. The more personal you can make a ceremony with your own creativity, the more powerful it will be for you.

"I'm all about people wanting to create their own rituals and just listening to themselves," Staci tells me when I ask her about sitting in ceremony. "The last ceremony I did for the Leo full moon, we made protection oil. I had everybody get some base oil, whatever they had in their cabinets, olive oil, almond oil, or anything else, and then add some essential oils of their choice and dried herbs or flowers. Then it becomes yours. You decide what goes into it, and what these things represent. It's not like it's my recipe that you have to follow. You're imbuing it with your own magic for protection. And what do you want it to protect you against? It all comes from you."

In most pagan traditions (which center on being in constant relationship with the cycles of nature), ceremonies are held on the pagan holidays, which correspond with the solstices and equinoxes. Each holiday honors the time of the year with different traditions—the harvest of the fall, bringing light to the darkest part of winter, celebrating rebirth in the spring (unsurprisingly, these sound a lot like more traditional holidays that non-pagans celebrate too—who do you think came up with the idea of putting a tree in your living room or decorating eggs?).

Another very potent time for holding ceremonies is on the full and new moons. Many witches keep track of where we are in the moon's cycle and base their work on what phase of the moon we are in. The new moon is seen as an especially potent time to set new intentions and call in new energy, while the full moon is a good time to release that which you do not want to bring with you into the next cycle.

I find that I sit in ceremony when I feel like I need it. If I am feeling particularly overwhelmed by big energies or hope to call something new in, I will check my moon calendar and plan accordingly. Often I can tell that a full moon is on its way, because the emotional energy has already become very heightened. (The myth of werewolves transforming on a full moon might just be a metaphor for all of us needing to face our more animal selves at this time of the month.)

I like to prepare for a ceremony by gathering things for my altar, which can be any place in your home that you have assigned for magical work. Some people have big elaborate altars that they clean and refresh every day, but even a small corner of a shelf or windowsill can be an altar if it is special to you. This is a place to keep meaningful objects and focus your magical work. It can also be a place for journaling or meditation, whatever inspires you to engage with your magic. For a ceremony with other people, you may want to create a larger temporary altar that you can all gather around in a circle.

If it's a holiday, I will choose things for my altar that relate to the particular time of year. Samhain, Halloween in non-witchy traditions, is the day that witches honor the dead and their ancestors. An altar for Samhain might include pictures or possessions of deceased loved ones or others whom you want to honor, offerings to them of food or flowers (marigolds are often used in the Mexican Day of the Dead traditions), and maybe a pumpkin or other fruit of the season. I like to follow the Wiccan tradition of bringing the four elements into the circle, maybe a stone for earth set to the north, a small bowl of water set to the west, a candle for fire to the south, and a stick of incense for air to the east. Sometimes I will also add two larger pillar candles for the Wiccan tradition of representing the god and the goddess, the twin energies of the universe. (To me they represent less of actual gendered deities, and more of a welcoming of balance in all things.) Then I'll add some favorite crystals and stones, usually rose quartz for heart-centered energy, selenite for energetic clearing, and black tourmaline for repelling bad energy.

The most important requirement for an altar is that it is meaningful to you. Make it beautiful, let it reflect your mood, your desires, your own aesthetic. If you are feeling called to keep it simple, maybe just lighting a single candle and setting out a crystal or stone that is special to you, then do that. If you want to turn it into an elaborate art project, wonderful! If you are gathering in a group, why not encourage the other members of the circle to contribute objects that are meaningful to them? Collaboration always makes for very powerful magic.

A common way to start a ceremony is by "casting a circle." To cast the circle, the person leading the ceremony (or the solitary practitioner) walks clockwise in a circle around the space where they will be holding the ceremony, and imagines a protective bubble or white light encasing that area and all the people and objects inside it, protecting the space from any interference from outside negative energies. They ask that only energies of the highest good be allowed into this circle.

I then like to light any candles and welcome in the four elements by mentioning them by name—earth, wind, air, and fire. This acknowledges that any magical work that we do in this circle is conducted in cooperation with and with the help of natural forces. I also welcome the god and the goddess—calling in the idea of balanced energetic forces. I then lead the group in a smoke clearing, in which each member of the circle stands and passes a smoking herb bundle up and down the body of the person next to them, picturing a clearing of any negative or stuck energy around their body. Sometimes we pass a soothing essential oil around and anoint ourselves with it.

Depending on the time of year, we will read something about the particular holiday or the astrology of the current moment. If this is a ceremony that is meant to call in new energy, we will write down what we would like to bring in during this next phase. I like to keep these papers folded up, and eventually bury them in the ground, like seeds that are going to sprout. If the objective is to let something go, we write that down and then burn the papers together in a firesafe bowl, depositing the ashes outside when we are done.

I like to end a ceremony with each person picking a tarot card and going around the circle to have the participants offer their interpretation of one another's cards. Even people who are not familiar with the traditional meanings of tarot cards can often offer very insightful interpretations simply based on their own intuition. I also like this practice because it erases any hierarchy in the circle. Every member of the circle is equally qualified to provide mystical guidance; there is no special knowledge needed.

When the ceremony is finished, it's time to release the energetic circle that you have created around your space. To open the energetic circle, I will then walk counterclockwise around the altar, imagining the release of that tight protective bubble, while still asking for ongoing protective energy for the members of the circle. After the circle has been opened and the ceremony is complete, it is traditional to eat and drink something to ground yourself back down into earth energy.

Participating in ceremony like this is something you can only really understand by doing it. Afterward, something shifts in you energetically. I feel the same way after ceremony as I do after a good massage or acupuncture, or after receiving a reading from a good practitioner. The sense is not only of relaxation, but also of being held and supported by very nurturing energy.

Sitting in ceremony by yourself is always an option, and might be something you want to try even in combination with working with others. It can be very helpful to develop your mystical practices this way, and to find out what you like and what works for you. You also never want to let a lack of other willing participants stop you from doing your magical work. Some people will form a committed coven of practitioners who gather together for ceremonies, but celebrating and practicing on your own is just as valid.

Solitary work might also be helpful if you are working through some difficult feelings that you need to process on your own first. This might be a moment when you just want to sit with your own tools—crystals, candles, a tarot deck, a journal—and see what kind of practice feels most helpful. Maybe you light a candle and meditate for a few minutes, then draw some tarot cards and journal on what kind of guidance comes up for you around them. Maybe you simply go outside and have a conversation with the moon. This kind of private witchy work is just as important as anything that anyone else sees.

I do urge you, though, to remember that sometimes a group can do an amazing job of holding space for us when we are going through something challenging. Even if you don't feel comfortable discussing the details of what's going on with you, a ceremonial circle should always feel like a comfortable place to bring that energy. I am often surprised to find that many people in the circle are experiencing similar challenges in that moment, and the energetic camaraderie of knowing that we are not alone in those difficult feelings is deeply helpful.

SPELLWORK AND MANIFESTATION

Whether you follow an outline for a spell that you find online or in a book, or you make up your own, spells are powerful ceremonies all on their own. And again they can function as deeply powerful metaphors, acting to sending a particular kind of energy out into the universe.

As always, the most important thing here is your intention, and you want your intention to always be for the highest good for all. In many witchy traditions there is a "rule of threes," which states that whatever you send out into the universe will come back to you times three. Of course this is a great motivation never to wish someone ill, but really we have to understand that we must always want the highest good for the collective, and harming someone is just not the way to get there.

When you are looking to do a spell, it might be helpful to journal beforehand, to examine more deeply what might actually help your situation. If someone is bothering you, the solution isn't to bother them back, but to ask that they simply focus their attention somewhere else. Maybe you even want to ask that they find happiness and fulfillment in such a way that their behavior changes for the better.

The same need for deep examination applies when we are looking to call something in, especially when this is something very specific. Always ask yourself, what do you really want and why? Do you want a new outfit? Why? Because it will make you feel cute and fresh and stylish? Why not ask directly to feel cute and fresh and stylish, and let the universe figure out how you'll get there?

At the end of any magical request that I make, I always say or write, "this or something better." I have found through experience that the things that I ask for might come to me in very unexpected ways, and that sometimes the thing that I think I want turns out not to be something that is meant to be in my life at all.

This is where the idea of manifestation has been co-opted by people who hope to simplify the concept in order to make it more marketable. Something very important is lost when witchy ideas of manifestation and focused direction of intent meet up with capitalism.

A witchy practice actually does not require anything other than you and your intentions. Sure, it's great and fun to have certain tools to work with—pretty candles or energetically charged crystals—but you don't actually need them in order to do this work. But capitalism is all about creating a false sense of need. And as we will discuss many times in this book, the best way to instill the idea of need in someone is to convince them that they are lacking, that there is something wrong with them that could be fixed if they only wanted it badly enough. Suddenly there is a very specific goal that has been determined by someone else, and if you do not meet that goal, then you have fallen short and you have no one to blame but yourself.

This is where things get tricky, because I do believe very deeply in manifestation and direction of energy. Spells are simply directed intention, clearly stating something to the universe and then backing it up with action. (As with everything, even if you do not believe in a mystical idea of magic, there is still metaphorical and psychological value to forming and stating your intentions, and then following up on those intentions with actions.) But the most important thing about manifestation to me is that we state our intention and then divorce ourselves as completely as possible from the outcome. If a spell doesn't work and you didn't get what you thought you wanted, that doesn't mean that you have failed. Manifestation is not about winning or losing; it is an ongoing conversation between self and the universe.

I don't mean to harp too much on the idea of new age "positive" thinking, but it's important to me to look closely at the ways in which an idea about working with magic can easily be manipulated. Ideas about manifestation that are commercially popular usually involve painting a pretty traditional picture of what someone should be asking the universe for—money, fame, fancy things, success, a certain kind of body. There is a false idea about personal empowerment here—a one-size-fits-all set of goals that has been purposely simplified so as to be easiest to sell to the largest group of people possible.

It's like someone saying to you, "You like nice stuff, right? I can help you get the nice stuff." Then, if you do not get the nice stuff, it must mean that you did not want it badly enough. You did not try hard enough. You are not good at manifesting.

Hooooo boy.

First of all, give me a break.

Second of all—a really great way to make money is to tell people who don't have much in the world that you can offer them a way to get more. Those who have the least are often deeply susceptible to promises of a quick way to abundance, because the actual ways to abundance have been blocked from them. Someone who was born into a situation with few resources may not have the money, time, or information that they would need to train in a profession that they care about and that would help them to better support themselves and their families and communities. Racism, sexism, ableism, and any kind of discrimination will unavoidably influence what someone is able to access and therefore accomplish in their lives, regardless of their ambition or goals. So are they not good at manifesting? Or are they part of a very complicated system of inequality that keeps resources and opportunities from them?

Capitalism thrives on the image of the empowered individual who is in charge of their own destiny above all else. The false narrative of meritocracy—that those who deserve it most will have the most success—tricks people into striving for a future that will glorify them as individuals, which nicely distracts them from looking around at the ways in which this idea of constant competition eats away at the well-being of the collective. Meanwhile, those who are held up as the success stories of individualism are silent about the many privileges that provided them with the tools they used to "manifest" their success.

I'll talk more about this in our chapter on career, but it's important to me to mention here that striving toward an unexamined goal that someone else has told you to value is not empowerment: It is brainwashing.

This doesn't mean that we shouldn't have goals in life, or that we shouldn't ask for things or hope to get things. On the contrary, if we are going to be in conversation with our own personal evolution, then we must. But we must also look very closely at what we are asking for, we must ask if it is in alignment with our highest good and the highest good of those around us, and we must remind ourselves that manifestation is a conversation, not a command.

None of my criticisms of mainstream manifestation practices are made to discourage you from dreaming big and believing that you can accomplish something. In fact, I think that one of the most helpful ways to use manifestation is to ask for support with something that you are already working on. In this way, the manifestation conversation includes you as an equal participant with the universe. You have to back up the request with the determination to show that you do truly desire this thing. If you are already doing your side of the legwork to manifest, you will be ready when the universe sends some magical opportunities your way.

"You can't want to manifest things and then not answer the door when somebody knocks on it, right?" Staci tells me.

"I find that sometimes it happens in a way that's much more complicated than we thought," I offer, "or it's not the way we envisioned it. The process of getting to that outcome can be super complicated. And maybe we need a couple of really intense life lessons on the way there."

"And then that gets all the triggers going and the shadows popping up," Staci says. "And that's hard."

I cannot tell you how many times in my life I have wished for something, attempted to manifest it both energetically and practically, poured my whole self into it, and just felt over and over that I was hitting a brick wall. These were incredibly frustrating times, when I felt like the Fool card standing on that cliff yelling up at the sky, "But this is a good idea!" My Scorpio moon would kick in hard in these moments, making me feel sorry for myself and angry that the universe had not kept up its end of the bargain and instead had thrown me into seeming chaos.

Every single time I ended up so deeply grateful that the things I thought I wanted did not happen.

Ideas around fate and your life path come into play here—what is meant for you to experience in this lifetime and what is not. If you keep knocking on the door of a goal or an opportunity that is not truly meant for you, the universe will eventually send you a very loud and unmistakable NO in order to get you to move on down that hallway to the next door, where inevitably something else is waiting for you. This is the manifestation magic of "this or something better." We remove our ego from the situation by admitting that we may not know all the options or implications yet.

Of course, knocking on a bunch of wrong doors is an important part of the process. I have been in unhealthy friendships that led me to healthy ones. I have had toxic work situations that led to beautifully aligned ones. I have evolved in much more complicated ways from my failures than I have from my successes. We never want to judge or discount the importance of that journey. But you can make it easier on yourself by paying attention to what the moment is actually telling you, even if it doesn't look the way that you thought it would, and even if things are not happening on the timeline that you wanted them to. I have often found that something that I was attempting to manifest had to come later than I expected it to, simply because I actually wasn't ready for it yet, even though I thought I was. There was so much more information that still needed to be revealed to me before I could take on the responsibility of what I was calling in.

As with all our work, we are simply erasing the binary—there is no success or failure in manifesting. The truth is far more complicated than that, and because it involves a very private conversation that you are experiencing with the universe, it is not something that is easily explained to other people, and that's okay.

Often when I work with manifestation spells, I focus on big

concepts like protection (for myself and those I care about), removing fear and self-doubt, and calling in joy and love. I find it can help to identify a feeling, and stay open to many different ways that this feeling may manifest in my life.

Of course I can write "fear" and "sadness" and "self-doubt" down on pieces of paper and burn them in ceremony on the full moon in order to banish them as many times as I want, but the truth is that they are part of the human experience, and will and should be part of an ongoing conversation in our lives. We can ask to deal with these things better, to have support in facing our fears and our doubts, but hoping to banish them altogether is not necessarily in your highest good.

Often those who hope to capitalize on mainstream ideas about manifestation will claim that having any negative thoughts or feelings will prevent you from manifesting good things in your life. The belief is that fear and other difficult feelings operate on a "low vibration," and not only bring you down but also keep humankind from evolving. The idea seems to be that if you are scared, sad, or angry, you're basically bringing down all humanity. *Now please enter your credit card number to enroll in a course in which you will learn to stop ruining everything for everyone.*

As we talked about earlier, one of the things I appreciate the most about the word "witch" is that, to me, it implies someone who is not going to discount the energetic roles of darkness and difficulty. A witch can see the darkness as an ally and a tool, and possibly even a friend. Some things are just sad. Some things are hard. Some things are scary. Some things make us angry. Some things can cause lasting trauma that requires a lot of hard work to heal. This is part of our experience as humans on this planet, and to claim that anyone who feels these things is somehow energetically self-sabotaging themselves is to set all humans up to feel like failures.

SHADOW WORK

Back to our old enemy "spiritual bypassing," the practice of discounting or avoiding difficult feelings in the name of "staying positive." Usually people who do this have simply not developed the tools to look directly at difficult things and therefore hope to discount the importance of those feelings by saying that they are not valid or helpful. It is unfortunate that a lot of well-meaning people can fall into this trap, especially if they are very sensitive, even empathic, and they have not learned how to cope with the overwhelming feelings that can come with looking directly at hard truths. Instead they simply shut down that part of themselves, while claiming to be chasing "high vibe" enlightenment.

What's really unfortunate is that people who tend toward spiritual bypassing have co-opted some actually helpful ideas and oversimplified and misrepresented them in order to serve their own agenda. Of course when we connect "positive thinking" to practices of gratitude, it can be hugely helpful in our lives. We always want to focus on the abundance available to us in the present moment, and learn to express gratitude for that abundance. We can imagine gratitude as a kind of full watering can, helping the abundance of the current moment grow and flower.

BUT!!!!!

We can express gratitude, focus on abundance, look toward our big, ambitious goals, and also acknowledge that some things in life are deeply challenging, and that no one is exempt from these challenges. To demonize this kind of hardship and the feelings that may come along with it is to blame ourselves for somehow not thinking positively enough to avoid it, and to unfairly minimize the role of many different energetic factors in people's lives.

We know from looking at our charts that the hard lessons are built in from the beginning, and to avoid learning to work with this energy is to set yourself up for a personal crisis. Back to our weather metaphor—this would be like refusing to own an umbrella because it is sunny for a few days. You have no control over the rain, and when it does start raining again, that is not a judgment on you. And you are going to be a lot more comfortable in the inevitable downpour with that sturdy umbrella handy.

Whenever you encounter any practitioner, you always want to closely examine the context for their practice, but when you encounter someone who is specifically claiming to work with manifestation through simplified positive thinking, I ask you to really get curious about why this person has developed a practice that insists on spiritual bypassing.

"When we talk about light and shadow, good/bad, black/white, there are always these negative connotations toward shadow," Staci tells me. "And I always say, honor both things for what they are. That dark shadow is not bad because it's the opposite of light."

"Shadow work" is a psychological concept in which we actively face and learn to work with the more challenging parts of ourselves.

"I'm definitely a person that does shadow work," Staci says. "I feel like that's one of my specialties, being able to be a good a guide and a facilitator for that, because I've been there so many times. When I hold space, I want people to feel like they're allowed to have emotional freedom. Whatever you're feeling is welcome."

"It makes me think of things like diet culture," I offer, thinking of spiritual bypassing, "where you're holding up this ideal of a certain kind of body, but instead the ideal here is love and light. So anyone who's not reaching that ideal is meant to feel like a failure."

"It's irresponsible not to acknowledge the darkness or the pain or the trauma that so many people experience," Staci agrees. "It can make someone feel like they shouldn't be experiencing what they're experiencing. Even when people cry, people are so uncomfortable with that. They are so quick to just shove a tissue in your face. And it's so unfair, because it makes us feel ashamed of our emotions."

Just as Lindsay was talking about holding space for someone in a tarot reading, holding space is a practice that we can also cultivate for ourselves in our witchy work, especially since this work is designed to be sensitive to nuanced energy and to embrace the idea of cycles. Sadness moves to happiness, back to sadness, back to happiness. We would never judge one part of the cycle as inappropriate. Facing something difficult is the first step to learning from our difficult feelings and integrating that complexity into our own evolution. Sure, happiness feels better, but that doesn't mean that the hard feelings aren't just as valuable and important.

A couple of years ago both of my beloved cats died within nine months of each other. They were both old, they had been with me and my wife for our entire adult lives, and they had lived very happy lives filled with many cuddles and much love and care. But these two cats were our companions and familiars, and the experience of caring for them through this transition was devastating. I still start crying if I think about them for too long, and there was a certain point in those years after they were both gone that I wondered if my grief was ever going to subside. Wasn't I supposed to get over this? Yes, I'm a sensitive person, yes, I lost my animal best friends, but when was I going to stop crying myself to sleep?

My friend and teacher Bakara, who was the one who brought me to the Brooklyn Fools tarot group that so deeply changed my life, was doing tarot readings every Sunday on Instagram Live during this time. They were attended by hundreds of people, and her words often delivered staggering wisdom. One Sunday she was talking about her mother, who died when she was young. "I will never not be sad about this," she said. The sadness was simply a part of her, something that had been integrated because it had been faced.

I found this way of thinking to be so freeing. I will always be sad about losing my familiars, and there's nothing wrong with that. It was, simply, very sad. The depth of my feeling exists in correlation to how deeply I loved them in life, and being sad about that loss does not take away from all the joy that I experienced with them.

A difficult period like this in our lives can contain all our complex feelings—grief, happiness, excitement, exhaustion. We have to allow room for all of this, or else we are judging and denying our own experience. This is especially true when difficult things are happening in the world—war, pandemics, violence, inequality. An empath is going to have to make room to process any difficult collective energy that comes their way, and learn to allow for the complexity of such feelings. We can mourn the state of the world, and also allow joy into our lives. We can experience extreme sadness, and still find ways to connect and celebrate with others. Anyone who brings judgment to the depth and range of your feelings is afraid of their own feelings overwhelming them.

I mention all this here in our witch chapter because centering this practice of acceptance and curiosity about feelings in a witchy, mystical framework has been the best tool that I have found to release self-judgment around these things.

"It's so important to me to give some dignity to that struggle," I say to Staci, "because I think, especially if we're in depression, it can feel really pathetic or really just, like, sad and small and weird."

"So many of us walk around in shadow," Staci notes, "and are just leaving it everywhere, and not realizing it because we're told not to think about it. And I think, like right now, we're in the winter months, and we can see the shadow around us in these cold days when things are literally dying, and everybody is slowing down. So how are you feeling? Most likely other people are feeling that too. And it's okay. Part of what you're supposed to learn about is how you're able to appreciate the light when it comes back again."

KEEPING AN EYE ON CULTURAL APPROPRIATION

There is another, even more complicated problem with the idea of holding up "light" and villainizing the concept of "darkness."

"There are so many people that identify as 'white witches,'" Staci tells me. "In their mind, they're meaning it as a 'good witch,' but that would mean that a 'black witch' would be a bad witch, or associated with 'black magic' and things like that. Being a Black woman, and a woman who comes from an African tradition, even my own family believes that the practices of our culture and our particular tribe is 'black magic.' That's all that they see. Voodoo is a religion that's primarily about healing, but we don't hear about that. And that goes back to slavery, and all this manipulation of saying that what you believe in is wrong."

This brings us to a very important issue of examining the cultural context behind certain practices, attitudes, and ways of talking about things, and making sure that we are being responsible if we are using any practices that come from outside our own personal heritage. Because mystical ceremonies and healing and manifestation practices exist in almost every culture, much of what we see today as "modern witchcraft" is an amalgamation of many different cultural traditions.

"People have been trading since the beginning of time, sharing recipes, sharing remedies, and sharing their spiritual practices and their rituals," Staci says. "And it is totally fine to partake in other traditions and other cultures' practices. But the difference is cultural appropriation is simply taking something from someone else and claiming it for yourself, without any sort of acknowledgment, or education about where it's come from. There are so many people teaching things that are of another culture, or of another lineage, and they don't know much information behind it. There are a lot of cultures that have taken on students in order to pass things down, but the only people who could have the privilege of being there were people who had money, and that isn't always people who come from that history."

"Do you recommend for people who are starting out on this path that they look into any magical lineage in their own ancestry and try to find their way through that?" I ask Staci.

"Absolutely," she says. "I would definitely encourage people to just dive into that. Asking their grandparents, if their grandparents are still around, or taking a pilgrimage if they can to where they come from, learn more about the foods that they ate, what they use to cure certain things. But it's hard. I mean, for me, as a Black American, it's very hard to figure out where you've come from if you're a descendant of slaves. I didn't grow up with something like that being passed down, like remedies, or recipes or things like that. And so even now it's been something that I've just had to slowly discover on my own."

"That's work that's important to do anyway," I say, "especially if you're going to have a practice that works with honoring ancestors."

"I also want to mention," Staci says, as her cat crosses the computer screen in front of her, "I've been challenged and questioned on this a lot. There are people that have been adopted into other cultures, there are people that have grown up practicing something—like how Tina Turner is a Buddhist and goes hard for Buddhism. I don't think that there's anything wrong with that, because she acknowledges what it is and where it comes from, but also how she deeply connects to it. So people can deeply connect to something of another culture, or religion, and it doesn't mean that you can't explore that. You just have to do it with reverence."

If we are going to be responsible witches, we must always be conscious of any privilege we possess, and any ways in which certain practices might be seen as insensitive. Throughout history mainstream culture has presented deeply racist images to us of many different cultures' religious practices. Staci mentioned the public perception of Voodoo, and of course when we look at the history of representation of Native American practices in popular culture, we are dealing with a white supremacist view looking in on the practices of a people that they are attempting to "other," minimize, make fun of, and much worse.

What we have seen in the last couple of decades is members of marginalized groups, empowered mainly by the communication possibilities of the internet, speaking up for themselves and their cultures. When this happens, those of us who are not members of that marginalized group are being given the opportunity to now hear the perspective of someone from inside this culture.

We want to be mindful of the painful legacy of a colonization mindset and the complicated history of people co-opting cultural traditions while having no concern for the people who created those traditions. Anger and frustration about people removing cultural practices from their context stems from this very complicated history.

"Using smoke cleansing as an example," Staci says, "smudging is a sacred Native American practice where white sage or sweet grass is used in cleansing and then in ceremony. It's such a sacred medicine and it's not just for people to burn willy-nilly. But people have always burned herbs for various reasons; it's not always sage. So what was around in the lands that you came from?"

The other important thing to remember when we are thinking about being anti-colonialist in our practices is that no single member of a group can, or should be expected to, represent a definitive perspective of an entire group of people. One person may find a non-Native American person burning sage to be offensive, while someone else might be okay with it if it is purchased from a Native American–owned business that harvests the herb responsibly, or even if you grow your own. There is no monolith of opinion, and something that can happen quite often, especially for white people, is that they are looking for someone to tell them what the "right" thing to do is, and the answer is not always simple. As Staci points out, there is a lot of complexity to the issue of adopting a practice that is not a part of your personal heritage, and that complexity can make people very uncomfortable.

"If you hear people are saying something is offensive or inappropriate," Staci says, "be curious about why they're saying that. Check in with yourself. Is this worth you diving into if it could possibly be offending someone?"

"It should be the beginning of a conversation," I offer, "rather than a moment of responding by saying 'How dare you accuse me of doing something offensive?' That defensiveness is what shuts down the conversation, which is a shame when the conversation is the most important thing."

Staci reminds me again of the idea of creating new rituals for ourselves to use in ceremony, bringing our own imagination into the process. We can take inspiration from older practices, but allow them to change into something that we have a personal connection to, like when Staci guided the members of her full moon circle to create their own original protection oils.

"It's different if you're doing that versus a hoodoo honey jar spell," Staci tells me. "Because that's very specific, and there are specific things that go into it. So you can't wing that and then call it a 'hoodoo honey jar spell.' But you can create a sweetening spell. You can do a honey spell. There's a huge difference between it being a particular sacred practice for a certain religion, versus just using what the action is."

Within this context, we also want to try to be the most responsible consumers that we can be. Maybe your first tarot deck came from a chain store, where you picked it up because you thought it was cute. That's totally fine, but as you learn more, you will probably want to shift your consumption to smaller businesses run by practitioners who are committed to sustainable and responsible practices. We want to use our mindfulness here, directing our attention toward the energetic makeup of the objects we purchase and the ways that we purchase them.

"I think that's where even well-intentioned people can get tripped up," Staci says. "Someone could buy something with all the best intentions and just think, 'Wow, this is so cool.' And it's this completely bastardized thing with no connection to anything."

Learn about different magical practices, get curious about the ways in which those practices are being represented to you, and at the end of the day, remember that a personal practice is about empowering yourself by making your own kind of magic. A witchy practice can look however you want it to look. You can be someone who works with the cycles of the moon, who just celebrates certain holidays, who creates an altar in their home with beloved objects and sometimes lights a candle and journals to connect to their unconscious magic self. All of this is valid. The more you follow your own imagination and intuition when it comes to creating your witchy life, the more empowered you will start to feel from it, because it will be completely yours.

THE TOOLBOX

With our witchy saying, "As above, so below," we understand that we are made up of the same stuff as the universe, and we are occupying space in this world and learning to work in harmony with its forces, just as the cells of our bodies learn to adapt to our energetic environments.

Working with this energy is truly a superpower. When you are comfortable interrogating your emotions, you become someone who knows how to understand what is important to you, what you want to nurture in your life, and what kind of energy you want to bring in. When you pay attention to the energy around you, you learn what exists in the present moment for you to work with, and how you can begin to manifest more of what makes you feel most alive and most in alignment. This does not come naturally to everyone, and if it is a part of who you are, consider it a gift, even in moments when that sensitivity can feel like a burden.

We spend so much energy fighting with "what is," and I find learning to work with the energy of our world's natural cycles can make you feel like you are no longer walking against the wind, trying to figure out why you can't get up a certain hill. You are no longer fighting "what is" but instead aligning yourself with it. You are not imposing your will on existence, but learning to work with it in the way in which it wants to be worked with.

Working with the natural world can mean starting to eat foods that are in season, learning about different herbs and flower essences and how they can support you, but it can also be as simple as taking a walk and grounding your energy into the earth under your feet or watching a sunset. Being in awe of the beauty of nature is one of the best forms of magical gratitude that there is. (I like to thank the sun after she goes down for putting on such a great show.) We show gratitude for the beauty and mystery of the world by fully taking in these mysteries and allowing their magic to change and nurture us.

We can also learn some really practical lessons from observing the natural world—plants can model a way to nurture and protect your immune system. We can look to the interplay of the four elements of earth, air, fire, and water to try to find a balance in our physical and emotional selves. Maybe after we have a conversation that is especially fiery, we listen to some watery soothing music in order to restore balance. You can even do this within your interactions with others. Maybe a friend is trying to solve a problem and everything she says is truly up in the air—can you bring in some grounding, earthy ideas to help bring her back into alignment?

Pagan and witchy traditions offer a way to connect to others, and also a way to nurture a connection with the natural world that can help support you, even when you are not in community. You are never alone, because you are always existing in a relationship with magic.

With this gift of an understanding of daily magic comes the responsibility of always acting from a place of integrity and the highest good for ourselves and those around us. Of course, we may not always completely succeed at this. Sometimes our emotions get the best of us and spill out onto other people. Sometimes we hope to manifest something that later we realize was ego-driven. That's all okay. As with everything, this is a process of learning and adjusting.

At the end of my conversation with Staci (I could easily

talk to her for four more hours), I ask her if she has a toolbox of strategies that she is able to pull out in emotionally difficult moments.

She considers this for a moment, then says, "The toolbox would probably be the archetypes within me that I call on. How would my Queen react to this in this moment? How would the Mother part of me react to this in this moment? What does the Child part of me need right now? And how does the Mother part of me offer some nurturing to myself? Where is my Warrior? Is it out of balance or in balance? Do I want to fight? Do I need to have agency and stick up for myself?"

This is such a beautifully witchy answer to me, because it's engaged with both the complicated psychology of our feelings and also the idea of magical empowered personas that can help restore us to balance. A witch is all these things—queen, mother, child, and warrior—and the more we can learn about the wisdom that all the parts of us have to offer, the more we can live in alignment with our own magic.

And remember—if being a witch is something that is calling out to you, it means that you are already a witch, and you are ready to get a closer look at the magic that has always existed in your life, and the magic that you will learn to make.

Exercises

FULL MOON CEREMONY

Look up online when the next full moon is and make a plan to do a small ceremony on that night, either alone or with a friend. Don't worry about casting a circle or anything too elaborate right now. Simply start by lighting a candle and writing down something on a piece of paper that you would like to get rid of. Sometimes it's nice to make this more about a feeling—would you like to have less self-doubt? Less stress? Less of a conflict with someone? Once you have written it down, fold it up and hold it in your hand and really think about what it is you are ready to release. In a firesafe bowl, in a very firesafe area (a bathtub can be good for this, or a safe spot outside) use your lit candle to set the paper on fire. Imagine this thing leaving you. When you are done, if you can, go outside and scatter the ashes, saying a final goodbye. If it's a clear night, look up at the moon and thank her for her help.

MANIFESTATION SPELL

Think about something that you would like to call in and manifest. Spend a few minutes meditating on what

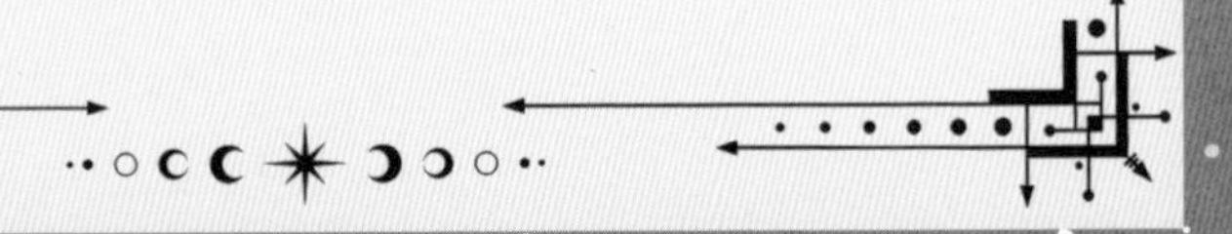

exactly it would look and feel like to manifest this thing, and what about this feeling is important to you to bring into your life. Now create an altar to what you hope to manifest. You can gather crystals, stones, candles, leaves, mementos, pictures, whatever feels relevant and helpful. Write down what you hope to manifest on a piece of paper, followed by the words "this or something better," and add it to your altar. Light a candle and sit and meditate at your altar periodically when you can over the next few days. If new insights about what you are trying to manifest occur to you, write them down and add them to the altar.

CREATE AN ANCESTOR ALTAR

This is a great exercise to do around Samhain/ Halloween and the Day of the Dead (celebrated on November first and second). Collect any pictures or mementos of family members or ancestors who have passed on. These can also be from chosen family, or just people who are no longer with us whom you would like to honor. Add things to your altar that they would enjoy, like flowers, trinkets, or even snacks (as long as they won't attract bugs!). Spend the week leading up to Samhain tending to the altar and asking your ancestors any questions that you might have for them. Write down any wisdom that comes through.

CHAPTER FOUR:
Energy and
Spirit Guides

I attempted to start writing this chapter approximately ten times, for some reason struggling more and more each time. It got so extreme and I plunged myself into such a deep despair over it that I had to stop, follow my own advice, and ask what was behind this resistance. And as soon as I stepped away and asked the question and made space to listen, an answer came.

Because this is the most vulnerable chapter for you to write.

Yeah, but why? Throughout this book I'm writing about my mental health, my experiences with therapy, my career missteps, my biggest anxieties. Why does this topic in particular make me feel so vulnerable?

Because it's the easiest to make fun of. Because it sounds the silliest. Because it's about your most personal connection to your everyday energy.

Because you are talking to your imaginary friends.

"Kids have imaginary friends," Aja Daashuur, otherwise known as the Spirit Guide Coach, tells me, "and some of those imaginary friends are spirits and guides and some of those imaginary friends are imaginary friends, and what is wrong with that?"

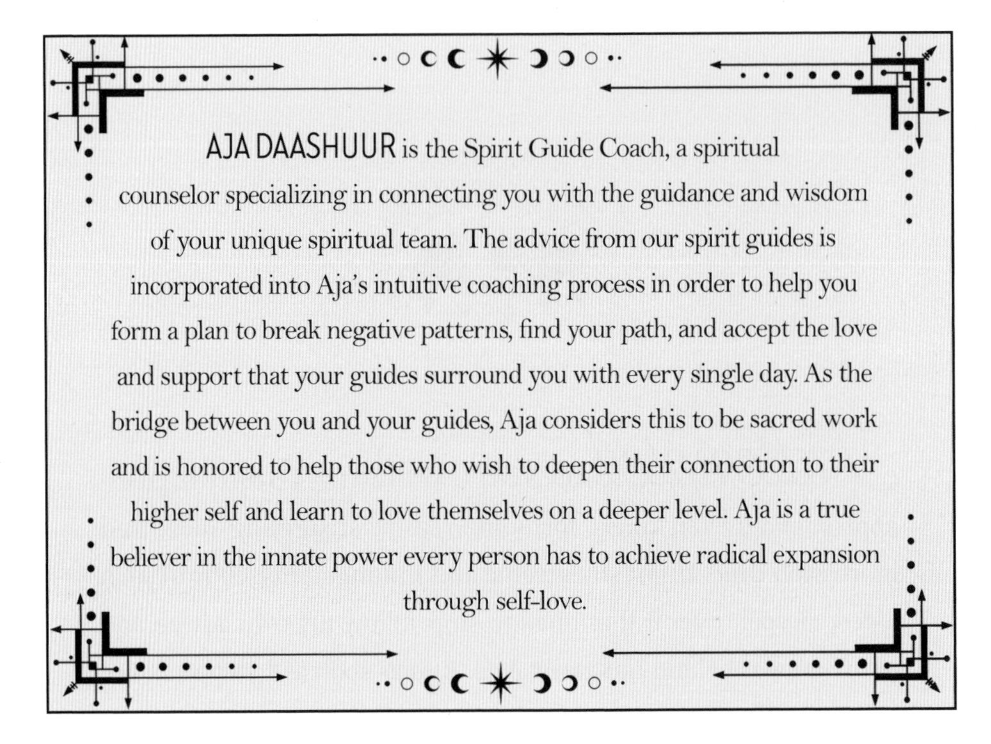

AJA DAASHUUR is the Spirit Guide Coach, a spiritual counselor specializing in connecting you with the guidance and wisdom of your unique spiritual team. The advice from our spirit guides is incorporated into Aja's intuitive coaching process in order to help you form a plan to break negative patterns, find your path, and accept the love and support that your guides surround you with every single day. As the bridge between you and your guides, Aja considers this to be sacred work and is honored to help those who wish to deepen their connection to their higher self and learn to love themselves on a deeper level. Aja is a true believer in the innate power every person has to achieve radical expansion through self-love.

In that first session with an astrologer that I had when I was twenty-two, he told me that I am a skeptic by nature. I am often too suspicious of human-made systems to blindly trust what someone tells me without experiencing something myself directly. But I've got a bit of an "I'll try anything once" attitude when it comes to mystical practices. So a few years ago, when I saw that one of my favorite mystical practitioners who I follow online was giving a workshop near me in Brooklyn, I figured I should check it out.

Aja is someone who has both a lovely online presence AND the goods to back it up. She inspires thousands of people on a daily basis with her beautiful words and guidance, and she possesses the rare gift of being able to create meaningful community through her deeply welcoming but no-nonsense vibe. The more I think about it, the more it makes sense that she would end up being one of the most important and influential practitioners in my life. First of all, she's from the same part of New Jersey as I am, so I felt an immediate kinship in Garden State sensibility; she has an incredibly high BS detector when it comes to people misusing and co-opting mystical ideas for their own gain; and she is in possession of an enviable caftan collection. She calls out spiritual bypassing and cultural appropriation wherever she sees it, and as a member of the BIPOC community, she continues to bring a much-needed political perspective to a wellness world that too often shies away from political engagement. She is also deeply practical, especially for someone who spends much of her days in communication with the spirit world.

"Be a skeptic!" Aja insists when I ask her if she thinks it's okay to be skeptical about the idea of communicating with spirits and energetic entities. "I'm a skeptic. I don't believe anything until I've experienced it. I think it's really healthy, especially when we're dealing with the spiritual realm, which is so smoke and mirrors."

The field of Spiritualism, most simply described as being in communication with spirits, has a long history of people taking advantage of an audience's gullibility. Two of the people who helped create the modern-day Spiritualist movement starting in the mid-1800s, the Fox sisters, Maggie and Kate, later called the authenticity of their experiences with spirits into question by claiming that they had made the noises that they attributed to spirits themselves, and then later reversing that to insist again that the communication was real. More recently, we have employees of TV shows for famous psychics revealing that they gathered information by listening in on the audience members' conversations. When it comes to communicating with the spirit world, it's easy to manipulate things for the sake of putting on a good show. The line between magic and magician gets very blurry.

It makes me sad to think that some bad apples could spoil the entire concept of spiritualism for some people, but of course I understand it. It's one thing to engage with a sense of generative, creative energy, and it's another to put names and forms to that energy.

As with our perception of witches, we can't help but be heavily influenced by the pop culture depiction of communication with otherworldly forces. This phenomenon is never depicted as something subtle and potentially helpful. In fact, it provides the premise for pretty much the entire genre of horror. Once again we are taught to actively fear something that exists in flow with magic, separating us from having an empowered relationship to this source of energy.

SPIRIT GUIDES

The simplest explanation of spirit guides is that they are energetic entities that support us in our lifetimes. There are many cultural traditions that practice a form of working with spirit guides, whether it's an honoring of ancestors, communication with the dead, or an experience of messengers or angels. Some people believe that guides were assigned to us at birth, or that we agreed to work together with our guides before we came to this current incarnation. Learning to communicate with these entities is another way of tuning in to the energy of the present moment and finding support for ourselves there.

But as with many of our tools, you can also experience this kind of communication as a metaphor, if the reality of magical advisors seems too far-fetched to you.

"You really can look at all of this as an exercise of your subconscious giving you information from the pieces of your mind that are either dormant or that you don't give the time to listen to," Aja offers. "All this psychic work is about getting to know yourself without judgment. Things in your subconscious that are saying, 'Hey, pay attention to me.'"

To me, working with guides is simply another way of looking at activating our sensitivity and intuition. It can even be as simple as what Staci described in our witch chapter—thinking of different archetypes that we can call upon in different situations. If thinking about spirit entities brings up resistance in you, or makes you think only of scary movies, I urge you to open your mind a little around what role these mystical forces might play in your life.

It is telling that our culturally acceptable connection to spirituality is almost always filtered through the hierarchy of organized religion. Only once a ton of human-made rules (which are often misogynist, homophobic, transphobic, and designed to make sure a few cis men retain power at all costs) are put into place, do we seem to be allowed to talk about things like the "holy ghost."

"That's what humans do," Aja says when I bring up my frustrations with organized religion policing our connection to Spirit (a word that can be used to mean both source energy and actual spirits). "We complicate things. I mean, I went to Catholic school, and I remember when Monty first wrote the words 'angel' and 'god.' I was like, 'Oh, look, I can't do this.' But he said, 'We're just using words that you can understand. Don't you kind of know what an angel is?' 'Yeah.' 'Okay, so we're going to use that.'"

Aja has very much modeled for me a way to develop an open-mindedness around these concepts while always staying conscious of the many ways in which they could be misused. She has helped me see the benefit of erasing the binary between even science and magic. Is it brain chemistry? Is it magic? Can it be both?

Oh, and Monty is the name of one of her main guides. He's very fiery.

I ask Aja what prompted her to begin to work with her guides, and I'm not surprised to hear that it was a search for help in a moment of mental health crisis that opened her mind to this kind of communication.

"I had been really, really depressed, and not knowing where to turn," she tells me. "I hit a wall and just thought, enough is enough. So I just started listening to my intuition. I'd be at work and think all of a sudden, 'I wonder if you can meet guides?' And I would Google 'meet your spirit guides.'"

Aja found a teacher who helped her further explore the concept of communication with guides. She learned about the practices of clairaudience (hearing messages), clairvoyance (seeing information), and automatic writing (channeling writing by allowing unseen or subconscious forces to move your hand).

"It opened up a door for me," she tells me. "Just trusting that if a thought entered my mind, I should follow it. I started having these tendrils of connection, like imagining them with me when I was walking to the J train, and then connecting to them through my daily meditation practice, which I had also had a lot of resistance to and made fun of people for doing. Those are the things that led me to ultimately opening a door for my spirituality, and this larger connection with my guides. It was a progression, like anything else."

It took Aja a while to get comfortable admitting that she was engaging in such a mystical practice.

"I didn't talk about my spirituality with anybody," she explains. "I think I was so scared that someone's opinion would derail this precarious stepping into a desire to understand myself that I kept it very close to my heart. And that actually continued for a few years."

Eventually Aja started offering sessions to people where she would communicate with both her guides and her client's guides in order to give them advice. It was only once she started to see the communication working when it came to other people that she felt she needed to take her practice seriously. She then started leading workshops to help others connect with their guides through guided meditations, and this is how I first experienced my own form of communication with such helpful energetic forces.

Before every session Aja always states what she has told us here—that even if you feel that a journey is simply leading you to connecting with your unconscious intuition, that's still a totally valid form of learning about yourself. To me, this is how all these tools should be presented, as deeply personal ways of connection that should be used in whatever way is helpful for you.

"When I first started meditating," Aja tells me, "I did it without anything, and it was really hard for me to just sit in silence. My brain is always going. Now the meditations that I do are a little bit different, because they really are journeys. We're just creating vibrations that allow you to discover new things about yourself, and what's coming from your subconscious, or the other side, or your guides or ancestors. Guided meditation can almost be like the crayons in the box. 'I'm going to choose this color or that color and see what happens and what opens up for me.'"

Working with guides has given me some of my most meaningful experiences of receiving messages from mystical forces. Aja provides the structure for asking a question of your guides and making space for helpful information to come through in her meditations, but you can do this for yourself at any time. Just as you ask a question of your tarot deck before pulling cards, you can ask for information from your guides and sit in meditation or journal and see if any helpful information comes through. Sometimes an answer will come in a tangible form, like finding a helpful book or receiving a phone call, and sometimes it will simply be a thought that presents itself.

But your relationship with your guides can be even more casual than that.

"First, I would say just start talking out loud when you get up in the morning," Aja says when I ask her how to get started. "Like, 'Hey, everyone, I can't hear you, but I know you're there.' We're just strengthening the muscle. And then you can start pulling oracle or tarot cards, you can ask, 'What are you like? Where are you from? What are you here to help me with?' I always want people to take them off this pedestal. I used to envision talking to my guides at the kitchen table, like, 'All right, what's going on, what's happening?' and let them all speak. I know it can get really iffy here. 'Am I just talking to myself? Or am I talking to other people?' And look, you know, it doesn't matter. Even if you are just talking to yourself, what's coming up? What's making you laugh? What's making you think? We can do this with our shadow self, with our higher self, our past self. We can do it with our future self and just hold court and sit and discuss things. And again, if you don't believe in these specific things, you can visualize them as different parts of the human psyche."

EMPATHS AND HSPS

Someone who is highly sensitive to the energies around them is going to be especially receptive to this kind of guidance, but it is also important for a sensitive person to learn about and establish energetic boundaries when doing this kind of work. Empaths are people who are very aware of the dynamics of the energies around them, especially the energies of the other people around them, to the point that they often have trouble telling the difference between their own energy and that of other people. Sometimes empaths are aware of when they take on the energy of others—like if a friend is sad and it makes you sad to see them sad—but more often the energetic load is more unconscious. An empath is often taking on energies without knowing it.

Another term that has become popular recently is HSP—short for "highly sensitive person." This is someone who is not only attuned to the feelings and energy of other people but also deeply sensitive to all aspects of their environment. Loud noises, bright lights, crowded rooms, and any kind of upsetting or potentially violent situation is overwhelming to an HSP. (This is pretty much what my mom was talking about when she would explain my childhood behavior to me by saying, "You're very sensitive.")

Everything in the universe is made up of energy—people, animals, nature, even inanimate objects. Everything is vibrating at a certain frequency, which is the basis for something called the "resonance theory of consciousness," which explores the idea that consciousness is linked to the ways in which something vibrates. Turns out that all this mystical energy talk has just as much to do with science as it does with magic (I happen to think science *is* magic, but that's a different book). So what this means is that your desk is operating on a certain vibration, your favorite outfit, your pet, your best friend, even your school is an amalgamation of all the vibrations it contains.

I like to picture the energy of everything around us interacting as looking like the colorful powder that gets thrown into the air during the Hindu festival of Holi. Clouds of color fill the air and everyone ends up covered in a rainbow. Everyone is subject to experiencing these colorful clouds of energy, but for HSPs the colors may be more vivid, and the aftereffects harder to wash off.

Something that HSPs often experience is a feeling of hypervigilance about their surroundings. Because they can't help but have access to a ton of energetic information about their environment and the people in it, they may come to feel that they must stay on alert all the time, continuing to take in all this unfiltered information. Many people who struggle with anxiety are HSPs who get in a feedback loop of energetic information. It's like the TV is playing every channel at once, and not only can they not find the remote, but they are also on a constant high alert because their nervous system is so on edge from trying to sort through this information. If they can't listen to every channel at once, they believe that they might miss some information that could threaten their safety or the safety of those around them.

One nonmystical, psychological explanation for this hypervigilance is that many people who have experienced trauma feel the need to be constantly monitoring their environment to protect themselves from further getting hurt. This has a relationship to PTSD (post-traumatic stress disorder), where a sensory memory of a traumatic experience is triggered by a situation, but being hypervigilant means having a kind of low-level experience of constant PTSD humming in the background. This is truly the clearest example of our cave person brains trying to protect us in a physical way. Back when a saber-toothed tiger might attack at any moment of the day, being hyperaware of your surroundings was the key to survival. And although it is true that people who have experienced trauma are more likely to experience compulsive hypervigilance, some people are just HSPs from birth. We know from studying our charts that some people were simply designed to have more open access to certain emotional and energetic information than others.

Like anything else in our charts, this is neither a good nor a bad thing, simply a tool that we need to learn to work with correctly. Knowing how to work with energy in your daily life is like learning to swim. You want to figure out the shallow end of the pool so that you know what to do when a big wave comes along. If we can learn to allow ourselves to tune in to one TV station at a time rather than allowing all energetic information to have full access to us at all times, we can begin to use our sensitivities as a tool. I find that the experience of working with guides allows me to learn to focus in on one kind of energy at a time—I switch the channel over from the tangible world in front of me to this intuitive realm.

It's sort of an easy target to poke fun at someone who calls themselves an empath, as if those saying they are deeply sensitive are declaring themselves to be somehow both superior and extra delicate at the same time. But the truth is that while everyone has equal access to the energetic information that is around us at all times, some people just grow to become more resistant to paying attention to it. Energetic conversations are always happening, and HSPs and empaths need to make themselves aware of these conversations so that they don't get overwhelmed by them.

"I believe that all of us are honestly born with a huge amount of sensitivity," Aja tells me, "and slowly through society and family it gets sanded away. But for some of us that sanding didn't take. The major thing here is that for kids, the more sensitive you are, the more you're made fun of. The more you're told that you're being overdramatic, you're being too loud. And I think that's the opposite of what we should be doing with kids."

If we are told that we shouldn't be so sensitive, then we try to ignore our sensitivities, which means we are not learning to use them or to create boundaries for ourselves. This is like being told that you shouldn't bother learning to swim even though someone throws you in the deep end of the pool every morning. Not only are we not learning how to take care of ourselves, but we are depriving ourselves of the joy of swimming!

ENERGETIC BOUNDARIES

When we think about creating boundaries for our energy, sometimes it can be helpful to imagine an actual physical boundary of protection. The energy within your imagined protective barrier is yours, no one can take it from you, and no one can cross that boundary. Some people use this as a chance to work with their aura, the energy field around each of our bodies that extends out into the world. You can picture closing off access to your personal energy field when you need to by visualizing your aura turning into a kind of protective shell.

"You're taught in grade school that everything is made of energy," Aja says, "so it's not surprising that people and things and places are going to affect you physically and emotionally. And being aware of that is only going to help you make better decisions, and feel more connected to your own truth."

Understanding how to have and maintain energetic boundaries is about learning how to create these boundaries with people, but also learning to create boundaries with your environment. An HSP who struggles with anxiety and is hyperaware of their environment may feel that they have a responsibility to make sure things are perfect and that everyone else is comfortable, to try to control the environment around them based on the intuitive information that they are receiving. Not only is this exhausting, but it also sets them up to feel as though they personally have failed when their environment and the people in it do not behave in the way that they had hoped. They are also scattering their own supply of energy, monitoring everyone else instead of centering in their own experience and providing for their own needs.

The truth is that what happens energetically around them is not up to them—they are dealing with other people, who are at various stages of learning to navigate themselves and the world. Those people are not always going to behave the way that you would like them to, and it is not up to you to dictate how their emotional and energetic development goes down.

"We are not here to heal other people," Aja says. "We can offer guidance, we can offer help, we can offer support, but at the end of the day, the buck stops with ourselves. And that's a hard realization, because a lot of empaths deflect from working on the self and instead turn toward thinking, 'Let me try to fix or help this person and put all my energy into avoiding what's going on here.'"

"And then it falsely feels like a noble distraction because you think you're trying to help someone else," I say.

"Totally," Aja says. "Meanwhile I'm withering away."

You always want to be asking yourself, "What is my actual responsibility to this person or situation?" Pay close attention to people who seem to come to you with a need that depletes your resources at the expense of your own energetic health. If someone is crossing an energetic boundary with you and asking you for something that you can't provide or that you shouldn't be expected to provide, you need to learn that you can say no. "No" is the ultimate boundary defender.

CHANGING THE ENERGY

As we observe the ways in which the people around us affect our energy, we can also come to learn how we affect others. Here's the complicated part of this—sometimes we actually can influence the energy around us, not by employing our HSP hypervigilance or need for control, but by being deeply grounded in ourselves and taking care of our own needs first. To make sure we are not extending our energy to help others at our own expense, we can think of the metaphor of filling our own cup first. If our energetic cup is empty, how can we be expected to give to someone else? It is only when we can feel that our energetic cup is overflowing that we are able to see the abundance of what we are able to give. Aja gives me an example of a way in which we can effect change in the energetic dynamics around us by zooming out our perspective beyond our own emotional states.

"You could be, like, 'Mom, I noticed that you always feed yourself last at the table. Why don't you sit down, and I'll set the table?' When you begin to notice the dynamics of yourself and the world you're in, everything can blow wide open."

When we start to tune in to what it feels like to truly take responsibility for our own energy, we realize that all the unconscious choices that we make throughout our days when it comes to our energetic relationships can actually be made in a conscious way.

There is a cliché in New York apartments (and all apartment living, really) that anyone who lives upstairs from you is the noisiest person who ever existed. They seem to be rolling bowling balls down the hallway twenty-four/seven. My wife and I have always been relatively lucky when it comes to this phenomenon. For more than ten years we lived below someone who we never heard. Every once in a while the floorboards might creak a little, but that was it. But then, at the beginning of the pandemic, our neighbor left and a friend was staying at her place, and we knew we were in trouble from day one. This woman's gait made our apartment shudder. I wish I was exaggerating. Day and night, she stomped back and forth, as we spent 99 percent of our time inside waiting out quarantine. We finally met this surprisingly small-statured person and asked if she could try to walk more lightly (as her friend had seemed to do naturally). She seemed enraged. She was walking "normally," we were told. There was no problem. What did we want from her?

There was a lot going on at this moment in time, of course, but when I tell you that this person made a bad situation much worse, know that I understand that she was not doing this on purpose. She actually believed that our apartment did not echo with footsteps every time she went to the bathroom.

This situation demonstrated to me more clearly than anything had before how complicated our interconnected energies are, and the many unintentional ways in which we affect each other without knowing it. Apartments and city living in general are rife for this kind of clashing of energies, where everyone may actually be doing the best they can, while still inadvertently causing energetic (and sometimes physical) distress to others.

It is an unfortunate reality that many people do not want to accept responsibility for the ways in which their energy affects other people, and if they don't want to face that, then there is no way to force them to do it. What we can learn to do is to create strong boundaries and maintain them the best that we can. And build up our resilience for the moments when we must navigate challenging energy.

Here we get back to our key concept—we are learning to be responsible for our own energy both because it will help us, and because it is our responsibility to each other. It is only when we truly sift through the complications of these energies and see what belongs us to and what belongs to others that we can begin to have compassion for others who are struggling, and start to figure out how to show up in support of each other. We must take care of our own psychic and energetic hygiene first, like taking a shower in the morning.

HIGH AND LOW VIBE

As we start to learn more about the nature of energetic fields, we inevitably come across the concepts of "high" and "low" vibe energy. Some people equate high vibe simply with "good" feelings—happiness, lightness, flow—and low with "bad" feelings—sadness, anger, frustration. But we already know that feelings do not exist on a binary. There is as much information for us in difficult emotions as there is in the ones that are more pleasurable. So in order to avoid assigning judgment to emotional states, I find it helpful to think about high and low vibe in terms of how much we feel tethered to the tangible world, to the point of not experiencing any magical possibility in the present moment, or how much we find ourselves experiencing the infinite possibility of source energy.

When I think about low-vibe energy, I think about the Devil card in tarot. I imagine devil energy not as something connected to vice or an idea about "evil," but as an energy that gets us so mired down in the tangible limitations of our physical world that we become completely cut off from our intuition and our experience of creative possibility. In this state of mind, there is no sense of commonality with other living things, no experience of a connecting energy bigger than our individual selves, no awe at the beauty and power of nature. The devil to me is one big indifferent "whatever." Not impressed. Not feeling anything.

I'll talk about my experience of depression more in our therapy chapter, but my concept of low-vibe devil energy is very much related to how I experience depression. It's a kind of dulling tunnel vision. It is anti-evolutionary, and against our individual emotional, spiritual, and creative progress.

On the other end of the spectrum, high vibe is all about magical possibility, about being open and receptive to possibilities beyond the tangible world. It is faith, creativity, and receptivity, feeling a part of expansive energy that is much bigger than just you.

To characterize moments of difficult feelings as "low vibe" might result in someone discounting the important information that is available to us in them. We know from our witch work that darkness is just as much a tool as light, and spiritual bypassing is simply a result of fear, not an actual attempt to help humanity evolve.

"There are so many practitioners, healers, people in the community," Aja says, "that when you bring something up about the shadow, or negativity, it's just like, 'Oh, no, no, no!' But we have to be able to look at the shadow. The shadow needs love. I imagine this little black cat in your hand, that's just going limp. So much of our shadow was born because we needed it in certain moments when we were growing up. In many ways it protected us. And just because those pieces don't fit anymore doesn't mean that they don't have information to share. So we have to be able to love those pieces of ourselves. Or we just forget about them and push them deep, deep, deep down inside. And then they begin to morph into something else much more toxic, and much more difficult to extricate from the body and the spirit."

When we stop rejecting these difficult energetic parts of ourselves and begin to pay attention to what is happening in more challenging moments, we are suddenly opened up to a lot of information about what we care about and what really matters to us.

"It's really important to understand that those low vibrational times can actually give you so much in preparation for that upswing," Aja explains. "What is this telling me about myself that needs to change, shift, and evolve? Because that's the whole point, that we're constantly learning and evolving, so that we can work toward being happier human beings, which then makes us able to share that happiness with others and spread that joy and love."

So how can we best use the energetic information that we receive in these difficult moments?

"I have been navigating depression for decades," Aja tells me. "When I'm hitting a little moment, it reminds me of the things that I'm now not doing for myself, like, 'Oh, I haven't gone for a walk in days. I haven't actually done anything for myself that brings me joy in several weeks.' Instead of just lying down in those feelings, use them as markers for yourself. Because humans need logic and patterns to make changes. And even those lower vibrational emotions have patterns within them."

HOW DO YOU WANT TO FEEL?

When we are tuned in to the energetic patterns in our lives, we can start to learn more about what we want to call in to our experiences. Just as we manifest by calling in something but letting go of the details of the outcome, it can be helpful to identify the way that we want to feel and focus on calling that in, rather than assuming that a very specific outcome will make us happy. This is something that Aja talks about a lot, and I tell her that I always really appreciate when she encourages people to be more focused on how they want to feel in their lives than what they want to do or to have.

"I don't think I was able to actually understand that lesson until I was in my thirties," she tells me. "Instead of, 'I want a job where my salary is one hundred thousand dollars, I want to buy a new car, I want to own a home,' asking, 'What does that mean, in terms of feelings?' I realized, 'Oh, I want to feel free, and that means feeling independent.' It doesn't mean that your idea of success is altered, it means that you're listening to yourself more, and therefore don't feel as much FOMO or feel trapped by the standards of others."

This is again where so much of new age ideas about manifestation get it wrong. So often they are not asking you to engage directly with your innate wisdom about your energy. They are entirely goal focused, and usually focused on goals that someone else told you that you should want to achieve. But so many people are so cut off from their own innate wisdom that the prospect of deciding how they want to feel, rather than what they want to do or be or accomplish, wouldn't even occur to them.

This quote that Aja received from her guide Monty really sums it up nicely for me:

"We can walk deeper into ourselves by being honest about the life we truly wish to live with when no one is watching. You can actually create your own rules of life engagement. So what are your specific rules for living?"

What starts to happen when you know what kind of energy you want to bring into your life is that you become able to identify it and truly appreciate it when it shows up. For years I was trying to find a collaborator to write music with. I would get yesses from people that turned out to be nos. A couple of times I tried to force a situation to work just because it looked good on paper, but everything about it felt wrong. I so badly wanted to write with other people in a way that felt fun and in creative flow, and it just wasn't working. I felt like a failure, and like maybe I was chasing the wrong dream.

But those energetically wrong experiences gave me the knowledge that allowed me to recognize something good when it finally came along, just by the nature of how different the energy was. When I finally found my collaborators, I immediately recognized the magic in how easily we were able to work together, something that had been missing for me in all those other situations. This has become my most cherished ongoing creative collaboration (our band the Witch Ones!) mainly because it brings exactly the energy into my life that I had been trying to call in for so long.

This doesn't mean that once you find these things, they will be easy and perfect all the time. We know that we are not looking to arrive at a point of happiness and stay there forever. But as we call in the good high-vibe stuff, we evolve along with it.

"I used to have a lot of anxiety in my twenties and early thirties around the idea that I should be able to arrive at happiness and stay there," I tell Aja. "I would have a great day, and then the next day be totally depressed, and I would think, 'Oh, I ruined it.' As if I had reached the goal and then messed it up."

"Or how about the fear when you've been happy for a couple of days," Aja offers, "and thinking, 'When is this going to go away? This can't last forever.' I think that's why everything we're talking about is so important, because we're really talking about listening, paying attention, making different choices, trusting yourself. Looking for those big feeling moments, knowing that even those smaller moments mean something."

"The thing is to pay attention when something feels good," I add. "Even if it doesn't make sense."

"It doesn't have to make sense to anybody else other than you," Aja agrees. "At the end of the day, remember that you are in control. You have the power to do whatever it is you wish, to make whatever changes you wish. You are your own guru, you are your own healer, your teacher and mentor, best friend, lover, all those things. Those you wish to seek out and connect with, they're the icing on the cake. I think we can all have wonderful mentors and teachers out there. But I really wish that I had taken more responsibility and trusted that I know what's best for me. Whether or not that feels right in my body, no one else can know that but me. And knowing that even if I make mistakes or things don't work out, there are literally a million more decisions I'm going to be making. And it's okay."

This trust in self requires a lot of faith. As two people who need to experience something for ourselves in order to believe that it works, both Aja and I reject the idea of completely blind faith, but embrace a kind of faith in the process. A faith that the magical energy of the universe wants to be in conversation and collaboration with you.

"There were so many times as a teenager where I felt unbelievably alone," Aja tells me. "There was so much pretending and affectation and trying to fit in and trying not to show pieces of who I was. Thinking, 'Am I going to be judged? Are people not going to like me? Am I pretty enough? Am I smart enough? Am I light-skinned enough? Am I going to go to a good college?' It felt so overwhelming and alone. But the idea is that you're not alone. There are several beings around you, rooting for you. And that unconditional love, with no judgment at all ever, can absolutely create space for you to love yourself more."

No one can define your relationship to energy for you, because it is meant to be a completely personal relationship. Just as your relationship to your internal wisdom, your intuition, and your guides is all yours. And the mystery of that beautiful connection is where all the magic lies.

I ask Aja if she knows the story of the blind men touching the different parts of the elephant, each declaring a different truth based on the limited information they were able to collect.

"We're all just touching parts of this elephant," I say to Aja. "And we're not going to see the elephant. Not in this lifetime."

"No," Aja says. "Not until we're on the other side. And then I'm sure we're all going to be, like, 'Ah, of course!'"

Of course! It's an elephant!

Exercises

TAKE STOCK

Think of a time when you felt particularly energetically depleted. Ask yourself what might have contributed to that energetic depletion—were you around a lot of people, didn't get enough sleep, had too many things to do in a day? Make a note of it, and when it happens again, sit in that feeling and really try to identify where and when you felt your energy leave you, and what might help you to restore it.

WORK WITH YOUR GUIDES

The next time you come up against a problem that you are really wrestling with, take a moment to sit down in a quiet place with a journal. Write out the problem in as much detail as you can, and then start asking questions. They can be as simple as "What should I do?" Keep the pen moving on the paper, even if what you're writing doesn't make sense. Keep writing until you start to get some answers.

CHAPTER FIVE:
Body

I recently learned about something called the "locus of control," which sounds to me like a giant science fiction bug that's about to go on a rampage, but is actually a psychological concept developed in the 1950s by a man named Julian B. Rotter. This is an attempt to describe where you place the main responsibility for what happens in your life. Are you someone who thinks that situations in your life are mostly under your control, caused and affected by you? Or does the external locus of control dominate your life philosophy? How much of your daily experience do you ascribe to your own actions?

There's usually a balance between how much we believe is under our control and how much is not. When we read tarot, we understand that possible outcomes that are being presented to us are not predetermined; they are dependent on the choices we make and the actions we take. When we look at our natal charts we see a framework for experience, a kind of lens through which we see the world, but we always remember that we are the ones doing the seeing. Even our relationship to nature and ceremony should be about this interplay between inner autonomy and outward circumstances. The moon will wax and wane, the seasons will change, but we get to decide how we interact with them, what we ask for, and what work we do inside those cycles.

The place where I find navigating the locus of control to be most complicated for myself is with my body. If we want to be good witches who are working in the magical energetic world while being deeply grounded in the tangible world, we need to consider our relationship to our bodies and how we view them as a home for this lifetime. Just as we are born with a natal chart, we are born with a body, and the more we can learn about it and learn to work with it, the more we can find it to be a source of comfort and nurturing, and not an enemy. After all, your body is the place where your spirit meets and interacts with the world. It is a conduit. And it is COMPLICATED.

When we talk about mystical work, there tends to be a lot of air element involved. We are often looking up to the stars or to the energy of the universe for some wisdom. Even the idea of something being "high vibe" is about a lifting up out of the tangible world and into a purely energetic one. But what happens when we forget to come back down to Earth? Or even neglect to make peace with Earth in a way that makes it a livable place for us?

The body presents us with the most literal and complicated meeting between the inner self and outer circumstances, which makes it a really difficult place to navigate this balance of the locus of control. Your true relationship to your body couldn't be more private—only you understand how it works, what it can and can't do, what it needs and how you feel about it—but then you are expected to take that body out into the world, where others will see it and may make misguided assumptions about you because of it. Your body is also deeply subject to the circumstances around you. Can your body get what it needs? Is there fresh air where you live? Nutritious food that you are able to access? Available health care? Often such things are also out of your control, moving your relationship with your body even further away from that personal connection.

For some people, paying attention to their bodies is too painful an experience, so they simply don't do it. Bodies can be strangely easy to ignore for something that houses our entire existence. But there are so many ways in which your tangible Earth form not only exists in relationship to your mystical practices, but also wants to be in conversation with your mind, spirit, and magic in general. Neglecting this connection will not only have unfortunate consequences, but it will also deprive you of getting to fully experience the phenomenon of what it means to have a body, which is your mystical birthright. When we really listen to what our body has to tell us without judgment, without wishing things were different from how they are, we ground ourselves very deeply in the magic of the present moment.

Part of the problem is that most people place their thinking about their bodies anywhere but the present moment. The worst-case scenario of this is someone who believes that good things won't happen (or they won't be happy) until they reach some kind of arbitrary body goal. For some reason, our bodies are especially susceptible to the kind of goal-based thinking that capitalism loves. Remember, capitalism's favorite thing to say is: "There is something wrong with you, you must fix it in order to be allowed to participate in the full range of human experience, and once you fix it you will stand on the top of the victory mountain and stay there forever. Oh, and to make this all happen, you need to buy a bunch of things."

But

What

If

There

Is

Nothing

Wrong

With

Our

Bodies

!!?!?!?!?!?????????

Nothing wrong. With all our bodies. Mine. Yours. The body of every person you've ever met, ever seen, could ever imagine.

If we can come to believe that there should be no good/bad binary for feelings and for how our minds work, can we learn how to extend that to the tangible world? Not to see our bodies as a burden, as something that should be controlled, wrangled into shape, or even able to do very specific things? Can we take every "should" that we have ever heard about bodies and tear it up into pieces and throw it out the window? Can we exist in our bodies with curiosity and tenderness? Can we be in conversation with our bodies and sometimes even enjoy that conversation?

HOW DID WE GET HERE?

Since the mid-twentieth century, we have more and more become a society that relies on images—watching movie stars in movies, then actors on TV, seeing people in magazines, advertisements on billboards. Our human experience, which had previously been mostly visually limited to the immediate world around each of us, was now being given an insight into the "rest of the world" through these images. Of course, the actual "rest of the world" has never looked like movie stars and TV ads. But our brains think that these images are telling us: "Just a heads-up from EVERYONE else, this is how men should look and behave and this is how women should look and behave and there is only heterosexuality and only two genders and bodies should be one way and whiteness is the neutral standard of existence and if you are not able to look and act and be this way, then you are probably going to be rejected by society."

It is not our fault that we are wired to try to "fit in." Cave person brain knows that belonging is important to survival. We all want to find acceptance and love, so being presented with information that implies that we do not fit the requirements of social acceptability can cause a real crisis in us.

But there are a few problems with this model.

The first is that you have to look at the people who are in charge of creating these images to understand what world they want to present to you. If society has created a situation in which an image-based experience of the external world is taken as objective "truth," it has put us in a position to be deeply manipulated by the people creating those images. And unfortunately, it is white, straight, non-disabled, cis men who have been the ones creating the majority of visual culture over the past century, and they have presented us with a version of the world that they know, and that appeals to them. They have historically had no obligation to present pictures to you that accurately represent the real world, in all its beautiful diversity.

Keep in mind that most of those creators over the history of our image-based culture were not crafting imagery out of an artistic desire to tell stories that would help humanity. They were interested in making money, or else they were in a position to have to answer to other people who were interested in making money. This was where capitalism shifted from functioning mainly because people were buying what they needed, to people buying what they want. And how do they know what they want? Why don't you show them? Show them how cool the thing is, and how everyone on TV likes the thing, and how the thing is in a movie, and wow, everyone's life just gets a lot better when they have this thing. Any complaints and difficulties that you have in your life are probably just about the fact that you don't have THE THING.

Why am I ranting about capitalism again? Because capitalism did an amazing magic trick of turning our bodies into A THING. Along with being shown what movie stars were wearing and eating and doing, we were also being shown what they looked like, what shape their bodies were, and what their bodies were capable of doing. This very narrow window of acceptability became so ingrained in us that we started to think that it was some kind of absolute truth, rather than the large-scale brainwashing that it is. Anyone outside that narrow window was shown to us in visual media to be unacceptable. But unacceptable to whom? A body of a different size, a person of a different skin color other than white, a person who did not act in accordance with society's narrow views of gender, whose body or mind worked differently from the norm, was shown to be inferior, dysfunctional, and even evil, if they were shown at all. Bodies became something that could be categorized into "good" and "bad."

Of course, the seeds of all of this were being sown even before we had TV and movies.

"As far as I understand it, the first real binary between able and not able was introduced by industrialists," my friend Erin Clark tells me over video chat. "They weren't trying to sell something, but to extract something—a workforce, and a work ethic. Then those people who did the work were rewarded with good standing in society, basically. The whole framework was that you were a good person because you were working. So you had values, you had morals, you had status. Anybody who wasn't was 'lazy.' But they couldn't just say that a person who couldn't work was lazy. So they had to create a category in which you were not valuable, but it wasn't your fault."

Most people who meet Erin Clark do it under some remarkable, fabulous, adventurous circumstances. In my case I benefited from a friend who is more adventurous than I am doing the adventurous thing that would allow me to meet Erin. My friend Laura had given herself a yearlong challenge to learn how to do aerial silks, going to classes multiple times a week and learning to climb up the hanging fabrics and balance in various wild positions. Because Laura is an appreciator of both celebrations and dramatic gestures, she planned a show to mark the end of her year and to demonstrate her new skills. And she enlisted a partner from her classes to be in the show with her.

I want to be very clear that I was deeply impressed with what Laura was able to accomplish in a year. Because she is very funny, she mostly made a joke out of the limitations of her newfound skills. She wore fairy wings and performed to a cheesy nineties Bryan Adams song. We all clapped and cheered her on and agreed that she had made huge progress in a year. And then Erin performed.

I believe the main word uttered by the audience during Erin's aerial silks performance that night was "whoa." Everything about her was fire. With her fiery red hair, you felt that if she looked directly at you, you might start to sizzle, but in a good way. It would be an honor. Erin and the silks were like twin flames wrapping around each other. It was one of those performances that make the seemingly impossible look effortless. It was poetry. The overall takeaway when she was done was, "Who IS that???"

Erin is an athlete and an adventurer (my word, not hers,

ERIN CLARK is the author of *If You Really Love Me, Throw Me Off the Mountain* and co-author of the upcoming *The Breakup Artist.* She is the current world record and gold medal holder for wheelchair para pole and two-time national champion representing Spain. And, as a paragliding pilot, she has a wheelchair that she can fly.

but it's the best way I can think to describe the way her life looks from the outside, as if she is a member of the Explorers Club, bringing wild tales home from far-flung expeditions). Because she is visibly disabled and uses a wheelchair, she gets a lot of reactions to her athletic endeavors and adventuring that someone who does not use a wheelchair would not have to deal with.

"You should read the YouTube comments on my videos," Erin tells me. "It's, like, 'You're such a light.' 'I cried watching this video.' And I'm pole dancing in my living room," she laughs, marveling at how much some people tend to put their own projected meaning on pretty much everything she does.

Whether she's pole dancing in her living room, winning a championship in the Spanish National Para Pole Competition, climbing mountains, or learning how to paraglide, Erin finds herself subjected to a lot of misguided projections that other people put on her.

"When people hear the word 'disability,' they think of particular things that have been invented by society," Erin says. "Disabling conditions exist across a very wide spectrum, and at a certain point a stigma gets applied, and that stigma is a separate thing from the state that my body is in. A disability narrative is, 'Oh my God, you've overcome so many obstacles!' And I'm like, 'None of those things were obstacles for me. You've invented this obstacle, you projected it onto me, then you see me accomplish this thing. And literally none of what was imagined even existed for me."

I wanted to talk to Erin about bodies because she has definitely experienced the phenomenon of having to learn to navigate the really specific needs of her own body, something that only she can fully know as the person in possession of that body, and then having people making very misguided assumptions about her based on their own preconceived notions and prejudices.

"I do experience obstacles," Erin offers. "The issue isn't that I'm not limited at all by my body. It's that when people invent the limits that fit their narrative, they ignore my real limits. They don't believe or listen to disabled people when they say what they actually want and need if it doesn't fit with what was projected."

The other reason I wanted to talk to Erin is that she is a powerful witch who tends to manifest some pretty amazing magic in her life.

"My sun sign is Aries," Erin reminds me when I remark on her very fiery way of facing the world, "but so is my Mercury, Mars, and Venus. So I'm made of fire. I mean, try to tell me whatever you want," she says, laughing.

CHANGING THE PICTURE

As we as a society move into the Age of Aquarius, in which the individual's relationship to the collective becomes heightened, we have found ourselves in a period of really complicated growth when it comes to how we relate to images. Social media has given everyone equal access to image creation and sharing. You can post an image in a second that is available for anyone in the world with a smartphone or a computer to see. All of a sudden we have an infinite amount of information about the visual world that exists outside our immediate surroundings, rather than a narrowly curated and controlled amount of information. The people who presented that very specific image of the world to us no longer have a monopoly on telling us what the world looks like.

There are a couple of problems here, though. One is that we may be entering into a new age of democratic control of images, but we have nearly a hundred years of society-wide brainwashing to undo, and the internet has moved a lot faster than our self-deprogramming has been able to happen. The result is that we continue to encounter that narrow view of the world as a standard that we are supposed to meet, often unconsciously. Those who do not fit into the narrow view are still seen as outliers who should probably explain themselves. They are either the object of scorn and disdain from those still stuck in that narrow binary, or they are declared "brave" by those who also do not fit into the narrow binary and continue to feel shame around that.

Because participating in social media can give us a sense of connection and belonging, especially when we feel isolated, of course it's understandable that we would want to participate in it. Finding people with common interests who you never would have otherwise met is magical in itself! But we have to be very careful about the energetic contract that we are entering into. Social media inevitably (and often unconsciously) puts a new standard of presentation on us. Suddenly we may feel that we are expected to be able to create an interesting visual representation of ourselves for anyone to look at. The line between the private and the public becomes very fuzzy, and it can feel as though the main value of the private self is to create content for the public self (never forget that you are, in effect, providing free labor for a very rich company that profits off the images and content that you make, and benefits from you spending as much time as possible on their platform). What may have started as an attempt to share your life with friends and family often turns into a game of status seeking. You are suddenly participating in a popularity contest that you may not have realized you were signing up for.

"I can trace a lot of my own good body/bad body experience to ideas about status," Erin says. "So in the same way that someone might feel like they need to go to Harvard or their dreams won't come true, we apply the exact same principles to how our bodies need to be for approval, for status. And so I think to some extent, unless you reckon with your thirst for status, and the way that that causes you to stigmatize yourself and others, I don't think rejecting capitalism is going to do anything other than just shift the dynamic onto something else. Because we will still be in an extractive relationship with the people around us, jockeying for status."

You can see people struggling with this desire to gain and maintain status while experiencing a conflict between the public and private in real time—influencers who break down in a post about how their lives are not as perfect as they seem in the pictures that they post, people attempting to post honestly about something difficult happening in their lives, a jarring switch from a feed that might normally be full of astrology memes and drag queens (or is that just my feed?). Whenever I come across a post like this, I always really sit with it for a while, wishing that I could communicate to this person that the internal conflict that they are feeling is not their fault. It's built into the system.

A person who is experiencing stress over how to present a fully authentic version of themselves on social media has already spent way too much time and energy thinking about this. They have put themselves into a complete existential crisis that is a waste of their time. And it's not their fault! Social media was designed to get people to spend as much time as possible on it, so why wouldn't it cause someone to spend hours obsessing over their public image? They have unconsciously entered into an energetic dynamic that does not prioritize their highest good. Their creative energy flows out, and they find themselves at the mercy of whatever uncontrolled energy might flow back at them.

This is what happens when we give over this level of control to others, or even to our perception of what we think others might think. We start to lose the thread of who we really are and what is really going on with us. And that can become especially painful when your body is involved, and when the private reality of your body may be complicated and difficult to explain.

But what if you didn't have to explain it to anyone? What if there is no public reckoning in which you will be asked to account for the way your body looks, feels, functions? What if all that matters is your own personal relationship to your body?

"One of the hazards of being in a stigmatized body, like for women, or queer or disabled people, is that the ideology about who you are is incredibly pervasive," Erin offers. "And sometimes it makes it feel like exploring your own parameters is the riskiest thing you could possibly do. Like, 'I'll just stay inside the bubble that they've created for me and hunker down.' But if you explore beyond that, you start to get a grip on what reality is for you."

To step outside what literally everyone you know has been brainwashed to think since visual culture was invented is to make yourself deeply vulnerable. It makes me sad that it is still a radical statement to declare that our bodies are allowed to exist on their own terms, in whatever way makes sense for each of us, but unfortunately it is. But I cannot stress this to you enough—you do not owe anyone anything when it comes to your body. You do not exist to be desirable to someone else. You are not a lumpy mold of clay that must be shaped into something very specific in order to be loved. You do not have to look a certain way in pictures. You do not have to be able to curate a popular visual representation of yourself. Your only responsibility when it comes to your body is to you and your own needs and your own pleasure in alignment with your own sense of balance and evolution.

This doesn't mean that you can't have a relationship to a visual representation of your body! Cute selfies, OOTDs, and flirty pics are all fun and should bring you joy! Dressing the way that you want in a way that makes you feel good is fantastic! Clothing and adornments are completely magical objects that can change the way you feel, manifest a creative persona for you, and allow you to express yourself through your interaction with the rest of the world. But with social media, we are asked think of ourselves aesthetically not just for our own enjoyment, but always in anticipation of being viewed by others. We are not taught how to first ground this public experience in a private relationship with self, and how to continue to return to our grounded place of self in our bodies when all that airy communication makes us feel ungrounded and unsure of ourselves. We are instead encouraged to participate in a literal popularity contest, presenting ourselves up for "likes," our only reward being a fleeting rush of serotonin that trains us to further mine our lives as aesthetic raw material.

I do think that, in general, we as a society are trying to get to a place where we have dismantled that damaging narrow view of what kinds of bodies and visual representations of bodies are considered "acceptable," but I think it's going to take us a long time to get there. And unless this is a cause that you feel passionate about and want to directly engage with, I don't want you using your precious energy up on having to think about anyone but yourself when it comes to how you look and feel. Because when you constantly offer yourself up to public scrutiny, it can be very difficult not to internalize the assumptions that other people put on you based on their prejudices.

WHEN YOU ASSUME . . .

Of course social media is a place that is primed for these kinds of prejudiced assumptions, but many people with bodies outside that historically narrow definition of "normal" have to deal with such things in real life on a daily basis.

Erin recently published a beautiful memoir called *If You Really Love Me, Throw Me off the Mountain*, in which she writes a lot about her experiences with disability as a child, having to navigate the misguided assumptions of the adults around her about her capabilities.

In the book she tells a particularly distressing story from when she was in fourth grade about being forced to allow a teacher to assist her in going to the bathroom, a process that, for Erin, involves using a catheter.

"I had been catheterizing myself since I was in preschool," Erin writes, "when I took the catheter from the teacher and did it myself."

But her new school had a policy that a teacher not only needed to inform her when it was time for her to go to the bathroom, but also had to accompany Erin into the stall and watch her insert the catheter and use the toilet. Erin told the teacher and the school that she did not want (or need) the teacher in the stall with her. Her mother asked the principal to stop the practice, and finally Erin, at ten years old, wrote a letter to the board of education stating that, "while it was important that the board provided assistance for the students who couldn't attend to their own needs, it was a problem that help was being forced on me against my will."

Her request was not granted. It was only when she moved to another school district that didn't have a teacher's assistant for disabled students that she was allowed to regain autonomy over her body.

"When people look me in the eye and say, 'You can't do such and such a thing,'" Erin tells me, "and I'm in the middle of doing it, it tells you the truth about how wrong other people can be about the world. So as a child, I knew then that I didn't owe respect to people for being in authority over me when they were observably wrong. If I'm in the middle of doing it, and if I do this every day, at home by myself, since I was two, who are you to decide now that I suddenly need assistance to pull it off? What has actually changed? Not me. Therefore, I'm not wrong."

"You actually benefited from experiencing something that was such an extreme case of people being wrong about you," I observe to Erin, "that there wasn't even room for a conversation there. You understood that they were wrong about this, so what else could they be wrong about?"

"Exactly," Erin agrees. "I think that my disability is great in that most [nondisabled] people won't have that sharp of a contrast. So if the first time it has occurred to you that ideas that you have about who you are or what you need are wrong is when you're sixteen, or twenty, or thirty-five, it's a lot harder to undo that, and also to sit with that. Because as much as it came from somebody else being wrong about you, it means you're also wrong about you, because you built up so much on that premise. So it's a very destabilizing experience. The more curiosity and exploration the younger, the better."

Erin's attitude is a great example of what happens when we start this questioning of other people's assumptions about us very early on.

"Eventually what happens is that it's really difficult to manipulate you," she says. "A lot of the ways that especially young women are manipulated is that they read a magazine and don't even realize that they're internalizing a beauty standard. It's not always about you, personally, it's just in the ether. And the more your sense of yourself is informed by experiences you have had of yourself, the less power that has passively."

Erin admits that it is partially her fiery temperament that has given her a natural comfort with questioning authority, combined with this lived experience of people's perceptions of her being so wildly incorrect. She tells me that the strange upside of people not expecting her to be able to do things freed her early on from having to follow anyone else's rules about how things should be done.

"One of the liberating things about my experience with being disabled," she says, "especially since it's very physical and people can see it, is that nobody expected me to be able to do anything, which means that they weren't holding me to any particular standard. And because I can't physically do it in the way that everyone else is, I have to think about how it works for me, or I don't do it at all. And so being Aries several times over, the not doing it at all was never an option for me. If I wanted to do it, I was going to figure it out."

This freedom that Erin has experienced in her life has allowed her to pull back her perspective to see the bigger picture, something that is much easier to do when whatever system you are questioning has already proven itself to you to be deeply flawed.

"My fear of embarrassment I think is a lot lower than it is for a lot of other people," she tells me, "because I never had access to status in society anyway. I had nothing to lose, because I could never gain it. People will always see the wheelchair, so no matter what I do, or who I do it in front of, that will always speak louder to people who don't know me than anything."

Erin's lived experience set her up to have a very clear understanding of the ways in which other people project their assumptions onto her not just in real life, but also on social media, which may be why she is able to navigate the world of social media with as much skill as she does. Erin is a joy to follow on social media. She posts videos of her paragliding, long beautiful passages of descriptive text describing her sensory experiences, and really expertly executed selfies and photo shoots. But of course, by posting these things, she opens herself up to the projections of anyone who comes across her accounts.

"People admire you for doing things they wouldn't let themselves do because they believe it's wrong," Erin says. "When we're talking about things like fearlessness, about following your own desires, about status, there's a very clear boundary that if you are uncomfortable, or admiring me, or shaming me, it's not my problem. Because when people say, 'Oh my God, you're such an inspiration. You're so fearless,' I don't take that on. I don't have to process that with them. I also don't have to process it for myself. I am clear on the fact that this isn't about me."

BODY POSITIVITY

This issue of projection on social media figures becomes even more complicated when we look at something like the body positivity movement. The body positivity movement was (and is) a well-intentioned attempted correction to the shame that has been forced on anyone with a body that did not fit into that narrow ideal promoted to us by capitalist media. If we have been told that bodies that are different from this standard are not beautiful, lovable, worthy of attention, then shouldn't the correction be to present those bodies as all those things? If traditional media representation got us into this mess in the first place, then couldn't the new democratized social media help us to correct in the other direction?

One of the problems with this is that the public/private conflict and confusion still exists here. What if a body positivity influencer isn't feeling good about their body one day? Does that mean that they have failed at being body positive? Are they no longer qualified to present themselves as a representative of body positivity?

We know two things already that are helpful here—we know how to give ourselves permission to experience whatever is happening in the moment, and we know that we need to step off the good/bad binary. The true body revolution exists in every person being taught to give their bodies permission to be exactly what they are today, in this moment. And to completely reject the external definition of which bodies are acceptable and which are not.

Of course, if someone wants to declare themselves "body positive" and is in active engagement with trying to present alternatives to that narrow view of bodies, that's great. But even by using the term, we are, in a way, reinforcing the idea of an unacceptability in difference.

"The line between shaming and admiration is often very thin," Erin tells me. "The irony was that people assumed I was 'body positive,' because I had a body that they didn't approve of. The message is, 'It's brave of you to be 'positive,' because that's a radical statement.' I've never had a specifically body-positive message. My relationship with my body, especially as it shows up in my self-expression, is very much about me enjoying what I enjoy. It isn't a political statement about what should be enjoyed, or a moral statement about how other people should feel about their own body. The idea that certain things are inextricably connected to insecurities is something that I have tried to prove as false. Disability is not inextricably linked to self-esteem, suffering, or body image issues. That's a social story."

The problem is that the idea of body positivity is still acting within that energetic binary, still playing the game of status in which we are attempting to prove to the existing system that other kinds of bodies are worthy.

Even though there have been many studies done that prove diets don't work, that people who lose large amounts of weight often gain back more than they lost, people still try them, because they are deeply susceptible to marketing promises of being able to achieve a certain outcome. But the whole problem with diets is that the outcome is the only point. If someone has a weight-loss goal, and they are making changes based on achieving that goal, they will either not achieve it, and feel like a failure, or achieve it and realize that not much about themselves actually changed in the way that they expected it to.

Once again in this situation we are asked to both look at our bodies as objects that can and should be changed, and to hold our bodies to a very narrow set of standards that may have nothing to do with who we actually are, or what is actually best for us.

The sad part is that the companies creating and marketing most diets, weight-loss plans, and gym memberships know that most people will "fail." They count on it. Because "failure" will make people go in search of another "solution," which they will have to spend more money on.

Your body can never be a marker of failure—that's not how it works. Your body does what it does. There is no good or bad—there is only the complicated truth. And it is only through a direct exploration of that truth that we can develop an experience-based relationship with nourishment, with movement, and with what our bodies need on an everyday basis.

To give over to some expectation that your body should be anything other than what it is keeps you brainwashed by a system that thrives on shame. Our anxious cave person brains may worry that if we don't have a system for control, we are just going to spin out into chaos, so we look for external rules to put on ourselves. But if you listen to your body and cultivate a private relationship with it, your aligned personal strategies are going to be far more complicated and nuanced than any diet could be, and they are not going to be about success and failure.

What can get tricky here is that often diets are masquerading as "self-care," still insisting on a system with strict rules and expectations, but paying lip service to an idea of nurturing yourself.

"I think one of the reasons we end up with 'self-care' the way that we have it now, where it's essentially empty," Erin says when I mention this to her, "is that's what happens when people need each other to give them permission, which means by design they can't be listening to themselves. People get so used to coping with the system, they tend to look for another system to give them permission. And I think being able to give yourself permission is a hugely valuable skill."

In order to be brave enough to live outside a system that someone else has created that is not in our best interests (and unfortunately, many are not), we must remember our truest witchy selves, that woman who lives on the edge of town mixing up potions, in full possession of her power, unconcerned with anyone else's ideas about how she "should" behave.

To claim power over your body, what you wear, and even how you move, is to make a potent political statement against patriarchy. We refuse to delay acceptance of ourselves and enjoyment of our lives until our bodies fit someone else's idea of how they should look. Why would we? We are the ones who are in possession of our own personal power and magic. Why would we listen to anyone else's opinion about the magical vessel that is our own bodies?

"I think a lot of the mentality of, 'I'm going to buy the dress two sizes too small,' is a way that you're denying yourself pleasure," Erin tells me. "You're denying yourself a desire you can fulfill by getting the dress that fits. Then you're wearing the dress. Yay, you look cute! And if it doesn't look cute on you, in the body you have now, it's not the right f***ing dress."

If your body is inspiring cute, fun vibes in you one day, fantastic! If another day it is frustrating you, changing in ways that are disorienting, or if you are simply feeling neutral about your body—that's just as fine! If thinking about "loving your body" seems like too much pressure, can you think of it as "working with your body" instead? "Staying in touch with your body"? "Respecting the needs of your body"?

This is the challenge, and know that it takes strength and courage, but it will leave you free to experience a life that is fully engaged in all the possibilities of the present moment—to step outside the system, to resist the pressure to put any kind of judgment on your body, good or bad.

"The idea that disability automatically means self-loathing is obviously false," Erin tells me, "because I never hated my body. Did I hate how people treated me? I hated the way that it was shaping what possibilities were available to me, how hard it was making things. But I never hated my body. I have always enjoyed being in it. My pleasure in my body is genuine. It's not a thing that I have to choose to do in resistance to a way that I'm feeling. I just like what it can do."

This removal of assumptions is something that we want to be doing both for ourselves and in our interactions with others. The truth is that there is very little that you can tell about a person's health, abilities, or relationship to their body just by looking at them, and you don't have to! If we know that we each struggle with that confusing combo of presenting a private body in a public space, we have to assume that everyone else is also going through something similar. Often people with bodies that fit that old narrow false ideal are experiencing something challenging that is not visible to those around them. Non-visible disabilities, body image struggles, and illness are not seen when someone posts a cute selfie. But they don't need to be shown, unless that person wants to talk about them. The point is for you to refrain from making a judgment about that person's body just as you will with your own.

Our goal here is acceptance and neutrality. Neutral is allowed. Neutral is not a failure. In fact, neutrality implies that you have successfully stepped off the good/bad scale and are existing deeply in the present moment, allowing your experience of that moment to exist without labels.

ILLNESS

The task of acceptance can be especially challenging to do for ourselves when our bodies are not functioning in the way that we expect or want them to. As someone whose periods of depression are closely linked to a lack of energy and physical ability, I've often found myself angry at my body for not behaving the way that I wanted it to. For a very long time I felt as if it was my body's main agenda to slow me down until I stopped moving altogether. In my twenties and thirties I had chronic Lyme disease and mono, combined with low blood pressure and thyroid surgery that left me with only half of what pretty much amounts to our bodies' gas tanks. Then I've got a pesky gene mutation called MTHFR that keeps my body from properly absorbing nutrients to make things GO. (MTHFR is weirdly common, and often an unknown contributor to depression.) All these things are very difficult to get a diagnosis for in traditional Western medicine, and cause symptoms that will usually prompt traditional Western medicine doctors to tell a patient something deeply unhelpful like, "Just lose weight," or "Just exercise more." So, thinking I had no other options to treat my symptoms, I would force myself to go to an exercise class, push myself as hard as I could in the class, and then come home and cry myself to sleep in the middle of the afternoon because I was so exhausted.

I am not telling you this for you to be impressed by my various ailments, but to tell you firsthand that bodies are very difficult to understand, even when we live our whole lives inside them. The sad truth of traditional Western medical care is that we as patients have to advocate for ourselves, especially if we are not straight white cis men. Even very well-intentioned traditional doctors do not have the time, or sometimes the skill, to sit down with you and help you unravel a complicated set of symptoms that you would like to at least improve if not eliminate. We can be told that we are imagining something, exaggerating, or straight-up lying. Experiencing medical gaslighting is not only an emotionally painful experience, but also can keep someone from seeking care or trusting doctors at all. Women, queer, trans, and nonbinary people and members of the BIPOC community have all historically been subject to this painful gaslighting, in which they are told that their symptoms are either insignificant or imagined. People with a BMI (body mass index) that categorizes them as "obese," based on a deeply outdated and biased system, are often told by traditional doctors that the only solution to pretty much any symptom they have is to lose weight. (I know women who were told that they would not be able to have a child because of their weight, delayed getting pregnant for many years, and then only discovered the doctor was wrong when they became pregnant and gave birth to a healthy baby.) All of this often results in people not being diagnosed for major medical problems, avoiding seeing doctors, and having to live with discomfort that could be treated.

I so deeply wish it wasn't like this. I wish that every person in the world could work with a doctor trained in many modalities who has all the time and patience to unravel the cause of complicated symptoms, but since that reality is not manifesting anytime soon, we have to learn how to do some of this work ourselves. The more we can listen to our bodies and pay attention to what is going on, the more empowered we can be in advocating for ourselves.

Unfortunately, Western medicine is also very dependent on its own binary of sick/well. You are either sick or not sick. You either have something that a test result tells you that you have or you don't. Luckily, we as witches are comfortable with the subtleties of the natural world, and our bodies are nothing if not our main form of participation in that world. Seasons change and cycle, and so do our bodies. So do our minds. We are observers and honorers of these cycles. We are here to learn about them and give them the attention and deference that they deserve.

What does this look like in practice? We use our mindfulness practices to get curious about the present moment. Is your body tired? Energized? Does something hurt? Is your stomach having trouble trying to digest a certain food? Can you get any kind of indication about what might help in this moment? Can you remind yourself that the way that you feel in this moment is not permanent?

"I'll talk to myself about it as though there is a friend or a therapist in the room," Erin tells me when I ask her about riding out challenging moments of dealing with pain. "I'll narrate—'Oh, I can really feel where that pain is, we're just going to be really gentle about that.' I'm giving myself affection, acknowledgment, and support in the places that hurt. I ask my body, 'What do you need?' It's a very literal practice of being guided by the body in periods of acute pain and limitation.

The body is having an experience, and it is what it is. So let's just be with that."

Something I have always struggled with is this idea of accepting the present moment while simultaneously hoping to change something when the present moment is unpleasant. When my fatigue was at its worst, I would become so tired that I couldn't function for long periods of time (even after drinking as much caffeine as I could stomach), and my overwhelming emotion was to feel sorry for myself. Why was this happening to me? Why couldn't I figure out how to fix it? Why were other people able to go jogging, climb mountains, take long bike rides, simply stay awake all day? Why, when my friends would do these things, did I feel like such a loser when I couldn't participate?

What's complicated here is that technically there was something "wrong" with me. A lot of things were wrong with me, and I spent years trying to figure out what they were and what I could do about them. But there is also a large part of the way that my body and energy levels function that comes from that mysterious mix of genetics, family, heritage, and good old astrology that makes us each so unique. Sure, there is a spectrum of functioning within my natural range of how my body works, but it is only through really trusting my own comprehension of my body that I can even begin to understand when something is wrong and what needs to be done to help.

So how to both have acceptance for where you're at in a potentially difficult moment and also allow yourself to want to learn to work better with a challenging part of yourself? If we are dealing with an illness or imbalance that is capable of being corrected or helped, of course we want to pursue that. But this does not mean that we shame the present for not being the future, and imagine the future as a place where we would much rather live.

This is where we are asked to hold more than one idea in our heads at the same time—the present moment can be difficult in a way that we need to be working toward changing, AND the present moment is here for us to accept it and learn from it. When we get angry at the present moment for being what it is, we add to our own mental and physical stress. What is happening in this moment does not determine what will happen in the next moment, or tomorrow, or next month. Not that there won't be challenges in the future, but we make addressing the present challenges even more difficult when we develop a false narrative around them.

"I know when I endure incredible pain, like migraines, it will pass," Erin tells me. "When pain isn't causing damage, I do the things that help my body handle it, but I don't feel any panic or fear. I don't enjoy it, but there isn't anywhere else that I need to be except with my body in pain. I know what is serious and what isn't, but not based on the drama of it. A migraine is dramatic, but isn't serious. Not in the sense of a threat to my life. I've had my life actually threatened by health concerns and it wasn't painful. It wasn't alarming or dramatic. So I know not to be overly caught up in the drama of the body. Because my body is very dramatic, but I'm okay."

Erin's ability to have compassionate conversations with her body in this way is something that we should all aspire to. In some witchcraft traditions, the body is seen as a separate entity from the mind and spirit, and the negotiation between the three aspects of self is about balance and attentiveness. If your body is feeling particularly vulnerable, are there ways in which your mind and spirit can reassure it? How would you treat your body if it was your best friend? Your younger sibling? Your beloved pet?

This connection between mind, body, and spirit can also mean that problems that we believe are only affecting a part of us may have bigger implications. Physical trauma can cause mental trauma, and feelings are often manifested in the body. Think of how anxiety feels in the body, what the repetition of that experience of stress does to your body over time. If you are only tuned in to your mind and ignoring the way that your body feels, you may not understand the bigger implications of this stress.

Traditional medicine is a fantastic thing when it helps us. As science comes to develop even more advanced ways of treating diseases, of developing vaccines, and of learning about how we can help our human bodies, we as individuals and as a collective benefit from the gift of getting to live longer, healthier lives. But we owe it to ourselves to develop a complex understanding of our bodies as constantly changing energetic homes for our minds and spirits.

ALTERNATIVE CARE

You don't have to look too hard to find information about the ways that the body is perceived energetically in different cultures.

Even a very mainstream Western yoga teacher will probably mention chakras, a series of energy centers in the body. Traditional Chinese medicine is also based in an understanding of the body through energetic pathways called meridians. Acupuncture, different kinds of massage, reiki (an energy healing practice), water therapy, aligning your eating patterns with the seasons, or other energetic patterns are all great methods to try when we are looking to bring different kinds of therapy and care to our physical and energetic bodies. We never want to attach a capitalist idea of the "cure-all" to any of these things, but instead to try things out and feel into what our bodies respond to.

To me all these modalities are magic. Lying in a warm pool of salt water in a completely dark, silent room for an hour may not sound appealing to everyone, but I challenge anyone to do a salt float and not come out feeling like their nervous system has been completely reset.

Even if bodywork or non-Western forms of medicine and healing are not available to us, we can use our skills as witches to figure out how to do this kind of work for ourselves. Our nervous system is what transmits signals based on sensory information to different parts of our bodies. So if our cave person brains are in that fight-or-flight mode of feeling threatened and stressed, our nervous systems are on high alert, scanning the environment for dangers. But when we stay in our cave person high alert all the time, we are maxing out our nervous system, which ironically makes us less ready to function in an actual emergency because we've so deeply exhausted ourselves. So when we talk about resetting our nervous systems, we mean actually pressing a kind of reset button for our body's experience of its environment. It's as if the system of taking in information has overloaded and needs to start again from zero. Remember that person who is watching all the TV channels at once? We have to turn the TV off, take a breath, and then turn it on again to just one channel.

You're the only one who can figure out what methods of nervous-system resetting work for you. For some people, vigorous exercise can serve to burn off excess anxiety and bring your body back to a neutral place. For others water always does the trick—swimming or soaking in a hot tub with some Epsom salts. Yoga, tai chi, and chi gong are all traditional energetically healing stretching modalities that can be learned through online videos and classes. Moving the body in gentle and loving ways, even if it's just dancing around your room, can be a huge help in working through feelings of depression and anxiety. Sometimes it's just about taking a long nap, letting yourself really, truly rest without feeling any guilt around it. Pay very close attention to how you feel after you try these things. Remember what feels good, what your place of reset feels like for you. You are giving your body the time and space to energetically clean house.

This is not to say that any of these methods are going to "solve" something that needs correction. Salt floats were never going to completely cure my Lyme disease. But they did help me relax around any narrative that I had invented about the way that my body was functioning, which then created a much more advantageous environment for healing. If we can use our energy to protect and care for our own nervous systems, then we can move through the world in a nurturing way, allowing us to stop being bogged down by unnecessary energetic narratives that we may be carrying around.

REST AND COMFORT

If you listen carefully, your body will tell you when it needs to rest, and when it's ready to go. For years I judged myself for the fact that I needed far more rest than other people seemed to. I worried that I was just lazy or that I needed to have more willpower. But if I had been tuned in to my witchy instincts, I would have remembered that all things happen in cycles, and sometimes those cycles are happening on very long timelines. Years where I needed a lot of rest were followed by years where I was more energized. The body will not lie to you—if it needs rest, it needs rest. If it is hungry, it is hungry. It wants to communicate with you. It wants you to be listening.

Unfortunately, our old friend capitalism in no way prioritizes rest, especially in the United States. While some European countries are famous for all employees taking entire months off in the summer for vacation, most people in the US fight for even a couple of weeks of vacation time a year. Parental leave after a baby is born is an afterthought. And forget the idea of building rest into a workday! Just as Erin was telling us about industrialists attempting to extract as much labor as they could from the workforce, our current capitalist system thrives on people working and producing as much as possible, without any consideration of the mental or physical well-being of those people. Most schools follow this same pattern as early as high school. Students are expected to work all day, participate in an activity after school, and then do their homework all night. Most of my high school friends and I usually operated on about five or six hours of sleep, a detrimental amount in a moment when our brains were still developing, our bodies were still growing, and we could have used all the rest we could get.

I tell you this so you understand that it is very likely that you are going to have to advocate for yourself in your life when it comes to rest. The institutions that you are a part of will probably encourage you to push past feelings of fatigue in favor of achievement, and there may be social pressure around you to compete in this way. Hopefully, this is beginning to change, as we learn more about the essential value of rest, but in the meantime, you need to know that you are allowed to rest, and that giving yourself rest in moments when you need it will allow you to show up as a stronger version of yourself when you move back into a phase of activity. Someone who sleeps eight hours before a hard test is going to be able to come to that test calmer and more focused than someone who crams all night and is operating on two hours of sleep. (The sad truth is we would probably have MORE productivity if we valued rest, and definitely higher-quality productivity.)

Just as we don't always have control over our schedules, we often don't have control over our surroundings. If you are an empath who is easily affected by the energy of those around you, a crowded subway, bus, or cafeteria may be a challenging place for you. You want to pay attention to the way that not just your mind, but also your body feels in these situations, and develop strategies to protect both your physical and energetic self. HSPs can find that they need to take extra care to recover after experiencing the demands of a highly charged energetic environment.

Most of us are socialized into the idea that it is not important to prioritize our own comfort, and the unfortunate consequences of this can be that we allow ourselves to stay in situations that make us uncomfortable even when we shouldn't. We need to reclaim autonomy when it comes to listening to our bodies, and the first step toward doing this is to become aware of what is going on in your body in different situations. When we don't examine the cause and effect of stress on our bodies, we might think that there is nothing we can do to help, and end up simply attempting to deal with the symptoms rather than the cause of becoming overwhelmed. This can lead to doing things to numb yourself out when these feelings get to be too much, causing you to distance yourself even more from the messages that your body is sending you.

If something feels wrong to you, that is enough of a reason not to do it.

LEARNING ABOUT OURSELVES

"Most non-disabled people I think are completely unaware of their body at all times," Erin says. "They don't actually feel it, let alone think about what it's doing. They don't remember learning to walk; it wasn't a conscious process. For me to do very basic things at a very formative age, I had to think about it. So there was always, 'How do I get from here to the other side of the room?'"

It can help to look at facing our physical challenges as opportunities to search for and discover things that we might not have found or examined otherwise, rather than as inconveniences. Your unique search for what works for you will give you a new perspective on the world around you.

I tell Erin that I have always thought in a similar way about my depression.

"I never would have gone in search of all these different modalities if it didn't feel urgent," I tell her. "The depression is what led me to all of this, because I needed to break the cycle for myself. Searching for solutions brought me so much that I would not have otherwise experienced."

"It's about being able to deal with the fears we have about getting very close to the source of the thing that has caused you pain in your life," Erin says. "The people who are willing to go there are the ones who find the medicine in the poison. It's not so much about solving the problem, because there really isn't one. When you make peace with complexity, what you discover is that the problem and the solution are often the same thing. There isn't one without the other."

As with our natal charts, we have to learn to look at even the challenging parts of our bodies as opportunities to learn and grow. And as with our charts, we want to become curious about not just the challenges, but also the strengths. Joy, enjoyment, and pleasure are all also a part of what it means to have a body. If we allow ourselves to be tuned in to what brings us comfort in our bodies, the next step is to begin to explore what actually feels good and makes us happy. The more you understand the good feelings, the more you can call them in and learn to use that positive magical energy as healing and helpful.

Does it make you happy to dye your hair green? To wear colorful muumuus? Do you feel amazing after a long ride in a kayak? Does certain food make your body light up? A certain place? This is all important information to pay attention to and to prioritize. As with comfort, our society does not tend to put much of a priority on pleasure. Pleasure may be seen as indulgent and unproductive. But to experience pleasure is productive for the one experiencing it, as it provides us with good, sustaining energy. When you understand this energy, you begin to be able to give it to yourself, a very important skill in a world that does not always provide enough joy and pleasure.

One of the things that I admire most about Erin is her relationship to pleasure, and to pursuing an exploration of where her physical body can take her. I mean, this is a woman who moved to Spain just because she had always wanted to live in Europe, discovered a paragliding school, decided she wanted to learn how to paraglide, worked with her instructors to create a flying apparatus that would allow her to fly solo in her wheelchair, and then spent some time just flying off mountains for a while.

"If I want to go on a hike, and my chair doesn't fit, I will crawl," Erin tells me. "Who gets to tell me that I don't get to use my body that way? The only reason not to do that is because it's a socially unacceptable movement, right? It's an embarrassing way to move. But who gets to decide that? Who gets to tell me that I shouldn't have access to an experience that I want, because I can't do it walking?"

Erin's experience of adventure is so obviously personal and really provides a model for how to let your conversation with your own body guide what you decide to do with it, rather than allowing yourself to be limited by anyone else's perceptions of you. Erin finds especially that when she competes in aerial silks or on the pole, people have deep misconceptions around the way that her body functions.

"Aerial stuff looks really impressive," Erin tells me, "but if you really look at the way my body is configured—my shoulders are very broad, and then I taper down to my waist where paralysis happens, and then my legs, which are tiny, weigh nothing. So other aerialists spend a year trying to learn how to do an inversion, and I had it in three days. Their center of gravity is in this really upright position, but my center of gravity has always been up here"—she gestures to the top of her body—"which means that I grab with my arms, which are the strongest part of my body. It's a completely natural movement for me. I'm paralyzed, but I'm also agile, and that's natural to me. I'm not doing the impossible when I do aerials, I'm just using my body in a certain way. And yes, the training, the beauty, the artistry is impressive. But when the reason people are impressed is that they don't think it should be possible, that's not meaningful to me."

I ask Erin about how she navigates her personal strengths

and weaknesses when she prepares as an athlete, especially for competition. How does she know when to challenge herself and when to rest?

"When I am at my limit, it's so clear to me physically, because everything else has already been so clear to me," she tells me. "Because disability is so misunderstood, even by doctors, a lot depends on my ability to articulate what my body is experiencing."

So the better we understand the unique energetic makeup of each of our bodies, the more we can know about our own limits and how to respect them. But this learning about our own limits will always be an ongoing process. Our bodies change our entire lives, and they are meant to. Just as we know to embrace the cycles of change, we come to understand that our bodies exist in that flow of change, and that we as witches must celebrate that. We are not meant to look or even feel the same way that we do as teenagers as we do when we are thirty or sixty. To fight this constant change is to buy into capitalism's brainwashing around denying us the pleasure of living in balance with the flow of the universe.

To exist as a magical being with a body is to exist in constant flow and change, to live as a participant in the natural world. Just as paying attention to the energetic rhythms of the world around us will reward us, so will learning to develop this magical relationship with our most important lifelong homes. When you think about your physical existence, think about the cycles of experience for animals, plants, entire ecosystems. Imagine shaming a tree for not having leaves in the winter! Imagine thinking a pink flower should be purple! Your body is no different from these other bodies, and just as you come to honor the miraculous magical energy of the natural world, so you can learn to see your body as the magical manifestation that it is.

Exercises

BODY SCAN

Lie down in a comfortable spot with your eyes closed, and, starting at your feet, slowly scan your body to see how every part of it is feeling right now. As you move your attention up your body, picture yourself as being in conversation with that part of you. Is some part of you feeling tight? Loose? Is there discomfort? Relaxation? Move slowly until you get to your head, not judging any feelings that come up, just taking stock and grounding in the present reality of your body. This is a great exercise to do when you are feeling anxious—you want to remind yourself what exists here in the present moment, and to take care of present needs, rather than projecting your problem-solving brain into the future. When you are done, ask yourself what would help your body right now, in this moment.

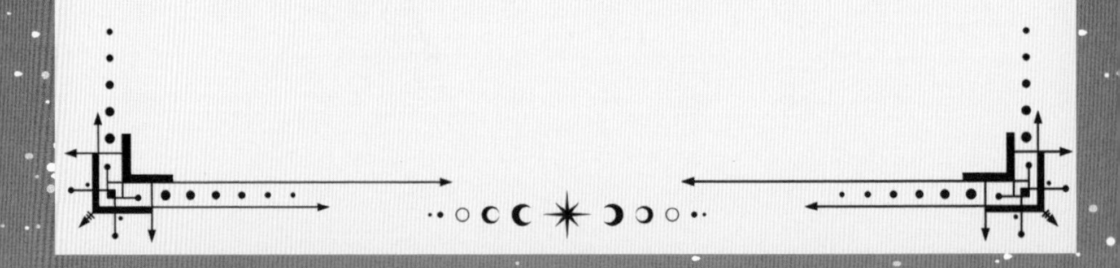

WORKING WITH YOUR AURA

Take ten minutes to sit in a quiet spot with your eyes closed. Deepen your breathing and begin to picture your aura, the energetic field that you carry around your body. Imagine yourself connecting down into the grounding energy of the earth, pulling up the earth's core energy, and letting it form into a protective globe around you. This is your magic, so get creative with the way that you imagine this protective energy. Is your protective barrier made of unbreakable glass? Is it a constantly flowing waterfall? Maybe it's made of fire on a day when you feel particularly vulnerable to outside energy. Throughout the day, anytime you need it, imagine recharging this protective barrier, bringing up more helpful energy as needed.

CHAPTER SIX:
Therapy

Sometimes before I start writing, if I find myself in need of some extra guidance, I like to pull some tarot and oracle cards to give me insight into the direction that my writing might take that day. Since I knew that talking about the idea of traditional therapy within the context of our more mystical tools would be complicated, I picked some cards to help clarify what exactly makes this just as magical a tool as any other. As usual, the cards had a lot to say.

I started with one of my favorite oracle decks—the Vessel deck by Spirit Speak. First I pulled Fire, then Structure. Of course! Therapy provides the safe structure for our fiery feelings.

Next I grabbed the Gentle Thrills tarot deck. First I pulled the King of Swords—authority, truth, clarity. Then the gnarly-looking Nine of Swords—literally the card of depression and anxiety. Okay—so a therapist is able to give us an outside perspective on our spiraling thoughts. In the Rider Waite Smith deck, the Nine of Swords is a person sitting up in bed, their hands covering their face, nine swords hanging dangerously on the wall about them. And here comes the King of Swords himself to manage all those precariously hanging swords!

And then things got even more intense. I picked up the Guided by Spirit oracle deck by our friend Aja. These are beautifully collaged and painted cards representing messages from her guides. First I managed to pull the most intimidating card in the deck—Entities. A blurry shadow figure with white eyes seemed to be staring directly at me. Okay, deep breath. Next—Hunger—a growling lion ready to attack. In the guidebook to the deck, Aja described the Entities card as energies from the past, generational trauma, collective angst, and/or energy that has attached itself to us that we need to break free from. She wrote of the Hunger card: "I demand more than I have been given. Scraps will only keep me where I am and not where I wish to grow."

Here not only is the lion of the Hunger card a therapist who can safely facilitate that journey into the shadow self, but it is also you, specifically the part of you that is brave enough to sift through your own messy brain and know that you will be safe while you do it. The question with therapy is, how do you create the safe space for yourself to take that journey? Can you ask for help in learning how to do that?

"How can I depend on people enough to take that risk, so that I can be vulnerable with myself?" I am talking with my friend Aram Jibilian, a therapist who has worked extensively with trans, nonbinary, and queer young people, over video chat. "You can't just do it on your own with shutting other people off," he says. "The bridge to yourself is other people."

As far as I'm concerned, therapy is as magical a tool as any other. Even if we are engaged in self-exploration by studying our own natal charts, the chart simply provides a map for our

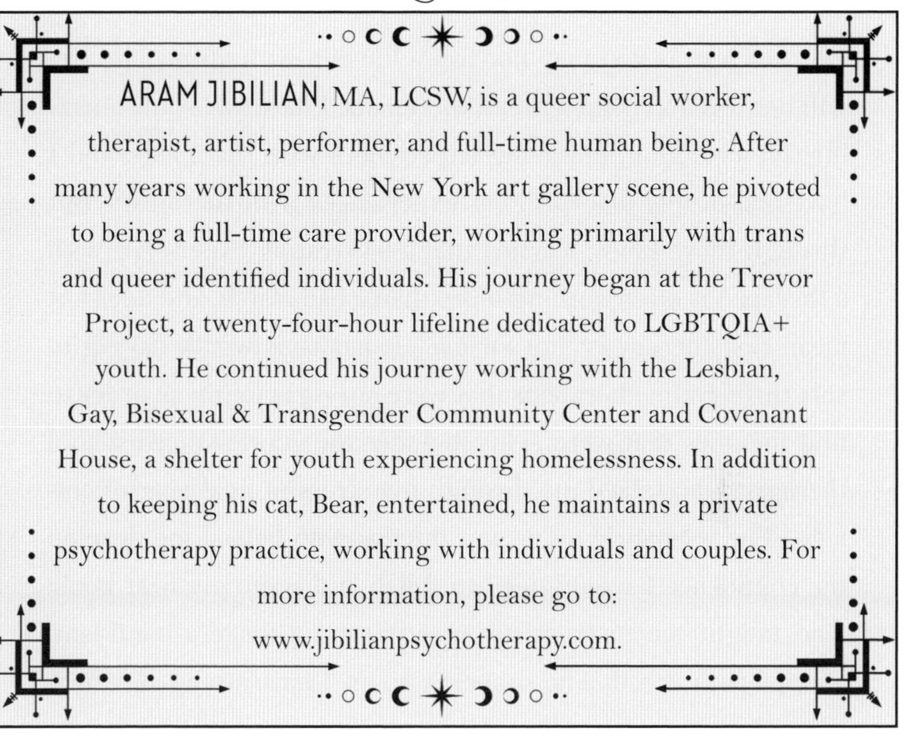

ARAM JIBILIAN, MA, LCSW, is a queer social worker, therapist, artist, performer, and full-time human being. After many years working in the New York art gallery scene, he pivoted to being a full-time care provider, working primarily with trans and queer identified individuals. His journey began at the Trevor Project, a twenty-four-hour lifeline dedicated to LGBTQIA+ youth. He continued his journey working with the Lesbian, Gay, Bisexual & Transgender Community Center and Covenant House, a shelter for youth experiencing homelessness. In addition to keeping his cat, Bear, entertained, he maintains a private psychotherapy practice, working with individuals and couples. For more information, please go to: www.jibilianpsychotherapy.com.

personality and experience. It can't talk back to us and help us interpret how these things play out in real life. It can't help us develop strategies for how to best work with the complicated parts of ourselves. It can't have a conversation with us about our identity, and help that identity form in a safe environment.

Of all the tools that I write about in this book, therapy feels the most complicated to me, and that's because it involves at least one other person. All our other tools are things that you can implement on your own and create a private relationship with, but the point of therapy is to get out of your own head and allow the most complicated parts of yourself to be witnessed by another person. This can be a very hard thing to do, and for good reason.

Therapists are just people trying their best to do a good

job, and just as you may not feel a kinship with all people, you will not feel a kinship with all therapists. I have had some amazing, life-changing, lifesaving experiences with therapists, and I have had deeply discouraging experiences with therapists. But through those I have learned that a frustrating experience with a therapist is often nothing more than a bad match, and does not mean that therapy is "not for me." It has been worth having to sort through the therapists that were not right for me in order to find the ones that were. This includes the gentle-voiced school therapist who talked me through my stressful final year of college. The woman I saw in my thirties who helped me develop the confidence I would need to finish and write my first book, who taught me to trust my creativity and forge a confident, aligned path ahead. The support groups I have attended, where through a shared kinship with strangers, you find comfort in realizing that you are not alone in a struggle. And my current therapist, who has talked me through the wild transitions of the past couple of years, all over video chat.

For me, therapy has been the next step after doing all this internal work with my other tools. It is as if, after working with the purely internal, I am now stepping out into the world, and here is someone who is out here too, who can be a guide through the challenges that the external world brings to us.

NAVIGATING IDENTITY AND SHAME

My friend Aram has the perfect demeanor for drawing out people who may not be used to talking to someone else about their problems in a sensitive way, so I am especially interested to hear about his work with young people who were experiencing homelessness at Covenant House in New York City.

"We created a whole special mental health clinic area, a soothing environment outside of the normal shelter vibe," Aram tells me. "A lot of the young people had reservations around talking to someone. My approach was very much to just meet them where they were. I let them tell me what they needed and what they wanted for themselves."

Because Aram was working with young people on a short-term basis, just for the amount of time that they were staying at the shelter, he would use very simple exercises to try to help his clients with practical tools for navigating the world.

"I call it the identity wheel," he tells me about one of his methods. "You basically write out all the identities that you are—a brother, a sister, a New Yorker, a resident at the homeless shelter, your race, your sexual orientation, all those roles that you play, and how being in certain places activates those certain identities and roles. Sometimes it's what you're really feeling about yourself, and other times it's really what other people are perceiving about you. And negotiating all that, finding a sense of home in it instead of feeling like a burden, is what it's all about."

We are always navigating the complications of our different identities throughout our lives, but this task can feel especially daunting when we are young and just starting to figure out what these identities are. This can be a complicated meaning point for our internal world and the restrictions and expectations of the external world, especially if we get a sense that there are parts of our identity that may not be accepted by the people around us. If we don't feel safe to explore these identities for ourselves, then we may have a hard time developing healthy relationships with those parts of ourselves. Especially if we are in a situation where we have been taught to people please and conform to the expectations of the people around us above meeting our own needs.

"If you're navigating an identity that you don't see reflected around you and that the society around you hasn't made space for, it can feel like a crisis," Aram says. "It can be a crisis with shame on top of it. And that element of shame keeps us isolated."

I recently became obsessed with a social phenomenon that is pleasingly called the "Streisand Effect." This comes from a real incident in which the singer Barbra Streisand sued to have a picture of her waterfront Malibu home removed from an online collection of photographs of the California coastline. The result, of course, was that the photograph ended up getting way more attention by her trying to suppress it than it would have if she had just let it exist anonymously in this government archive. Before she sued, the picture had been downloaded six times. After, it was viewed almost half a million times. Babs wasn't ashamed of her waterfront mansion—she was just exercising a control-freak need for privacy—but I appreciate the very clear cause and effect here. Sometimes when you try to hide something, it just gets bigger and more insidious.

When we decide that a part of us should not be viewed by the outside world because it is shameful and will not be accepted by those around us, we tend to devote more energy to trying to suppress that part of ourselves than we would if we looked at it head-on and examined what about it is so threatening to us. We see this play out over and over again in public life in really unfortunate ways—without fail, a right-wing politician who spends all his energy fighting against rights for queer people will turn out to be a closeted queer person. (Okay, maybe not "without fail," but this happens A LOT.)

Shame is a very exhausting energetic state to exist in, and to allow it to play a role in our lives is to cheat ourselves of having access to the full potential of our life's energy. Someone who lets shame continue in their life unchecked is also much more likely to take their frustration with their inability to eliminate that shameful part of themselves out on other people—this is how we end up with our closeted homophobic politician causing very tangible harm to other people. Not only does he feel shame about this part of himself, but he resents those who have faced any issues of shame directly and now dare to live their truth openly.

Such difficult energetic exchanges can happen on a much smaller level. If there is something about you that you have been taught to view as shameful, you will inevitably see constant examples of it in the world around you and judge them just as harshly as you are judging yourself. It's like saying to someone, "Don't think about a giraffe." The more you try not to think about a giraffe, the more you are going to see giraffes everywhere you go, and be very annoyed at them because why are they reminding you of the existence of giraffes when the one thing that you are trying to do is NOT think about giraffes!?!?!?!

The only thing that you are doing wrong is spending any time at all feeling shame about any part of yourself.

(I'm going to say that one more time, just to make sure you've got it.)

The only thing that you are doing wrong is spending any time at all feeling shame about any part of yourself.

We already know that we need to learn how to view the more complicated parts of us as allies rather than as things to be eliminated, but this is much easier said than done. And to let someone else help you navigate this path to acceptance can be very challenging, because first of all you are letting them witness this seemingly shameful part of you, AND you are admitting how difficult you find it to navigate this part of your psyche, which can bring on further feelings of shame.

"I mean, that is the journey of becoming a human being," Aram says to me. "It's not about asking, 'How do I figure this out on my own?' Implicit in that question is a faulty belief that 'I should know how to figure this out on my own.' This belief maintains our profound shame that keeps us feeling separate from others. We have to task ourselves with 'Who can I reach out to?'"

What we are doing when we begin to examine our unconscious ways of thinking is to interrupt a harmful leak of energy. Have you ever seen that infomercial where a guy is standing next to a container of water that is quickly leaking out of a large hole? He turns and slaps a heavy-duty patch over the hole and suddenly the leak is fixed! In order to learn how to slap that magical patch on that leak, we first have to acknowledge just how quickly that water is spilling out of us. (Remember that we are not fixing a part of ourselves, we are fixing the waste of time and energy that we devote to feeling shame about a part of ourselves.)

It can be very hard to look at just how severe that leak is. But when we avoid looking directly at the size of the leak, we may find ourselves surprised when we are suddenly depleted—which means we will have no energy left to give to ourselves or the people that we care about. To further avoid the pain of looking, we may blame the depletion on something or someone else. This can provide a brand-new activity to help further distract us from the scary task of self-examination—now we can spend time telling a new story about what is happening, or turn to self-destructive behaviors to busy ourselves and create new problems that have clear cause-and-effect narratives.

If we are HSPs, this process of looking at our feelings can seem even more daunting, because we sometimes don't even know if our feelings are our own, or if we are picking up on someone else's energy, or projecting something onto a situation based on a complicated energy that is affecting us. Then, just to make things worse, we can get mad at ourselves for being so sensitive.

"This is something that I latch onto in therapy," Aram tells me. When people say, 'Why am I so sensitive?' I'll say, 'Take out the why and just say that as a declarative sentence. I'm so sensitive.' And just that alone, in just that small redirection of getting rid of the 'why,' people are finally able to feel their pain and just be in it.

"I remember when I was a teenager, my thing was, 'Why am I so hairy?'" Aram says. "'Nobody else is so hairy around me.' It's like, [the truth is just that] you're Armenian and you're hairy. But the 'why' was me saying, 'I'm being told that it's not okay.' Nobody ever says, 'Why am I so beautiful? Why am I so heterosexual? Why am I so athletic?' We know what we're *not* supposed to be. And we somehow are not allowed to experience that difference without shame."

THE ANGRY KITTEN INSIDE YOU

Let me pause here to tell you a little story about my mom's cat Jackie. Jackie was part of a litter of kittens that I got tricked into rescuing one summer, and he was a mess. He was tiny and dirty and obviously hungry, but he would hiss and spit anytime anyone came near him. On top of that, he couldn't open one of his eyes and he had lost part of his tail. I took him to the vet along with two of the other kittens we had rescued, and came home with about five different medicines for him—one that had to go in his eye, one on his tail, and a few in his mouth—and this for a cat that would not let anyone get near him. I had no idea what I was going to do. I already had my two cats at home, and two others that I needed to find homes for, and I wasn't going to be home enough to give this poor little guy his medicine three times a day. Part of me wanted to just let this kitten out into the backyard where I found him; the problems seemed that insurmountable.

Enter my saint of a mother. I called her in tears, explaining the situation and asking what I should do, and she told me to bring the kitten to her house and she would see if she could help him. So I drove him out there.

We put him in the bathroom, where he immediately ran behind the sink and stayed there, hissing if we came too close. The only way to catch him in order to give him his medicine was to throw a towel over him and quickly wrap him up in it like a burrito—just pulling the body parts that we needed to access out from under the towel one by one. The first two days he hissed and struggled the whole time, immediately running back behind the sink as soon as I let him go.

And then on the third day, something changed. We had given him his medicine, and I kept holding him in the burrito towel a little longer afterward to see if he could start to get more used to people.

"What is that noise?" I asked my mom, who was washing the three kinds of cat medicine off her hands.

She looked over at me holding this cat burrito.

"He's purring," she said.

It was a stressed-out purr, and as soon as I put him down he ran away again, but I have never experienced a clearer or more profound level of communication from an animal. He was scared because he was sick. And he was thankful that we were trying to get him to feel better.

A week later this cat was sleeping next to my mom on her pillow every night, following her everywhere, and loudly purring like a malfunctioning engine. He couldn't talk and tell us what was wrong with him, but as soon as we directed our attention toward his healing, it became very obvious what we needed to do to help him. Now he weighs eighteen pounds and is the happiest, most spoiled cat in the world.

The parts of us that have been neglected, hurt, or malnourished are inevitably scared and nonfunctioning. It is not their existence that is the problem; it is that we have not been able to give them what they need. We haven't put in the effort to find the right medicine and spend the time and give the attention that will be necessary for healing. But I promise you that once you turn your healing attention to a neglected part of yourself, it is going to reward you with the equivalent of some loud kitten purrs.

"This is not a process of self-improvement," Aram says, speaking about therapeutic work in general. "It's a process of self-acceptance. Until I am able to accept every situation and every problem as exactly what it needs to be in this moment, I will not be able to accept myself, and that keeps us feeling apart from ourselves and others. That's where your mindfulness practice comes in. Just accepting the moment as the moment and saying that I have everything that I need right now, in this moment, in this life."

As we will talk about in our mindfulness chapter, our brains are often very loud without us even knowing it, and often they are saying not very nice things very loudly. The trick is not to fault your brain for being loud, but to acknowledge it, to say, "Hi, I see you." To ask that loud brain what would help it to build resilience in this moment. It's only once we have acknowledged the existence of that voice that we can start to get down to the nitty-gritty of actually working with the complications of our minds.

Remember that you are not trying to "solve" anything with therapeutic work, but you are learning to spend time with the complications of your own mind and spirit. What that means is that you are able to become much more resilient to the changing circumstances of your life. The idea is not to prevent issues from ever coming up again, but to develop the self-awareness to recognize them and strategies to manage them when they do. The more we do this, the more we are not afraid of these issues, the more we can put them in perspective. We learn that things pass and we can help them pass. And when we find ourselves afraid, we don't get angry at ourselves. Instead we let that fear point us in a direction of inquiry.

About once a day I think about the Buddhist teacher Pema Chodron and this quote from her book *When Things Fall Apart*: "Usually we think that brave people have no fear. The truth is that they are intimate with fear. When I was first married, my husband said I was one of the bravest people he knew. When I asked him why, he said because I was a complete coward but went ahead and did things anyhow."

Being brave does not mean doing something that comes easily to you. It often means feeling afraid and facing that fear anyway.

LEARNING TO RIDE THE WAVE

Depression for me often feels like a lack of possibilities, as if anything I ever had enthusiasm for has been shown to be stupid and not worth anyone's time. This is a very different feeling from sadness or experiencing grief. For me, sadness and grief just need to be felt. It is important to remember that when something very sad happens to you, you do not need to Get Over It. You are allowed to be sad for as long as you are sad. In situations of grief, it is possible that you will carry some part of this grief with you for your whole life, especially if it involves losing someone that you care about. But even within this experience of grief we can be finding a way to talk to this sadness, to integrate it, to investigate it. Can we use it to make something? Can it allow us to have empathy for other people who are going through a hard time? Or can we just sit with it, in awe of its power as much as we are in awe of beauty?

But when it comes to depression, I find that a way to counter this feeling of a lack of possibilities is to get curious about why I feel stuck in this one way of looking at my life. What is there in the present moment that can give me a hint about what is really going on and how to work with it? If we are built for evolution and growth, and depression is about feeling that the growth is no longer happening, we need to open ourselves up to the possibility that progress doesn't always look the way that we expect it to. Often progress happens much more slowly than we want it to, and involves long periods of quiet and processing. Think of the idea of planets in retrograde—to the untrained eye they look like they are actually going backward in the sky—but that's just how they look, it's not the reality of the situation. We use these times of planetary retrogrades to go over the lessons we have learned in relationship to that planet, revisit information, make the necessary adjustments, and find ourselves more prepared to move forward when the planet goes direct. And the real secret is that the planet was moving forward this entire time—it just looked like it wasn't.

What a great metaphor for these moments in our life when we seem to be standing still and not making any progress! There is often really important work happening in these moments that would be missed by an outside eye. So if you're worried about what it looks like from the outside when you are struggling, then you're missing out on digging deeper into the true progress that you are making in addressing your mental health.

The key for me often is to learn to face these moments of dips in my mental health without panicking. As a compulsive problem solver, my instinct is to try to find an immediate solution, and I then push myself further into despair when one isn't readily available. Mindfulness comes in handy here, where we stop and look at the truth of the present moment, rather than bringing old information into a new situation and making assumptions about how this is going to go down. Here is our old cave person brain, trying to pull up old files of info to identify as much as it can about a threat. We always want to learn from the past, but sometimes we bring more to a current situation than it needs. Sometimes the real solution is just about giving ourselves the time and space to ride out a wave of bad brain chemistry.

When things are difficult, we can always ask ourselves, What is the medicine here? What am I learning from this situation? What knowledge do I now have that I did not have before, even if it is simply "I can survive this"? Having these realizations MUST be seen as an accomplishment. We should give out trophies for this. Straight As in self-understanding. Even if that understanding is a private one that might be difficult to explain to someone else.

"It's so hard because you just want someone to say to you, 'It's okay,'" I say to Aram. "'It's okay that you are the way you are.' But you kind of don't even know what you're asking for permission to be for a long time. I think when I was younger I felt like I was going to be called to make some sort of report of myself that would make my existence seem comprehensible. But there's no test. And maybe some things about me don't need to be explained to others."

"Also we're in constant change," Aram says. "We're in constant flux. So how can we just stay in that curiousness?"

"And not be threatened by it," I say, jumping in. "In those moments we may even need to move beyond language. Into creativity, like music or painting. We can let it be about pure feeling."

The reason why I often turn to creativity to counter depression is exactly because of this element of mystery. For me it works in a similar way to connecting with nature or the energy of animals. To be in "awe" is to stand in front of something that you don't understand but don't need to—to feel yourself as a part of a bigger energy and release the need to control or be able to fix everything. It gives me a tangible understanding of the fact that not everything is up to me, and that some things are far more amazing than I could have imagined. Awe exists outside the realm of linear narrative, and when we engage with it, it allows us to step outside that need for linear narrative as well, and to experience a moment of pure existence.

Here we have another example of a kind of nervous system reset. When our internal narratives are not serving us, we find that reset button and make a mindful choice about what we want to pay attention to.

If I have learned that I cannot and should not try to fit the way that my brain works into any kind of present expectation I may have, then what is my personal, private standard for functioning? Basically, as long as I can write, I'm okay. We'll get into this more in the creativity chapter, but this has been the place where I have found the strongest connection to Spirit energy, where, if I take care of myself by engaging in my magic/awe/generative practice, everything else with my mental health becomes much easier to work with.

I ask Aram how he feels about using mystical tools in his practice, and I'm not too surprised to hear that he has used tarot with his patients.

"It was with a young person who was having a really hard time identifying content to bring to his session," he tells me. "He was describing this dream that he had, saying, 'I feel like I'm just sort of like throwing arrows into the sky. And I am sending out all the messages and the signals and they're just not landing anywhere.' I had pulled this card that morning, the Eight of Wands, the ones that are all flying through the sky."

Aram shared this convergence of the meaning of the Eight of Wands with his patient, and asked him if he would be interested in pulling cards.

"Twice he pulled the same card—the Five of Cups, which is the best card to pull with somebody who's had trauma. The

Five of Cups is totally the 'what else is true?' card. He's this guy who's staring at these three fallen cups, and behind him are two cups standing upright. And so we identify, what are the fallen cups for you? And how can we turn and pivot ourselves to look at these two full cups? Again, it's not to say, 'Don't feel that, don't feel those bad feelings,' but instead saying, 'We can hold both truths—the grief and the anger over what's been lost *and* the strength and joy in what is still present.'"

"One of the things I feel like tarot and therapy actually have in common," I say, "is this thing where you've got something going on that is so tangled up in your own brain, that you literally want to pull it out of your head and put it on the table in front of you so you can look at it and organize it. And therapy allows you to have someone else look at it and say, 'Okay, here are a couple of different ways to interpret and approach this.' This idea of externalizing this thing that feels so painful or incomprehensible in your head and having someone mirror back to you that, yes, this is complicated, but also we can look at it."

"Exactly," Aram says. "We can bring it into language. It doesn't have to stay primal, it doesn't have to stay in the solar plexus, like, vibrating panic. It can actually be externalized."

I am glad to hear that Aram approves of combining different tools to approach mental health (since this is the entire basis of this book!). I think of how the therapists who have helped me the most have been the ones who were open to accepting these different tools of self-exploration.

"It's something I tell people when they say, 'I don't believe in therapy,'" Aram says. "I'm like, 'Well, neither do I, if you're making it a god, and you think that it's the only thing that's going to help you.' It's a slice of the biggest pizza pie ever. And I encourage other slices. If you want it to be your only slice, you're going to be really disappointed."

"Capitalism likes us to believe that there's one magical solution," I say, bringing up my favorite topic, "and if you follow the path of that singular solution, then everything you've wanted to 'fix' will be fixed. We are taught to think, 'If I can just find the right puzzle piece, I'll solve it, and then I'll win!' And that's just not the game we're playing here."

"It's very child mind," Aram says. "Capitalism keeps us like children, because it's all about short-term gratification. 'I need it, I get it. Mine. Me.' It's that narrative of, 'I went from being sad to a happy Hollywood ending.' But it's not like that. We're not in a happy-ending story. We're on a journey."

"It's like we're supposed to be in competition with everyone around us to self-love the best," I say. "It's completely counterproductive to actual mental health. Can't we allow ourselves to live in neutral sometimes? Can we say, 'It's fine. I'm living, I'm getting through my day. Things work pretty well'?"

Usually when capitalism co-opts a self-help narrative, the inherent idea of competition and achievement not only sets people up to experience failure, but also inflicts a very damaging erasure of both complexity and vulnerability. So much of Western culture was designed to see vulnerability and weakness as unacceptable. This is where a lot of stigma around the idea of therapy comes in—maybe an idea that someone should just "tough it out," or "grow a thicker skin," or "get over it." But anyone who feels this way about therapy is revealing their own fears about their mental health. The idea of uncovering the role of the unconscious in their own lives is so terrifying to them that they believe that no one should do it, or that there is some kind of badge of honor in not asking for help. And as my mom likes to say, "You don't get extra points for suffering." Again, no one is keeping score, and even if they were, how could anyone fault someone for taking responsibility for their own mental health?

ASKING FOR HELP

So how exactly do we go about asking for help, especially if traditional ways of getting help don't feel particularly open to us, or if we come from a family that we worry might not understand what is going on with us?

"The best referrals come from people who know the person," Aram tells me. "If you don't want to talk to your own parent, just find somebody who you think is kind of cool. Is there a teacher? A social worker, your pediatrician, or even your dentist? Someone at your church, or the parent of one of your friends? They might know someone who's a therapist. If somebody had to do it alone, let's say if it was a queer person, they might call the Trevor Project [a nonprofit focused on suicide prevention for LGBTQ young people]. And that person might help them find someone in their area who works specifically with LGBTQ kids. [When I was young] I would call helplines left and right, because I didn't feel comfortable talking to people in person. Even when I was twenty-two and looking for therapists, there was no way I was going to look for one by myself. I asked my uncle who had been a therapist, and he connected me."

A nasty trick of depression and anxiety is to convince us that not only are we alone with these feelings in this moment, but also that no one has ever gone through something similar before. Even though asking an adult for suggestions for help can feel daunting, keep in mind that it is extremely likely that this person has had to ask for help at some point in their lives, and will understand how vulnerable you feel in that moment. It's also very possible that there is a person in your life you wouldn't necessarily think of who might be in a position to offer you guidance.

"I remember at Covenant House," Aram tells me, "I worked with a resident who said, 'No one's going to understand that I'm gay.' I said, 'Okay, well, who are some people you grew up with?' 'Oh, I had a cousin and she had a girlfriend.' 'Was she cool?' 'She was the best.' 'Have you ever talked to her?' 'I can't call her, that'll be weird.' 'I mean, for you it will be weird. But I bet it would mean so much to her if you reached out to her.' So a lot of it's just helping them think it through. They're telling you they feel like they don't have anyone, but they may not literally have no one. There might be another way to think about it."

If you do feel comfortable talking to a parent or other caregiver about what's going on, definitely do that. I know it can be difficult, even with very supportive and understanding parents. Sometimes our parents may be hoping to be able to protect us from the more difficult parts of life (an impossible task!) and we might feel bad admitting to them that we're having a hard time when we know that they want the best for us. It is very, very likely that your parent will be glad you confided in them and will work with you to decide what kind of help you need, but again, if this feels too daunting, do not let it stop you from talking to someone.

Imagine if a friend or family member came to you asking you for help. If they said they were having a hard time and wondered if you could help them navigate finding someone to talk to, wouldn't you feel honored that they trusted you so deeply? And wouldn't you be proud of them for having such initiative to take care of their mental health? I promise you that if you ask a friend or teacher for help now, you will have an opportunity in your life to repay this service and help someone else. Someone will see you as a safe space to come to. Is it possible for you to even create that safe space for yourself?

"Something I often do with clients who are struggling with being kind and compassionate toward themselves is to ask them to think about themselves as a child," Aram says. "Imagine yourself as a seven-year-old, or imagine if your little brother or sister was going through this. What would you tell them? Everybody has that inner wise self inside them that is capable of kindness and compassion."

Even in writing this book, I knew I needed to ask people for help, that I wouldn't be able to communicate everything that I wanted to say without these other voices contributing their invaluable wisdom and perspectives, and yet I was nervous to ask! Every time a friend that I have interviewed here emailed me back to say that they would be delighted to be involved, I was hugely relieved. The asking for help felt deeply vulnerable, but the help that I received as a result of asking was so valuable and important that it made being vulnerable completely worth it.

When you give yourself the tools to figure out what kind of guidance and support you need, you are engaging with the world in a way that helps to reinforce your sense of self and personal empowerment. Life can seem helpless and hopeless when we feel at the mercy of forces that are beyond our control, so by figuring out what we can do to help ourselves, we call in a feeling of autonomy and hope. We are constantly looking for the balance on the locus of control, understanding that the mysteries of fate are often out of our control, but that we are always able to learn how to navigate our feelings within that.

But what about those situations where, for whatever reason, talking to someone is not an option, and we have to figure out how to manage our mental health on our own? Because the truth is that even with outside help and someone to point you in the right direction, only you know how things feel inside. So how can we self-soothe? What is in our bag of tricks that can help our brain chemistry ride out a bad wave? What is the practice of helping yourself that you can nurture, so you can show up feeling supported even when you are scared?

It's actually a good question to ask yourself in moments when you're not feeling in need of immediate help, in order to have a strategy in your mind of what you can do for yourself when things feel challenging.

"You don't just brush your teeth when you have a cavity," Aram says. "It actually probably hurts to brush when you have a cavity. It hurts to all of a sudden meditate when you're having a panic attack. So there's a difference between things I do when things hurt and things that I do on a regular basis. And if you know something's going to hurt, you can be open to accepting those things about yourself. Like I have to accept that my birthday, even though it's supposed to be a great day, is really triggering for me. And if I accept that, then I'm able to take care of myself. If I don't accept that, and I expect myself to be happy, then I'm going to be miserable and not know why. So we have to become sort of cartographers of our emotions."

I love this! Cartographers of our emotions! Just as we map our experiences with the planets, the cards, the seasons, our bodies. Here is another part of that giant elephant to explore!

As with all our work on our minds, bodies, and spirits, our personal evolution has a huge impact on the world around us. Unjust power structures have benefited for a very long time from people not feeling safe to explore the complications of those power dynamics and keeping their mouths shut about what they know to be true. As the Pandora's box of reality gets forced open in these first stages of the Age of Aquarius, we must each examine the parts of our own lives and selves that previously felt too dangerous to show the world. What about your individual truth is a threat to capitalist power structures? In my opinion, the best thing to do would be to find it, treasure it, and add your own voice to those who refuse to avoid the tough questions any longer.

We know that as above, so below. The way to be responsible for your individual energy is to be willing to look into the whys of your feelings and behaviors. The more you allow the truth of yourself to feel free to reveal itself to you, the more the world around you will start to make sense, and you will be able to see how essential your role is in our human energetic conversation. The magic of therapy is allowing that direct connection with another person or people to serve as your guide through this process, recognizing that we can learn so much from each other when it comes to more deeply understanding ourselves.

Exercises

YOUR TOOLBOX

Make a list for yourself of resources you could call on in a moment when you might need some mental health assistance. This should include contact information for people who can help you, but also those things that lift your spirits and comfort you no matter what. Is there a favorite book or TV show? Certain music? An article of clothing? Along with thinking about how you could employ your mystical tools in those moments, create a toolbox of things that bring you joy. When you find yourself riding out a bad wave, you will see the care that your past self has put into this list, and recognize that you will cycle back to a place where you will soon be adding more joyful things.

SOMETHING "WRONG"

Take twenty minutes to journal about a time when you didn't have the reaction that you expected to have to something (or that others expected you to have). What about the situation affected you differently from how you thought it would? Did that feel bad? Good? Why? Did something else present itself even though things didn't go the way that you expected them to? Did you give yourself space to have your feelings or did you try to suppress them? What would it look like to have let the truth of your feelings fully exist in that moment?

CHAPTER SEVEN:
Mindfulness

So how do we actually get these noisy minds of ours to be quiet enough for us to be able do all this excellent cartography of our emotions? How can we give ourselves a tool that allows us not only to drop in and see how we are feeling, but also to decenter our ego-driven narratives about what is going on in our lives and why? It is time to turn to one of the one of the oldest spiritual practices of all time—mindfulness!

To talk about exactly what the practice of mindfulness involves, I needed to go to a person who inspires thousands of people on social media on a daily basis to learn self-love practices, my friend Jeffrey Marsh.

"Almost nobody has the ability to sit quietly with themselves," Jeffrey tells me over video chat from their home in Los Angeles. "It actually becomes a superpower. Because if you're able to sit quietly with yourself when anything happens within you—emotions, boredom, whatever—you can sit through anything that happens outside."

I first met Jeffrey in one of those magical, "universe making moves" ways (although Jeffrey is deeply practical and tends to reject my magical musings). I was sitting in the front row at a small theater in downtown New York next to my wife, who had made the costumes for the show we were about to watch. The show, which involved our friend dressing up as a giant vagina and hosting a talk show, was pee-in-your-pants funny, and the vibe in the room was more party than show. At some point during intermission my wife had to go help with some malfunction on the giant vagina, and I was sitting alone. The man sitting next to me turned to me and said, "Hi, what do you do?" I told him that I write books for young adults.

"Oh, you have to meet my friend Jeffrey," he said. "They're an internet sensation. They get literally mobbed in the streets by teenagers."

I went home and spent hours watching Jeffrey's videos, completely charmed by this glamorous nonbinary internet superstar and deeply comforted by their method of self-assured wisdom. When Jeffrey speaks, you want to listen.

"Your friend says I have to meet you," I wrote to Jeffrey. "We were sitting next to each other at a show about a giant vagina."

Jeffrey, unfazed, suggested a date for us to meet at the statue of Gandhi in Union Square in New York City. Since this first meeting, whenever I am around Jeffrey I feel the way that people talk about feeling when they meet the guru that they then follow to a commune, where they spend the rest of their life wearing matching caftans and chanting all day. You know—that person who people meet and say, "They had the most amazing eyes! They looked into my soul! They truly listened to me!"

I have a feeling that if I told Jeffrey this, they would just smile at me in an amused way and say, "Okay."

But today they have met me over video chat to tell me about how they came to become a student and teacher of Zen Buddhism for the past two decades, a practice that has deeply informed their messaging about self-acceptance. As practical as they are, it turns out that mysticism was their gateway to a mindfulness practice.

"I went into what my mom would call a 'woo' bookstore, a spiritual bookstore in Philadelphia," Jeffrey tells me. "I loved going there. They had fun crystals and all kinds of books I had

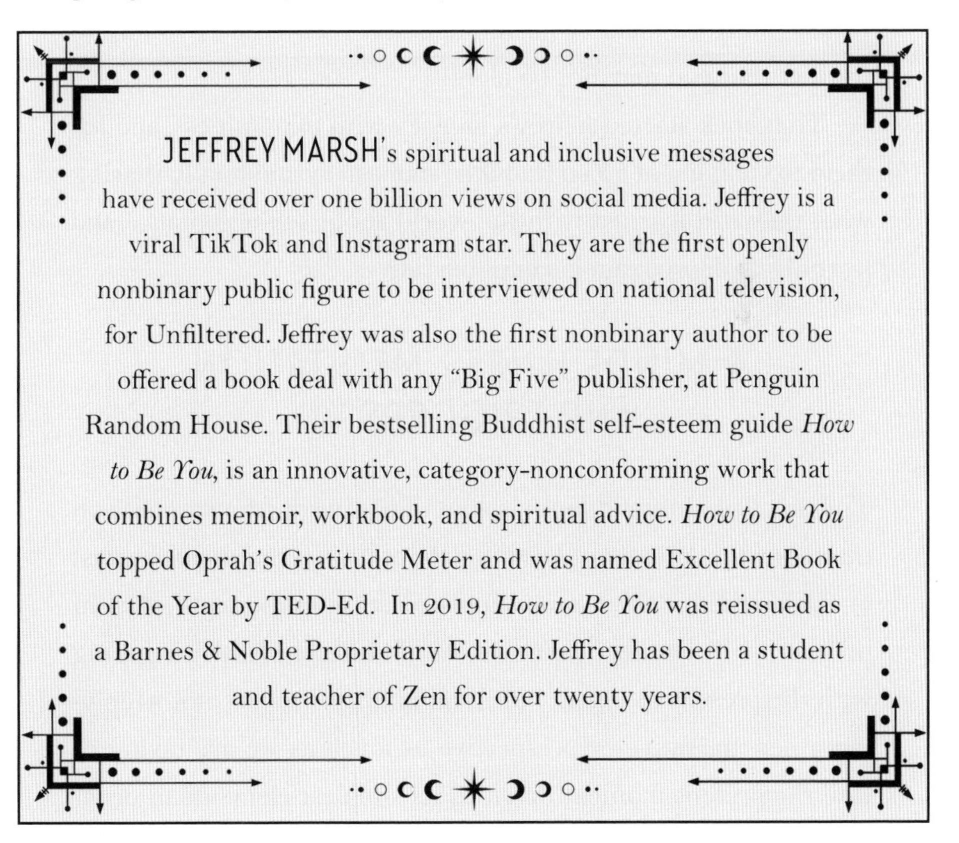

JEFFREY MARSH's spiritual and inclusive messages have received over one billion views on social media. Jeffrey is a viral TikTok and Instagram star. They are the first openly nonbinary public figure to be interviewed on national television, for Unfiltered. Jeffrey was also the first nonbinary author to be offered a book deal with any "Big Five" publisher, at Penguin Random House. Their bestselling Buddhist self-esteem guide *How to Be You*, is an innovative, category-nonconforming work that combines memoir, workbook, and spiritual advice. *How to Be You* topped Oprah's Gratitude Meter and was named Excellent Book of the Year by TED-Ed. In 2019, *How to Be You* was reissued as a Barnes & Noble Proprietary Edition. Jeffrey has been a student and teacher of Zen for over twenty years.

never encountered growing up in rural Pennsylvania. So it was just a wonderland for me. And I remember going in one day, and seeing a book across the bookstore. The cover said in handwritten letters, *There Is Nothing Wrong with You.* It was like it called to my heart. And my head started to argue [with that]. But luckily, as my brain was saying, 'You've got to be kidding. Of course there's something wrong with me. Here's the list,' my feet were already walking over to that book. I opened it up, and it was the experience we sometimes have, where you feel so alone, and like what's wrong with you is so singular, so you're constantly trying to hide it. Then you read a book that tells you what's going on inside your mind, and it really wakes you up to the fact that you may not be alone."

That book started Jeffrey's journey with mindfulness, and led them to studying at a Zen Buddhist monastery and finally sharing what they had learned with the world about self-acceptance and learning to deprogram harmful narratives.

MINDFULNESS, MEDITATION, AND TRIGGERS

The practice of mindfulness is about focusing your awareness on the present moment, not thinking about the narratives of the past or the worries of the future, simply existing in the truth of right now. As with our other practices, we are intentionally reengaging with the present moment, but in mindfulness we are not supplying a new narrative or perspective as much as we are trying to take the present moment down to its simplest elements in order to accomplish that nervous system reset we so often need.

Most mindfulness traditions recommend accomplishing this by bringing our attention to our breath, since our breath is always existing in the present moment, and it can anchor us back into our bodies when our brains start running off with various narratives based on what has happened or what we think might happen.

"So many traditions follow the breath," Jeffrey explains. "The breath is always happening at this second and the body is always happening in this second, so the body is a real friend when it comes to mindfulness. But so many people are taught to hate, reject, and judge their body. This comes up a lot in talking to trans people with dysphoria [a feeling of distress caused by the difference between the gender someone is assigned at birth and their gender identity]. But it's really common for all humans to feel that way."

No wonder mindfulness is hard for most of us! If the solution to experiencing unnecessary stress is to return to feeling grounded in our bodies, and we've been taught by society that our bodies are not positive, happy, nurturing places to be, that our bodies are something to struggle with, to mold into a shape, to exist primarily as a way to present ourselves to others, then how could we possibly start to find a retreat of safety and comfort in our bodies?

But we know that we are able to engage our bodies in an energetic conversation at any time. If we sit quietly in meditation for five minutes, asking our bodies to be a safe place to do that, we will begin to find a home in that present energy. And even if our relationship with our bodies feels complicated in the moment, there's room for that, too.

If mindfulness is the practice, then meditation is the container. Meditation is just creating an opportunity to practice mindfulness. You can even think of mindfulness as the magic and meditation as the ceremony. Just as a ceremony for the full moon creates a space for the energy of that moment to flourish, sitting in meditation allows the energy of any moment to settle and reconnect with you.

When we sit in meditation, we devote a certain amount of time to stillness and to focusing on the breath—it could be five minutes or five hours—and we watch our busy minds at work, always gently bringing them back to the present moment. The idea of meditation is not to eliminate thought; it's to observe our thoughts and learn how to avoid attaching ourselves to any thought in particular. We can picture our thoughts like clouds in a sky, slowly blowing past and revealing the bright blue again, or as sticks tumbling down a stream. We simply label them "thinking," and then tell them we will get back to them later. We acknowledge them, and we let them pass. With this practice (and it does take practice), you begin to realize that you have the power to shift and adjust your attention at any time, and that this ability to shift your consciousness is as magical as any other tool that is available to you.

In popular culture, meditation is often depicted as something that is part of relaxing self-care practices, and meditation can be relaxing, but often it is not, and we should not expect it to always be. Because meditation is actually training us for a much bigger task—learning to practice mindfulness in everything that we do.

"You're going to be sitting in meditation," Jeffrey says, "and you're going to get the trigger from your brain—'Oh, my God, I have to do the laundry right now. That email, I was supposed to send it by two o'clock, it's two fifteen!' There's a lot that's going to happen in your brain that's supposed to trigger you to get up off that cushion. And if you learn not to, that's a very practical skill. The outside world is filled with things that trigger us. So learning to see how triggers work is extremely valuable."

It might be true that you do need to send that email! But in meditation we actively practice not letting that trigger thought derail us. The email can wait until we are done meditating. We are practicing not being thrown around by every single thought that arises. Because the truth is that most of us are being tossed around by our thoughts all day long in ways that we may not even realize. If we can start to observe that phenomenon, we can start to sort through those triggers and begin to determine when something is actually important and when it's not.

"I think that for highly sensitive people, those triggers can become especially overwhelming," I offer to Jeffrey, "and mindfulness can give us a chance to extend the time after a trigger. Not that an emotional reaction is wrong, but just that, especially for people who are hypervigilant about their surroundings, it can feel like life or death in that moment, when it maybe isn't. And you're putting your nervous system through something by letting your body think that it's life or death."

"Oh, absolutely," Jeffrey agrees. "And if it feels like life or death, your brain is going to react like it is. Whether it is or not."

The word "triggered" has come to have a watered-down

meaning in popular culture, so much so that it is easy to make fun of it. What started out as a term for a sensory experience that can affect someone with PTSD and force them to feel as though they are dropped back into a traumatizing experience, is now sort of a catch-all term for getting upset. But I actually find the word "triggered" to be very useful—it's as if a starting gun goes off and your brain begins running around a wild track without you even knowing there was a race—but there are other terms we can use here too. Buddhist teacher Pema Chodron talks about "not biting the hook," as if we are a fish presented with particularly juicy bait who will then face only suffering as a result of allowing ourselves to indulge. In her book *Taking the Leap* she introduces us to the Tibetan word "shenpa," which she describes as "that sticky feeling" when we click back into an old pattern of anger, hurt, or general dysfunction that accomplishes nothing other than hurting ourselves.

This practice of learning not to bite the hook is not about keeping quiet when you witness injustice. Instead, it's about telling cave person brain to slow down with that fight-or-flight response and take a look at what is actually happening, because we know that unless you tell it otherwise, cave person brain is going to think you are literally being attacked by a saber-toothed tiger.

"For you to revoke access to your buttons takes discipline and it takes practice," Jeffrey tells me when I ask them about dealing with a triggering situation, "but it's completely possible."

They offer up an example: "A family member is on the phone with you and really judges you for something. Says, 'Why can't your partner get a job? Why would you be with somebody like that?' You are supposed to start defending, start staking your claim, start being aggressive. But if what you really want is to defuse the situation, is to have a nice life, you say, 'You know, you're right. I'm going to think about that. Goodbye.' You don't have to actually agree with them. But you're revoking access to what they want from you, which is that conflict."

For some people this may feel as if they are not honoring the truth of their anger—of course you have every right to be angry at your family member criticizing your partner! But the secret to this practice of allowing yourself to pause and let your stress response calm down before you act is that you will actually be in a much better place to face the situation if you are not in your shenpa stress response. You might even be able to see that what this person is saying is probably more about themselves than it is about you. So this is not always about completely walking away from a situation that is hooking you, because sometimes that's not possible. Most days of our lives we will experience something that causes us to have a stress reaction, so we need to know how to work with it.

WHEN OTHER PEOPLE DON'T BEHAVE PROPERLY

For many highly sensitive people, the part of us that becomes stressed is the part that wants everything to go according to a perfect plan that we have in our heads, and that plan has often been subconsciously designed to make sure that we and the people we care about feel safe. But there are some tough lessons here that mindfulness can help us work through. The first is that you do not have the power to control everything that goes on around you. And it is not your responsibility to even try to do that. We know this from our spellwork—we can have a vision for how we would like things to go, but we must keep a very light grip on that vision, and always be ready to trade it in for something new and maybe even better.

By extension, I find that when I really get angry at someone, it is usually because they are not acting in the way that I BELIEVE they should act. I KNOW they can be better than this, so WHY DON'T THEY DO IT?!?!?!? Do I have to EXPLAIN IT TO THEM??? If I EXPLAIN IT TO THEM, will they then come to understand that they SHOULD NOT ACT THIS WAY?!?!?!?

Maybe things would be a lot easier if you could program everyone around you to act the way you want them to, but that is not called life, that is called *The Sims*, and even those guys go off the rails every once in a while. It's a very harsh lesson to learn that you can't always help the people around you, and you certainly can't expect them to change just because you want them to. If there are changes that need to happen, they are not going to happen until that person feels very deeply for themselves that they need to change. The way that they are acting is happening for a reason—it is a coping mechanism that they have developed to deal with the world. It may not be a healthy coping mechanism, and it may be negatively affecting the people around them, but it probably serves a purpose for them that you can't understand, and it's not your job to understand.

This doesn't mean that we don't help someone who needs our help, or that we don't try to work out problems in friendships and other relationships. Communicating with someone close to you about the way that you are feeling can be hugely powerful. You may be surprised to find that they had no idea that you were feeling this way, and they will change their behavior based on this new information. Or you might find yourself in a situation where someone talking to you about the reasons for their behavior helps you to have a deeper compassion for what they are going through.

But the key here is acceptance. If we are to participate in the magical process of our own evolution, we have to take a good, curious look at how we are feeling and why. If someone has hurt us, of course we want to protect ourselves from being in a position to be hurt again, but we also learn the most by tending to ourselves in that moment. You are your best caretaker, because you know best what you need.

I ask Jeffrey their advice about dealing with someone who is resistant to stepping into the truth of a moment with you and continues to throw triggers your way.

"The way that you know you're dealing with someone resistant," Jeffrey responds, "is because you know what resistance is in yourself. It's always helpful to remember that we've acted like that, at least in our past, if not very close to now. But the second thing is that, in interactions like that, they likely want something from you. There's a role that you're supposed to play in response. And in my experience, if you play any other role, anything at all, except the one they want, they don't get what they are looking for from you. And they move on. Absolutely easier said than done, because they're trying to push your buttons."

"It involves a kind of self-commanding awareness," I say, "to be able to stand strong in a storm. Especially when we're young, and we're forced to give away a lot of power to families, friends, social circles, the system of school. All that external stuff starts to feel so much more important than what's going on inside."

"Not even much more important," Jeffrey insists. "It's like our needs don't even exist. And if they do, we better pretend that they do not."

When we meditate and practice the magic of mindfulness, we start to realize not only that we are being triggered by things and people outside us, but also that our frustration often turns in on ourselves, causing our inner monologue to turn to criticism. Because we may be so used to the way that we talk to ourselves, we might not even realize that we are judging ourselves more harshly than anyone else until we take a moment to ask the monologue to pause.

"It's not something adults talk about very often," Jeffrey says, "these incessant voices inside our head that always talk to us about how horrible we are. But it's something we're all going through. We're really taught to keep it to ourselves, and I am a strong advocate of not doing that."

Why do we talk to ourselves in a way that we would never dare talk to a good friend? A sad secret that I have discovered about people who are quick to say deeply judgmental things to others is that this is simply the tip of the iceberg of how they talk to themselves in their heads. Their inner judgmental monologue is so loud that it is actually slipping out of them onto other people.

All this judgment of others and judgmental self-talk tends to overlap in really harmful ways. Other people put their negative, unexamined self-talk on us, we internalize it and unconsciously claim it as our own, and then we have the potential to project it out onto others.

"We begin to police ourselves in the exact ways that we were policed by outside people," Jeffrey adds. "We are trained by the system to fear what we will find, so we stop looking. But you get to say, 'I'm no longer going to allow you to do the programming. From here on out, I decide what goes into this brain and this heart and this beautiful person. And you do not.'"

"PAIN IS INEVITABLE, BUT SUFFERING IS OPTIONAL."

"It's one of those things that is fundamentally true," Jeffrey says when I ask them about this popular quote that often comes up when people think about Buddhist principles of nonattachment, "and of course, it's also one of the most enthusiastic ways that self-hate perpetuates itself. Because we feel like we're inadequate if we still suffer. It happens to be true that you can learn not to suffer with these things. And a huge part of that is changing your self-talk to be something kind. And if that's hard for you to do, if it's hard to make this a new habit, if you stumble, if you can't do it for a while, all of that is absolutely wonderful."

So the key here is that even when we do get hooked, and

believe me, we will, we don't judge ourselves for that.

"You talked about standing strong in the middle of a storm," Jeffrey adds. "But I would encourage any- and everybody to stand 'accepting' in the middle of anything. So if you're in the middle of a storm, and you're, quote unquote, 'weak' and you get swept up into the storm, it's about just learning that that happens to human beings sometimes."

"You can't feel bad about it," I say. "To start feeling bad about feeling bad. Like there are these many layers of suffering . . ."

"A baklava?" Jeffrey offers.

"Exactly!" I laugh. "It's a pastry of suffering!"

"A phyllo dough of suffering!"

"There's the thing that's happening in the moment that is distressing," I say, now enjoying picturing our pastry of suffering, "then there's our reaction to that. And then hopefully you can eliminate this third voice of, 'I wish I hadn't reacted that way, or I reacted the wrong way, or I'm mad at myself.' The judgment on top of all of it. Because that negative voice talking to ourselves comes from somewhere. We're emulating the outside world."

What this means is that there is a separate, higher form of self that is able to step out of stress response and judgment and act as a helpful witness to our lives. Now, this to me is an incredible superpower—to serve as your own witness in life, to help yourself along the journey just as you would help someone that you cared about, and to stay curious and interested in this life path that you are on. If we have a basic human need to be witnessed, can we give that to ourselves, rather than looking for outside validation from institutions or other people? And if you can act as your own witness, how is your witness-self communicating with the rest of you, and how would you like it to communicate with you?

"What I've found in doing Buddhist practice is that the line between what's me and what's the life accepting me gets really, like, blurred out," Jeffrey tells me. "You begin to realize that you may not be the small, scared self who is hoping to impress everyone. You may be the kind, loving, gentle, wonderful energy that's ready to give that person whatever they need. And making that transition is the chef's kiss of Buddhism."

"For me, in hard moments, I do feel that I have this witnessing self," I admit, "that's sort of saying, 'Oh, this is an interesting thing for a human to go through. This is what humans go through, and here you are going through it.'"

"What you described, though, is a little too detached for my taste," Jeffrey says. "Because to me, I want to get in there, and I want to be kind to myself. You know, today I was angry at my partner for something. And my partner is a saint, so I know it was not his fault, but I was triggered into this angry response. And I heard inside my mind, 'I love you, Jeffrey.' Just like that. Immediate. And at this point habitual, because I have trained to be able to do that. What I did not hear in my brain was, 'Oh, anger is so interesting. Human beings get angry.'"

"Like an alien scientist with a little pen taking notes!" I insist, laughing at Jeffrey's disdain for the way I picture my witness self.

"I do not want an alien scientist," Jeffrey says. "I want a friend, somebody who likes me, who wants to hug me, who wants to be with me while I'm going through these things."

"I love that," I say. "I'm going to try to get one of those!"

So although my alien scientist taking notes is not exactly Jeffrey's vision of a helpful witness, I think they might approve if I made my curious alien just a little more loving and friendly. For me, the important thing is to give yourself a strategy for how to sit with moments of discomfort and know that you are not alone in them. In fact, it is especially in moments when things are difficult that you are connecting with an experience that everyone goes through, and keeping that thought present in your mind can be a huge help toward developing compassion both for yourself and for others. The more we can each normalize letting ourselves experience the full spectrum of feelings without judgment, the more we can do that for other people too.

"With a lot of people who talk about mindfulness, it really gets analytical and logical," Jeffrey says. "'You should be able to logic your way out of feeling things. You're supposed to be that detached observer.' For a long time I felt extremely inadequate because I tried, and I could not do it. To me having a kind, loving, nice person with you, no matter what you're going through, is a really handy definition of mindfulness. I think there's a lot of queer phobia or femme phobia with all of this, or fear of being soft. 'Having emotions is weakness!' But it just makes me sad, because people don't have nice things going on inside their mind."

NON-ATTACHMENT

The concept of non-attachment can be interpreted in different ways, but for me it's about our witchy understanding of letting go of expectations around the way that something might happen. We want to allow for our positive magical intentions, but to remember that we are not meant to become attached to a particular vision of how something "should" happen, so much so that we are no longer open to the possibilities that we couldn't have even imagined. Mindfulness helps us provide space for the unexpected magic to creep in. If we become overly attached, what happens is that the gap between our expectations and reality makes us start to shut down. But if we are using our tools of paying attention to the present moment, we are always looking for what new opportunities may present themselves.

In our therapy chapter, Aram talked about how he knows that he usually feels down on his birthday, so he has learned to allow space for that. He does not expect it to be the most fun day of the year, and he doesn't beat himself up about the fact that it "should" be and it's not. This is a common experience for many people with birthdays and other holidays. We have such a collective expectation about how we "should" feel on these days that we can't just sit with how we actually feel without judgment. There is the societal expectation that you should have a great time on your birthday, and maybe sometimes you do. But if you set yourself up for a very specific expectation and it is not met, you suddenly get plunged into that gap between expectation and reality, where you either blame yourself for things not going according to plan, or you blame the world around you. The reality is that blame is usually beside the point. What is happening is what is happening.

So we allow the feelings—disappointment, sadness, stress, even grief—but we do not let them take over forever. We let our loving witness-self step back and say, is there something else going on here? Is there opportunity in the unexpected way that this is happening?

This practice is very difficult—to allow yourself to have dreams, make plans, but keep a very light grip on how it all goes down—so we return to our spellwork to support us here. Always asking for "this or something better." Sometimes the something better is way more complicated than what you had originally imagined, but there is always something in there for you, even if it is something that is challenging you to grow in ways you never imagined that you could. We'll talk about this more in our career chapter, but the reality is that often even when things do go according to plan, they may not "feel" the way that you thought they would, and there's so much to learn in that, too.

We also learn through this practice to accept that most things are never all good or all bad. The goal here, as with all our practices, is to step off that good/bad binary, to stop needing to categorize experience in this way.

"You used the word 'binary' first. I thought for sure it would be me," Jeffrey says, smiling at me when I propose this to them. "There's a whole tradition in Buddhism of calling it the Middle Way. It's not choice on or choice off. It's the Middle Way. There's some other choice."

We can even use this practice in moments of uncertainty (which is every moment, really). The inability to know everything can be an opportunity for relief rather than anxiety. The inability to control is exactly what is asking us to turn to that magical unknown and search for things that feel even better than control—like joy, lightness, surprise, fun, love—all things that you can look for right now, in this moment. If we started out knowing how everything in this lifetime was going to go and going to feel, what would be the point? It would be like playing a video game that you've finished a hundred times already. The excitement is in the discovery! In the face of this knowledge, how could we possibly fail to realign our priorities away from a false sense of control and toward a very real and present enjoyment?

"I think I recently realized how tightly I was holding on to ideas about my life," I tell Jeffrey, "where I wanted it to go and what I thought that was going to look and feel like. And letting non-attachment liberate me from even some of that is so surprisingly relaxing."

"Of course it is," Jeffrey says. "To me, having non-attachment is not as important a goal as accepting that you are attached. You can notice that you're attached to things and accept that you're a human being and attachments are what we do. Of course you care about things because of course you care!"

"Right?" I nearly cheer in agreement. "We are here to have this human experience. We're not here to reject it!"

"Hello!"

"Why would we be here if the point wasn't to say, 'All right, let's do this!' So the idea that enlightenment should be about some kind of separation from that is like, no, we're supposed to do life!"

So can we learn to allow all the dreams, hopes, and emotions to have their place, to celebrate our beautiful brains and spirits that can contain all this magic, and also let ourselves stay open to all the possibilities of the present moment? It seems worth a try!

IDENTITY AND EGO

What we're also doing when we allow ourselves to be mindful of our attachments is examining the role of our egos in our lives, that part of us that seems to have a lot invested in figuring out the rules of the material world and then being praised and lauded for figuring them out.

"Ego" is a word that comes from psychoanalysis and is defined in contrast with "superego," your higher moral conscience, and "id," your primal instinctual self, with "ego" existing as the moderator between the two. But it has come to mean our sense of self in relationship to the world, often a part of ourselves that has some very big ideas around who we are and who we think we "should" be, which becomes difficult when your life and world and identity inevitably change over time. Your ego does not like this! It thinks that there must be a fixed version of you that popped out of the womb knowing everything, doing everything right, and posting the best pics to show it all on social media!

"I think some people find it very threatening to consider that an identity is not a stable thing throughout their life," I say to

Jeffrey. "Because then they don't know who else they are."

"What you're talking about is asking, 'What is the timeless?'" Jeffrey says. "What is the eternal? What is the thing that is beyond this Jeffrey or this Kate?"

We know that we are meant to grow and change; it is one of the fundamental things that we are here to do, and if we are going to make that process easier on ourselves (it's usually hard enough on its own), then we have to tell the ego to stand down sometimes. We're never going to get rid of our egos completely. They are a part of who we are, and they are another tool that we are meant to work with. But when we practice mindfulness and shift into that witness mind, we are giving ourselves little breaks from letting ego run the show, and it can be very powerful to get to feel that, even for very short amounts of time. We can start to see what is helpful about ego/thinking mind and what is not, where it serves us and where it takes us down roads of false narrative and unnecessary stress.

For example, let's go all the way back to the scenario of failing a test at school. If an important part of your identity is that you are an excellent student who always gets straight As, failing a test is potentially a huge blow to your ego. You have an idea about yourself that you are simply not someone who fails, and this probably then spins off into a much bigger narrative about how smart or hardworking you are and how you believe achievement "should" happen for you. Your ego is managing to spin out into an entire narrative about how a situation that is different from your expectations of it is incompatible with your view of your life and your identity.

So mindfulness can bring us back to what is actually true here. We sit in meditation, we breathe and let the thoughts fly by, practicing releasing them one by one, until that ego-based narrative starts to lose its grip on us, and we can reset and observe without judgment.

What's actually going on? You failed a test. You are disappointed and frustrated with yourself. That's okay. Are you still you? Of course. Has anything major changed? Nope. Can you study and try to do better next time? Absolutely. Is it dinnertime and a delicious meal is waiting for you to enjoy with your loved ones? I hope so!

If our ego fears a loss of a certain identity, we have to ask why—what is threatening to our ego about that loss? And is that identity something that was even our idea in the first place? Who told us that we had to be that way? Why is that the way to be?

"Being where I am has given me this great advantage," Jeffrey tells me, "because I was never really an insider. I never could ever get the feeling that I was doing it 'right,' with the house and the two point three kids and all that. People get on that track and then they discover the track is fake—I just was raised with knowing the track was fake. I'm not saying it was easy to be ostracized my whole life, but that was definitely an advantage and a boost in spiritual practice. Because I'm already outside the system."

I think about what Erin said when I interviewed her for the body chapter. "My friend Erin said almost the exact same thing," I tell Jeffrey. "Because no one was ever going to look at her and not see her disability, she was given an out from the beginning. 'There's no chance to participate in this, so I'm not going to. I'm going to go live my life.'"

"Yes. I'm going to just go do some other things," Jeffrey says. "[On TikTok] there are these men who will come into my comments and say things like, 'You're the ugliest woman I've ever seen. You're not even trying.' And I'm nonbinary. I am not a man. I'm not a woman. I'm *not* even trying. But misogyny is so ingrained that they try to hold me to these impossible catch-22 standards that women are held to. And I can see so clearly that I have nothing to do with that. But if I was a heterosexual cisgender woman, I could imagine it being much trickier to undermine misogyny. Those systems are so pervasive that any tool we have to be able to break free, we should appreciate."

This makes me think of a meme I saw recently that said something like, "In the end, love yourself, in spite of everything." It took me a minute to realize why this well-intentioned meme felt so wrong to me, and of course it's because we should love ourselves BECAUSE of everything, not in spite of it! Everything about you is part of your humanness and worthy of love! Even the parts that are hard for you to navigate, or the parts that have made mistakes, or the parts that you wish you could change.

Think about all the things about you that other people sometimes struggle to understand. As we do when we look at our charts, you are learning to work with those parts of self, but can you go one step further and celebrate them? Can you see them as gifts that save you from participating in the fruitless attempt to fit into someone else's ideas about who you should be?

It was only when I started writing, and letting myself express as fully as I possibly could all the very emotional and sensitive parts of me, that navigating my own emotions no longer felt like an inconvenience. When I started writing songs with my writing partners (for our band the Witch Ones, thank you), I felt for the first time that this emotional part of me was a gift. Not even something neutral that I could tolerate, but a part of myself that had a place in this most emotional of art forms, to write songs that would express the way that I feel.

It took a long time for me to go from just accepting that part of myself to celebrating it, but arriving in that place of celebration, fueled by no outside force, simply by your own relationship to yourself, is amazing. And believe me, even though I have a much stronger relationship with that part of myself now than I used to, it is something that I have to tend to. It is not a given. And when in doubt, I turn back to that place where I can let that part of myself exist as freely as possible.

"There's the cliché of 'there's only one you, you're uniquely special,'" I say, "but it's real! You have come to this planet in this lifetime. This person—if she likes wearing a velour muumuu, she should wear it! So don't wait! What are you waiting for?" (I am pointing to myself when I say this; earlier Jeffrey was admiring the oversized tie-dyed pink velour dress I am wearing.) "This is who you are! Enjoy finding out who that person is. That could even be fun, too!"

"Of course," Jeffrey agrees. "It's not just fun. It's your job in life."

This all must begin on a very small scale, with a practice of daily acceptance. When we feel ourselves getting caught up in self-judgment, we allow that witness mind to help us observe and let the judgment pass. Allow for the discomfort to exist, and watch as it goes out the way it came in. Bye-bye!

"I say kind things to myself every single chance I can get," Jeffrey tells me when I ask them about their daily mindfulness practice. "I'm just washing the dishes, saying, 'I love you. I appreciate you. Thank you.' That's my mantra. Because why not? So many people choose something neutral as their mantra. Why not choose something that just makes you feel lovely and accepted?"

As self-care and self-love have become more of a trend in pop culture, capitalism has tripped all over itself trying to keep up with how to still make money when people aren't being taught to hate themselves. It runs up against the fact that if there is nothing wrong with you, then you don't need to buy anything to fix yourself. Capitalism also does not like more than one thing to be true at a time, and it flounders in an environment where we are looking at the complex, multilayered truth of reality. You can't convince someone to buy something by saying, "This might work. Something else might work too, but, um, try this!" (Consider that politicians do not like this either—they like to easily manipulate people by promising them the comfort of one unfaltering truth, even when one does not exist.)

As we saw in our body chapter, capitalism wants there to be something wrong with you, for there to be one answer to how to fix it, and for you to spend all your energy trying to meet that arbitrary goal. You must produce results! You must have something to show for yourself! But mindfulness is a tool that allows us to step out of this focus on goal-oriented tasks. For even a few minutes, we intentionally stop whatever it is we are doing. We stop working, stop studying, stop producing, stop planning. And it is only within that quiet, non-goal-oriented space that we are able to listen to the gentle heartbeat of our lives. We are able to understand what true evolution of self can look like. There is no outer reward for this—no trophy for best meditator—and anyone who seems to be seeking this nonexistent trophy is deeply missing the point.

The idea of a pause is also so important when we think about personal evolution. It's all well and good to learn something new about yourself or gain some new mystical understanding, but in order to integrate it into your consciousness, you need to give it time and space to sink in. Believe me, you will continue to receive the same information over and over again until you learn to really use it. That's not meant to sound like pressure—the universe will be quite happy to continue to send you the same information in different forms; the universe has all the time in the . . . well, universe! You, however, might like to learn about how deeply connected you are to energetic abundance sooner rather than later.

One more quote from Pema Chodron: "You are the sky. Everything else—it's just the weather." Meditation and mindfulness are the quickest, most accessible tools available to us to access that true sky self. All you need is your breath.

"To me, mindfulness is perhaps the most important thing you will do in your entire life," Jeffrey tells me when I ask their advice about how someone should go about starting a mindfulness practice. "And not to be overly dramatic, but most people are living in an emergency situation in regard to self-hate. So I would not worry about making the wrong choice. Just try every book, every meditation class, every kind of assistance. Some stuff will stick and some won't, but I would just go dive right in. And the books and stuff that worked for me may not work for you. Just don't avoid going for it."

If we look at meditation and mindfulness as magical practices, we can view them as casting an immediate spell to connect with energetic abundance. The magical mystery of life is happening to you in every single moment, the joyful ones where you are laughing with friends and the more difficult ones where you are experiencing stress or grief. The same life brings you all of this, and it will always bring you both. You may be checking in with your friendly alien with a clipboard, or that gentle loving presence that says, "I love you"—whatever metaphor makes sense to you. But meditation and mindfulness will give you the practice of knowing that this abundance of energy does not go away, and that it is yours to claim for whatever kind of healing you need in any moment.

Exercises

WALKING MEDITATION

Pick a path that you can walk for ten to thirty minutes alone and in silence. Don't talk to anyone, don't listen to music; simply focus your senses on what is going on around you. What is the scenery like? Is there nature? Are there other people around? Animals? Buildings? Cars? What sounds and smells do you notice? Feel your feet on the earth as you walk, grounding you in this place and this moment. Afterward, check in with how you feel and what you noticed.

BOX BREATH

Find a quiet, comfortable place to sit and set a timer for five minutes. Slowly begin to extend your breathing, silently counting to four on the in breath, holding for a count of four, four on the out breath, and holding for a count of four. Allow any thoughts that come up to drift away as you return to your counting.

CHAPTER EIGHT:
Creativity

I sometimes wonder how many successful artists and writers are secret devotees of the book *The Artist's Way*. It seems to be something that is whispered about or reluctantly mentioned, only because it lies pretty deep inside the slightly hokey old-school self-help canon. A super-hip artist in the most stylish clothes selling artwork for millions might not be ready to admit that their entire career hinged on a self-help workbook that they now hide at the back of their bookshelf.

But I display my (multiple) copies of this book proudly! I give it away to any friend who demonstrates a whiff of a creative and/or existential crisis! Why? First of all, because I gave up on being afraid of cheesiness a long time ago, most likely the day that my life was transformed by getting a natal chart reading among a collection of pewter fairies and ren faire corsets, but also because that book led me to find a way not only into my creativity but also into an entire way of thinking about magic, energy, and the universe.

I was twenty-five when I finally caved to *The Artist's Way*. I had picked up the workbook many times in bookstores, opened it to see that the word "God" repeated many times, and promptly put it back on the shelf.

I was raised by parents who are staunchly against organized religion. When my dad was a teenager, he had been so devoted to his Catholic faith that he had decided to leave home and join a seminary to study to become a Jesuit brother. As the activism of the sixties started to take hold of the world outside the seminary, my dad found that his vision of a utopian commune based in faith and kindness was maybe not what was actually going on around him. The final straw for him was finding his precious personal book collection, which he had donated to the library in the spirit of sharing all that he had with his community, on a private bookshelf in the office of one of the brothers, who had decided to keep the books for himself. Dad packed his bags, headed home, and started a radio revolution (but that's a different story).

My mother's family is Jewish, deeply secular, and suspicious of the kinds of divisions that institutional spirituality intentionally fosters in people. We always celebrated holidays as a reason to be with family. "God" was not part of the picture.

So, as is true for many people, the word "God" brings up a lot of complicated feelings for me. When I first saw it used in *The Artist's Way*, it seemed like someone signaling to me that they were part of an institutionalized faith-based system, not a space that I normally find to be very welcoming.

So I had to be feeling pretty desperate to keep reading past page one.

I was in the basement of the downtown Shakespeare and Co. bookstore on Broadway in New York City. It no longer exists, but it was one of those magical haven places when it did. A place to escape from the busy NYC streets and just breathe in books for a while. It took me years to even realize the downstairs existed—that's where they kept plays, textbooks, general nonfiction, and self-help. This was around the time when I received that natal chart reading, and I was on the verge of some new kind of understanding that I hadn't fully figured out how to access yet. I was also dealing with an onslaught of grief. Within a year, between my wife's family and mine, five family members had died. It suddenly felt like going to funerals was a part-time job, and it was sparking a not-insignificant existential crisis in me. I seemed to be waiting for something to happen, and the only thing that was happening was that we kept experiencing loss.

So I picked up the book, and I read past the first page.

When you read more than one page of *The Artist's Way*, you are introduced to Julia Cameron's motherly, nurturing voice, which reassures you that if you don't feel comfortable with the word "God," you should substitute something else. Like "good, ordered direction" or "the universe" or "creative energy." Fresh off my mystical astrological experience, I felt my mind open enough to bring the book upstairs to the checkout counter and hand it over. What did I have to lose?

Talking to my friend, the artist Amy Khoshbin, it makes me smile to hear that she had a very similar formative experience with this book.

"When she talked about creativity, she said, 'I'm going to reference God in this book,'" Amy tells me about her own first Julia Cameron impression. "That turned me off a little bit. But then she said, 'God can be the creative spirit.' And that was kind of a revelation for me, because I had never heard that before."

I met Amy about a decade ago when she came with the theater company that I worked with on a tour to Prague. The company was appearing in a performance art festival being held in a public square in a makeshift structure of white cube rooms. (I know it sounds like I am making up these ways that I meet people, but I promise I am not.)

Amy is an artist who works in many forms—video, installation, writing, rap music, even tattooing. She is someone who has found a fascinating balance between the deeply personal and the widely political, both in subject matter and in the experience of art making, so I knew she would be a great person to talk to about making a creative life.

Since this book is about the magical energy of possibility that exists in every moment, I am going to stick with the word "energy" in talking about creativity, but understand that I mean the grandest energy possible. The energy that moves planets and erupts volcanoes and creates a moth with wings that look like eyes. That is the same energy that moves my fingers across the keys of my laptop in this very moment. It is both unimaginably grand and the simplest, smallest thing.

In *The Artist's Way*, Julia Cameron describes a process that is one step away from channeling. She instructs us to open ourselves up to an energetic flow of creativity that exists around us at all times by putting aside as much of our own egos as possible. Her view of creativity is deeply democratic—everyone has equal access to it. How could they not, if it exists

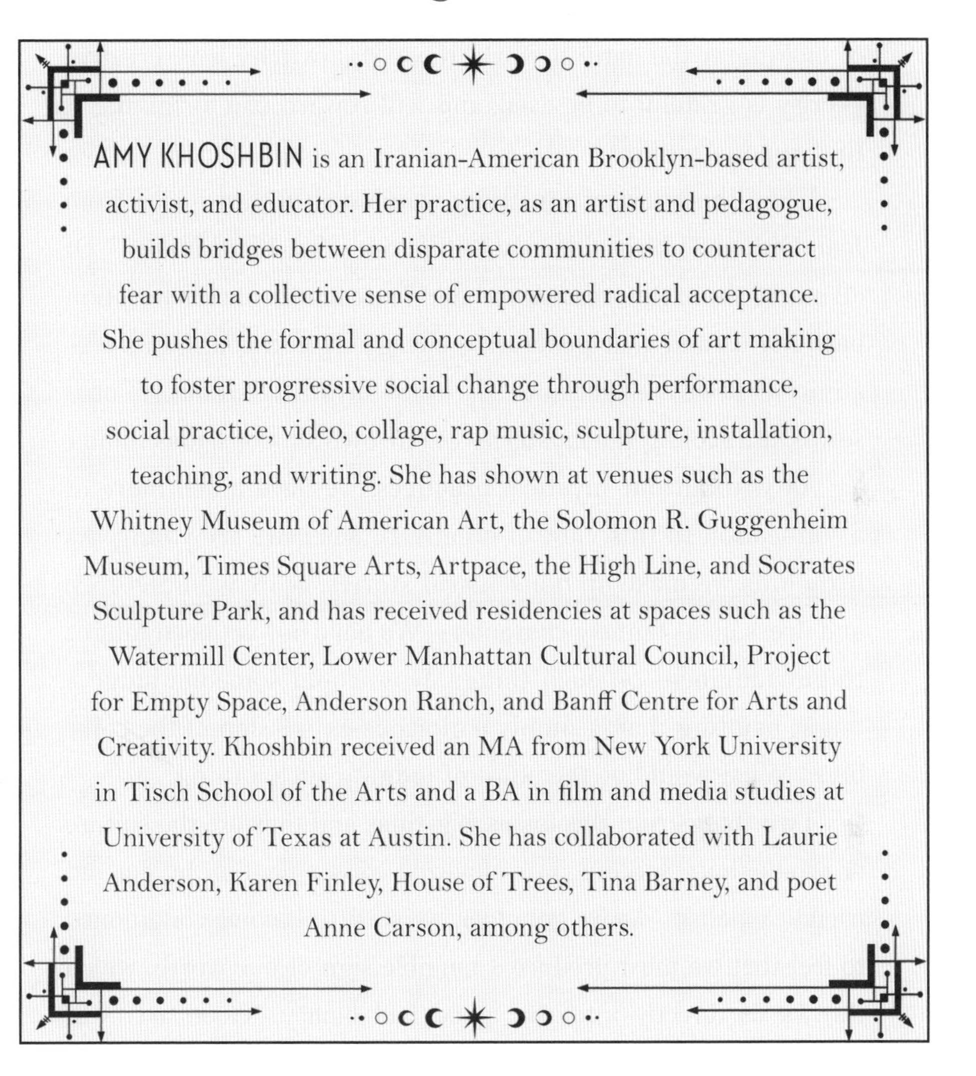

AMY KHOSHBIN is an Iranian-American Brooklyn-based artist, activist, and educator. Her practice, as an artist and pedagogue, builds bridges between disparate communities to counteract fear with a collective sense of empowered radical acceptance. She pushes the formal and conceptual boundaries of art making to foster progressive social change through performance, social practice, video, collage, rap music, sculpture, installation, teaching, and writing. She has shown at venues such as the Whitney Museum of American Art, the Solomon R. Guggenheim Museum, Times Square Arts, Artpace, the High Line, and Socrates Sculpture Park, and has received residencies at spaces such as the Watermill Center, Lower Manhattan Cultural Council, Project for Empty Space, Anderson Ranch, and Banff Centre for Arts and Creativity. Khoshbin received an MA from New York University in Tisch School of the Arts and a BA in film and media studies at University of Texas at Austin. She has collaborated with Laurie Anderson, Karen Finley, House of Trees, Tina Barney, and poet Anne Carson, among others.

all around us and can be harnessed at any time?

Elizabeth Gilbert has a similar spiritual view of creativity, which she presents in her book *Big Magic*. She believes that creative works want to be made, that they are floating out there in the ether waiting to be discovered by a collaborator who will bring them into the tangible world. Here, as with our discussion of looking at the natural world through a witchy lens, creative energy is grateful to be used, and will reward you for giving it the proper attention.

I like this view of creativity, combined with a quote from Joan Didion: "I write entirely to find out what I'm thinking." Of all our tools, to me creativity is the clearest area of collaboration between us and that generative energy. It is through our creativity that we connect not only to the mystical but also to ourselves, unraveling the mysteries of our own subconscious minds.

As with all our mystical practices, we have much more of a connection to this view of creativity when we are young. As little kids we make up nonsensical stories, draw wild pictures, and dress up as fantasy characters. We have not yet been taught to put judgment on such things. How could someone judge a finger painting that is simply a glorious expression of the color blue? What would be the point of judging such a thing?

Two things ruin this for us, big-time, and they are the culture of productivity and our individualized egos, egged on by our old friend capitalism. As we get older, we start to become conditioned to feel that we must produce a tangible sign of our worth, which throws us directly into that good/bad binary. "Good art" will get you praised—maybe a perfectly rendered copy of the Sistine Chapel? But does your true expression of your creativity manifest in making a pile of toilet paper rolls and covering it in green Silly String? That is just ridiculousness and you should probably give up any creative endeavor altogether. Can you sing beautifully, hitting all the high notes with ease? You are good! Do you love to sing but emit a kind of Tom Waits grumble? Bad. Never do that again.

(The biggest problem with this phenomenon is actually that it is the artists who do something deeply unexpected who have a huge impact on our culture, and it is a testament to their tenacity that they continue to make work in the face of a world that they have to reinvent in order for it to understand them.)

When it comes to creative endeavors, as with so many things in our lives, sometime around adolescence we find that we have been thrown into a kind of contest, and that skill plus ego plus work will allow us to win this contest, which will further boost our ego, and will lead to bigger wins of bigger contests.

Except we already know that there is no There there (as my mother likes to say by way of Gertrude Stein). Any contest, any measuring, any declaration of good or bad, worthy or unworthy, is the business of the world outside you trying (and usually failing) to make sense of itself. These measurements have very little to do with how you feel about yourself or what will actually make you happy. So why not spray Silly String all over a pile of toilet paper rolls and sing the alphabet in the style of Tom Waits?

You may right now be thinking, "Okay, maybe there's not a reason *not* to do that, Kate, but what exactly is the reason *to* do that?"

Thank you so much for asking.

MAKING A CREATIVE SPACE FOR YOURSELF

Let's talk first about what this connection to magical creative energy can look like. Julia Cameron is famous for writing about the idea of "morning pages" in *The Artist's Way*: three stream-of-consciousness handwritten pages, ideally written first thing in the morning, before your conscious brain has had time to fully turn on. You start writing and you don't stop until you hit the bottom of page three. It doesn't matter what you write, and you should be as unprecious about it as possible. If you can't think of anything, start writing "this is dumb" over and over. You don't have to show the pages to anyone, and you don't have to ever look at them again. You can even throw them out when you finish them.

What this practice does is provide a space in which you can train yourself to turn off the ego part of your brain, the part that doesn't want to write a sentence unless it comes out perfect the first time. The part that says you can't make anything unless it proves something about your worth. The part that will keep you from getting to the really wild and fun side of creativity because it wants to keep you safe above all else.

We acknowledge that this goal of keeping us safe is a noble one. Stretching outside the boundaries of what we have known or been shown is scary business. But the reward is too great to let worries about safety stop us. It is that push past discomfort that can lead us to some pretty profound personal evolution. So we say, thank you, Judgmental Editor Ego, but we are busy with magic right now, we'll talk to you later.

In many mystical traditions there are practices around channeling—opening yourself up as a vessel to receive information from the universe and letting whatever wants to come through come through. This is one way of communicating with your spirit guides—automatic writing is where you clear your mind and simply begin to move your hand across the page and see what comes out.

The early-twentieth-century Swedish painter Hilma af Klint famously used automatic writing to receive instructions from her spirit guides about a massive set of paintings that she was to channel. The queer fifties poet Jack Spicer described writing his poems as taking dictation from Martians. So whether it's coming from Mars, guides, universal energy, your own subconscious mind, or ghostlike ideas floating around waiting to be grabbed and tethered down to the earth, you have access to a deep channel of expression as your birthright on this planet. You just have to allow it to come through.

Having access to this channel all the time isn't possible, but the more you practice, the easier it becomes to return to this state of creative permission, in which you are able to experience the exhilarating freedom of creative vibration.

Now what does all this have to do with our mental health?

Giving ourselves full access to our own creativity provides us with a tool that can help us navigate two pretty big areas of human experience: joy and healing.

There is nothing quite like the feeling of being in the flow of creativity. And within the exhilaration of this connection to creative spirit, you are free to explore and ask questions of yourself and of the universe.

"It can be about the process of self-discovery," Amy offers. "The process of understanding who you are. The process of understanding how you interact in the world, or what pleasure is for you, what joy is for you, what happiness is for you. What pain is. What anger is."

In this way creativity is able to provide a container not only for the good, joyful feelings but also the more difficult ones. Just as we may use ceremony to begin to transmute our shadow, creativity can provide us with safe boundaries in which to sort out feelings that may overwhelm us, or feel too complicated to understand. I can't tell you how many times I have started writing morning pages with an impossible question on page one, only to have my question answered clearly and concisely by page three.

How does this work, you may ask?

You know what I'm going to say.

Relax, kid, it's magic.

But also . . .

If we are in fact tuning in to a higher universal wisdom when we allow ourselves to open as channels for creative energy, wouldn't it make sense that some wisdom that we don't consciously possess will come through to us?

HEALING THROUGH CREATIVITY

For an empath, using the tool of creativity to come back to yourself can be immensely helpful. To me it almost feels like giving your mind and spirit a long, hot bubble bath. By allowing yourself to focus on your own connection to your creativity, you will find that extraneous energy that does not belong to you will begin to fall away. You are turning down the volume on all that outside noise—energy that you picked up from someone else's emotions, expectations, or even by simply being out among people—and turning the volume way up on the conversation between you and existence, you and life, you and yourself. Even though I often use my real life as inspiration in my writing, and I find that writing is a great way to learn about and process our experiences, I also find that the everyday problems of the world seem to fall away when I am fully engaged in creativity.

An empath may also find that a creative practice is a great place to put their emotional sensitivity to use. All of a sudden that hypersensitivity to your surroundings, to your own emotions and the emotions of the people around you, becomes a huge asset. Your deep understanding and experience of emotion can be used to create a piece of music that will invoke joy or sadness in anyone who listens to it. You can write characters who other people will relate to and care about. You can make a painting that expresses emotion through color. All the nuances of feeling that you have come to understand become tools for representing the world in a way that will be deeply meaningful to other people.

Developing a creative practice is also a way to provide yourself with a healthy form of escapism. The author Jennifer Egan talks about how, when she is deep into a writing project, her fictional world feels just as real, if not more real, than the tangible world around her, and she feels like she is living a secret double life, walking around and thinking about her fictional people.

By switching into ways of thinking that are beyond the everyday visible world, you are also bringing yourself into a new mental space where new kinds of solutions and strategies may present themselves to you. Even within a creative practice, you can learn to activate these different parts of yourself, experimenting with how you feel when you draw a picture versus sing a song versus write a story. What parts of your brain light up? What can you understand more deeply through accessing the energy of these different forms of creativity?

"I've always known that art is a healing practice for me," Amy tells me. "Feeling like an outsider growing up and having these thoughts related to my queerness, turning to art making would feel really super healing. To work with my hands, get off my screen, be in my body again."

I have found that creativity is my quickest and most reliable way out of the depths of a depressive episode. Because my depression is so closely related to my energy levels, I count on creativity to serve as a spiritual and mental boost for my lagging state of mind. It doesn't always work, but at least 80 percent of the time working on something creative, even for a little while, functions like putting gas back in the tank of my sense of self.

There are a lot of reasons why I think creativity works for me in this way. One is that I become activated just through the process of bringing something new into the world. Participating in the act of creating brings hope, as I reengage with the energy of the present moment. I am very literally taking what is in front of me right now (a paintbrush, a pencil, a notebook, a laptop, a loom, a potter's wheel) and exploring the possibilities of it. In doing this, I begin to engage with the possibilities of self.

In the book *How to Change Your Mind*, author Michael Pollan writes about how our brains are incredibly active with possibility when we are kids. When we look at a tree, we don't just see a tree. Maybe we see a face in the bark, or holes that fairies might hide in, or shimmering leaves. We literally perceive the world differently. And then as we get older, these variations and possibilities start to fade away. Now the tree is just a tree. It's ordinary, uninteresting. Just another tree in the world. We may barely even notice it.

There are surely evolutionary reasons why our brains develop this way. If we spent all our time looking at shimmering trees, we wouldn't be able to drive cars, buy groceries, and pay our bills. The adolescent-into-adult mind is meant to settle into a fixed understanding of the world around it so that it becomes more possible to manage it.

But what if it didn't have to be that way all the time? What if we could give ourselves a break from logic and once again see shimmering trees for a little while?

Pollan writes that people who are depressed often suffer from the most extreme cases of lack of possibility, which extends from how they look at a tree to how they look at their lives. Suddenly their lives look like a regular, uninteresting tree. They no longer feel like they have options ahead of them. They simply can't picture it. They literally have dreaming shut down from them.

Depression can take many different forms, but for me this idea of a lack of possibility really hits home. I am someone who usually has a ton of ideas floating around in my head, more than I could ever actually accomplish, and thinking about all these different ideas gets me excited about my life. This can be as simple as the idea of reorganizing a room—think of all the possibilities!

You could paint the walls a different color! Hang up a tent made of tapestries! Grow one hundred plants in your window!

I know I am in trouble when all those thoughts suddenly get shut down, and a voice in my head starts telling me that those were all stupid ideas anyway and I was stupid for thinking they were fun or cool and who even cares and why would they? Sometimes this is caused by a moment when I'm experiencing a particularly harsh rejection of my work. Sometimes it's more internal and physical—a result of SAD or my various bodily ailments acting up. But when I reach into my toolbox of strategies, the one that is able to slowly open back up that door of possibility the most is creative practice.

Often the work that gets me back into balance is not something I am being paid for or even something that I will show to anyone. Sometimes it is fun and silly and simply gets my mind off my troubles, and sometimes it helps more to actively engage with the way that I am feeling and mine it for material.

This is where we come back to the territory of transmuting the shadow. There is a quote I love by the writer and director Nora Ephron: "Everything is copy." She meant that all life experiences, good or bad, can be used as material in your creativity. This may sound a little mercenary—as if we are all trolling the world for material to claim for our artwork—but I do find that it can really help to put a framework around a difficult experience. Grief, for example, can be a very powerful subject for creative work, and when I have experienced it, it has often helped me to try to write about it, to describe how it feels, as though I am making a record of what is happening to me.

"I don't think I couched art making in the realm of spiritual practice and full healing methodologies until after my dad passed," Amy tells me, "and then it was really true that it was the only way out of my depression on some level. I've struggled with anxiety and depression my whole life, and the only thing that was really getting me through was making or talking about making or thinking about creative ideas."

"You made a whole project about your dad, didn't you?" I ask Amy, remembering seeing pictures where she dressed in her dad's old suits.

"Yeah, and that was a huge catharsis for me," she tells me. "I made a quilt with my mom out of handkerchiefs of his. I wore his suits and took photos. I made sculptures out of his suits. Being able to embody him as a spirit, as someone that created me, as being part of me, it really allowed me the first step toward healing from that grief. It gave me the realization that through embodiment, through art making, there was a pathway through the grief."

"A creative practice can provide this container almost in the same way that an hour of therapy provides a container," I offer. "It can be a safe place to put difficult emotions. This is where all the hardest and ugliest stuff that I don't know how to deal with can go."

"I think that that's true," Amy agrees. "I've always used art as a container to dump depressive, even wild ideas that might be completely out there. Even if it's writing in your journal, drawing, being out in the world and moving in a different way, being in your house and dancing to your favorite song.

Whatever it is, it's allowing you space to work through whatever it is that you're experiencing. It's not about product all the time, but you can look back on that and use it as inspiration."

"It's hard," I say, "because superficially, people can judge therapy or even astrology as narcissistic or self-obsessed, because it's about studying your own chart. But then the next step, of course, is taking the work that you've done there and going to your family, to your community, to the world."

Amy brings up the famous Audre Lorde quote: "Caring for myself is not self-indulgence, it is self-preservation and that is an act of political warfare."

"You have to do an internal vested investigation to be able to show up, period," Amy says. "So if you're thinking about your astrology, if you're thinking about crystals, plants, meditation, yoga, creativity, making things with your hands, all that is necessary for that process of self-discovery. If you're in the world a lot, and you feel overwhelmed by that, you have to have some kind of practice to be able to get you through this journey of life, essentially. You're not going to be able to show up for others until your cup is full and able to overflow. And it's hard to get that cup full without providing for the full range of experience of self-discovery and allowing yourself to go there."

One of the reasons why I so admire Amy's work is that she always has bigger goals of systemic change in mind, while still prioritizing the importance of the very private and personal work we need to do in order to get to that bigger place of effecting change. In 2020 she ran for New York City Council as both an art piece and a sincere bid for participation in the democratic process. One of my other favorite projects of hers was a series of bright, bold, collectively made banners that were displayed in Times Square that said things like, "I was born for love, not hatred," and "Quiet lives inside noise."

"Then through this act of self-discovery," Amy offers, "you're able to have the conversations that slowly dismantle systemic oppression, queerphobia, xenophobia, racism, because you're able to come to those conversations with strength and knowledge of self and others."

So creativity gives us another way to access one of our essential truths—through connection with magic, we can begin to not only nurture ourselves, but also the world.

LETTING IT BE PRIVATE

If you are going to use creativity as a way to work with and through difficult feelings, it is imperative that you give yourself as much privacy as possible to do this. In order to give ourselves full permission for self-discovery—to let something out that might feel weird or stupid or embarrassing—we have to feel safe to know that we can express these parts of ourselves without worrying about an outside eye judging it. The writer Virginia Woolf talked about having "a room of one's own" that you can escape to and claim as a space for yourself. Sometimes this is an actual room, or maybe it's just a favorite notebook, or a particular park bench, or just a state of mind that you are able to conjure up for yourself where you owe nothing to anyone other than yourself, where you are beholden to no one's rules but your own.

Maybe it's partially because I'm an only child, but I also find that my creative practice is a way to savor and enjoy something private that is all mine, that I don't have to explain to anyone else. There is something lovely and mysterious about going into your little creativity cave and coming out at the end of the day exhausted and covered in purple paint with a mischievous smile on your face. It brings me back to the idea of being the witch in a little cottage on the edge of town, cooking up something mysterious in her cauldron. So much of our lives forces us to live in an outward way in which we are constantly being witnessed by others, needing to account for ourselves, defend ourselves, and even justify ourselves. What a relief to give yourself a break from that energy and turn back to something that is all your own.

This gets extra complicated for us, since we live in a moment in history where we are sharing more about our lives than ever, and where we may feel a responsibility to somehow account for ourselves and our time on a daily basis. There is nothing more outward facing and enmeshed in judgment than social media, and the easiest way to kill a creative vibe is to share something vulnerable about yourself or your work in a setting that is designed to make you feel judged. This doesn't mean that you can't post about your life or even about your creative practice, but you always want to be considering the energetic implications of posting. Is it an okay time for you to have energy flowing out, not knowing in what way it may or may not come back? Or is it a good time to devote your attention to creating that safe space for self that is not asking for or needing approval from anyone?

I find that the energetic conditions that my creativity requires are frustratingly fragile, and there are certain things that I need to guard against in order to protect my creative practice. Some of these things sound kind of silly, but they make a huge difference. One is that I can't watch a TV show or a movie until I have finished my writing for the day, because if I start watching something else I will lose the train of thought of my own work. I become so absorbed in this other thing that already exists (even if it's something that I've watched one hundred times) that the delicate wisp of whatever story I was trying to create can't survive in the face of someone else's finished product. Sometimes this even means limiting what I read while I work on a project. If I read someone else's finished book, the imaginative world of my work in progress starts to fade.

This can happen to us on an even bigger scale with social media. We can know objectively that no one's social media presence shows the full picture of their lives, and that everyone is creating an edited version of their own experience, but sometimes our own sense of self can become murky in the face of someone else's seeming self-assurance. Telling ourselves that this is a fiction isn't enough; we have to actually re-ground in ourselves, bringing our full energy back to understanding and honoring where we're each at in our own journeys.

So just as we allow ourselves the privacy to experience a tarot reading, spend an hour in therapy, or conduct a witchy ceremony on the full moon, we want to give our creative practice the same respect, so that it can give us the full magical experience of creative discovery. This is a practice of devotion in showing up for yourself, and giving yourself permission without needing it from anyone else.

"It's the power of being alone," Amy tells me. "Being off your screen, and having fallow time just walking in the world. Sitting without any mediation and just experiencing nature—experiencing wind, air; if you're in the city, seeing what's around you in terms of people."

"It's tough for some people to be alone with their own thoughts," I say. "So they distract themselves from the solitude by engaging with social media, which they may see as a place where other people seem to have figured something out."

"I'm totally unmotivated for large swaths of time," Amy tells me, "and totally hating myself for it and looking at social media and thinking, 'Compare is despair.' Then being out in nature and being like, 'Oh, my God, these are ancient mountains.' Thinking, 'We're specks on the earth, part of a cosmic continuum.' So who cares? Just do something. Hang the weird shiny stuff!" Amy gestures to the shiny fabric hanging behind her as a background for her video calls. "Do whatever makes you feel happy! If you need to make an altar, if you need to hold a stuffed animal, if you need to pound into a pillow, whatever it is!"

Having privacy for your period of creative incubation is so important, and so undervalued in this moment when we are expected to be public, to present an aesthetic vision of ourselves, as if we are a branded product that someone is trying to sell. The longer I can sit alone with something and not feel that outside pressure, the more I can allow myself to dig around for the really good stuff that only comes when you are in that protected flow.

"I think as a teenager," I tell Amy, "even without social media, I felt like, 'There are weird things going on in here that I can't explain to anyone.' And I guess eventually I told myself that that was okay. But no one else told me it was okay."

"I grew up in the suburbs, and it was very much about normalizing," Amy says. "This also relates to queerness and coming out. Having all these ideas in your mind where you feel a certain way and it might not be what's socially sanctioned. I would feel like I'm having all these wild ideas, and I didn't know how to output that yet."

Even taking social media out of the equation, we may still feel that sense of pressure to be able to explain the weirder, more complicated parts of our creative practices to anyone who might ask. As if we are going to be stopped in the hallway of our school by a teacher who will demand to see our terrible poetry and send us to detention if it is incomprehensible.

But here's the thing—you are allowed to write incomprehensible poetry. In fact, you may need to write a ton of incomprehensible poetry in order to get to the good stuff that may become a final product that you would want to show to people.

This process of "getting to the good stuff" happens when we allow ourselves to be in "flow." Both athletes and creative people talk about the idea of flow, and you can picture it as a kind of physical and sensory experience. It's the equivalent of running effortlessly, adrenaline rushing through your body, the wind blowing at your back, helping you along. Flow is complete engagement in the elevated magical potential of the current moment. This is where we are channeling like Hilma af Klint. Where we are taking dictation from Mars. We are completely caught up in engagement with a creative power that is bigger than we are. We are in collaboration with the universe.

But often the reception coming in from Mars isn't perfect, and we shouldn't expect it to be. Sure, every once in a while a piece of work comes to you fully formed. Dolly Parton purportedly wrote her hit songs "Jolene" and "I Will Always Love You" on the same day. ("That was a good writing day," she has said.) But the alternative to writing two of the most iconic songs of all time in one sitting is to allow yourself to write terrible first drafts. I am talking very, very bad. Just the most embarrassing prose, the dumbest ideas, the silliest nonsense that is coming through. This is the point of entry through which we can access Flow Self.

(I actually find that closing the door to a room and intentionally doing something completely ridiculous that you would never voluntarily show another person can help to kick-start this freeing energy. For example, I just did a very vigorous "chair dance" to "Blinding Lights" by the Weeknd. Please do not attempt to picture this.)

This is where you want to distinguish between Flow Self and that Judgmental Editor Self. You want to your let Flow Self be delusionally grandiose. Flow Self should be painting in giant brushstrokes, scattering paint everywhere, making tons of those terrible first drafts. Hopefully, what can happen through this process is that Flow Self is able to kick Editor Self out of the room completely, and those terrible first drafts start becoming something else, a way of conducting creative energy. In these moments, Flow Self might even start thinking to itself, "This is actually the greatest thing ever made!" And why not? When you are in true creative flow, of course you are in awe of what you are making. You are doing a magic trick—pulling something completely new out of your own mind, heart, and soul! When you are in flow, you don't notice time passing. Hours seem to disappear. Afterward you feel accomplished, often lighter. You feel that you have done something worthwhile.

I cannot stress this enough—when you can, please revel in this Flow Self completely and indulgently, and only when you have let Flow Self run itself out do you invite in Editor Self. I recommend that you wait as long as possible to do this. Of course, if you have a project due, you might not have much time to rework something. But I like to put projects away in a drawer for at least a year. Then when I take them out again, I am far enough away from that initial flow experience that I am no longer as influenced by it. I am coming to it more as an objective observer, closer to what my audience would be. It can be embarrassing to look at what's in there that doesn't work—maybe something clunky or cliché. But if I'm the only one who's seeing it, who really cares? You're simply facilitating a conversation between Editor Self and Flow Self.

I like to picture Editor Self as looking like a very stern librarian. She's got her fifth cup of coffee in one hand and a red marker in the other.

"Okay, that is really cheesy," she says. "How did you think you were going to get away with that?"

Meanwhile, Flow Self is in a sparkly caftan gathering

flowers in a field. "I don't know. I was just *feeling* it, you know?" she says as she skips through the grass.

TO SHARE OR NOT TO SHARE

So let's say you have given yourself the space of your own to work through feelings, create new worlds, hang all the shiny fabrics, and channel all the beautiful mysteries of the universe that are available to you. And now you're ready to show someone else what you have made. After doing such a good job of protecting your private creative magic from outside judgment, how can you now safely switch into having a public-facing moment with work that is important to you?

Let's just acknowledge now—this will never be easy. Never. And the wilder and more out there you allow your creativity to be, the more likely you are to feel vulnerable when you share it with others. That's totally normal! And there are a few things to think about to help you with this.

The first is not to let that fear stop you if it is important to you to share your work. Remind yourself that the fear is normal, and not a sign that you shouldn't share with someone. You already know how important it is to push through certain places of discomfort in order to allow for your own personal evolution. Consider that this might be one of those places.

Something else that will help you is to have more than one project happening at once. Maybe one is in the very early stages and not yet ready to be shared, and another has gone through a few iterations already and is far enough away from the emotional space you were in when you made it for you to be able to look at it more objectively.

This is also a reason to always be taking notes or collecting ideas and material for possible use in your creative practice. The notes app on my phone is filled with phrases or ideas that I can look back on when I feel stuck and need to mine for new material. If you are making work that is vulnerable and engaged in communicating emotion, it can be so helpful to create as many little systems of support for yourself as you can. I often thank Past Kate for writing down something that Current Kate can use when she needs a prompt.

Be careful, though, that you are not compulsively starting new projects without ever finishing any! This happens to a lot of us as our brains attempt to work around our perfectionist tendencies. If we never finish something, then we can never be disappointed that it doesn't live up to some "perfect" idea of it that we had in our heads. But the truth is that we know that "perfection" doesn't actually exist, and by holding ourselves back from seeing something through, we are depriving ourselves of the beautiful surprises in store from the universe that we couldn't have even imagined. Your work is being created in collaboration with magical energy, and if you refuse to show up and see something through to the end, then your creative partner isn't going to show up either! Our idea for the next project is always "better" because it doesn't exist yet. It gets to stay in a kind of unborn ideal holding pattern. The grass is always greener on the project that doesn't need your attention right now!

If you are someone who is lucky enough to be overwhelmed

by ideas, why not sort through them and see what wants to be born first? What is the present moment calling for? Write the others down; you will come back to them.

A huge source of support in fostering your creative practice can be having one or two trusted feedback givers who you feel comfortable sharing early versions of your work with. This can be another creative person who wants to trade feedback with you, or just a friend who really gets your sensibility. You may even want to consider making a feedback group, like a coven of like-minded witches comparing notes for spells. There is nothing that helps me more than when I have given some chapters in progress to my friend Laura and she wants to know what is going to happen next, so I'm forced to find out for myself.

This is why it can be a huge help to approach receiving (and giving) feedback as a process that is grounded more in talking about your impressions of a work than whether something is "good or bad." Remember, we are off the binary here! And anyway, a book that you don't like might be someone else's favorite read of all time, so judging work by defining it as "good" or "bad" isn't helpful or even accurate. Someone who is skilled at giving feedback will be able to judge a work on its own terms. Your ideal feedback giver will be able to see what you are trying to do and help you get there. A painting does not need to be the most glorious artwork of all time. Instead we look at it and ask ourselves if it accomplished what the creator wanted it to.

Back to the artist Hilma af Klint, who was receiving instructions for her paintings from her spirit guides—she was very private about her work, showing it to very few people. But in 1908 she invited a prominent member of her Spiritualist community who she admired to her studio, to advise her on showing the work to the public. This man's feedback was to tell her that the work was embarrassing and that she should never show it to anyone. (Of course, he took pictures of the paintings with him, and somehow very similar abstract work began showing up from other artists in his circle.) Meanwhile Hilma was devastated and stopped painting for four years.

More than a century later her solo exhibit at the Guggenheim Museum was their most attended show of all time.

There is so much vulnerability involved in showing your creative work to someone. You are facing down a very primal fear of not being seen or understood. And the truth is that many people will not understand you or your work. And that's okay! You are not making work that is for everyone (an impossible task anyway—is there anything that EVERYONE likes? Videos of cats playing the piano? Maybe?). The more far-out and original your work is, the more it's going to take people by surprise. You are not looking to win over the general public here. If you are interested in sharing your creative work with people, the goal is for it to find the people that it's meant to find. Remember that your work will go on to have a life of its own separate from you, and your only job is to create something that you want to see in the world. But it takes a very long time to get enough emotional distance from your work not to feel personally misunderstood when someone does not like it. The drawer method helps a lot. Put it away—let it incubate on its own.

And if you show your work to someone and get tough

feedback, show it to someone else and see if they give similar feedback. Sometimes a piece of work may just not be accomplishing what you hoped it would. And sometimes not even all the revision in the world is going to get you to where you want it to be, and it's time to put that project away. But because you are a creator with a creative practice, the failure or success of one of your creations will not dictate how you feel about yourself as an artist. That identity is yours alone, and it is strong enough to withstand a failed project.

The truth is that even helpful criticism can be difficult to hear. But if you want to become someone who works on your craft, it will be an essential part of your growth process.

When I sold my first book, I had no idea how much revision would be expected of me. I had naïvely figured, "Well, if you like my book, then you must think that I'm brilliant, and everything I write is brilliant, and so let's go to press and it'll be an instant bestseller!" I knew of course that polishing my work was important, and I had reworked my manuscript for a year before showing it to anyone professionally. Then when I found my amazing agent, she had me do rewrites for another year. And although every time she gave me notes I felt complete despair over the fact that my book still needed work, I could tell that it was getting better with each new draft. Then we actually sold the book to an awesome editor who loved it, and then I spent another year completely rewriting it multiple times.

I can say with absolute certainty that there are fewer than five hundred words in the published version of my book that were in that first draft. And I am so glad that none of those earlier drafts was published.

The reason why revision is so tough is that you are very literally coming up against your own limitations. There can be a tendency, especially for someone who was a determined student in school, to feel as though notes are coming from a teacher telling you that you did the assignment wrong, then assigning you new tasks that you have no idea how to do. This feeling has lessened for me with experience, as I started to learn that the relationship with your editor has to be much more about compromise and an ongoing conversation about your vision for your work. But sometimes you get that hit of frustration, and you just have to sit with it, let it pass, and then get to work.

This is why it's so important to find people whose opinions you trust to give you feedback. I knew to take the feedback from my agent and editor seriously, not only because it was my job, but also because I trusted their opinions and I knew that they were motivated from a place of wanting my work to be as strong as it could be. It can take a lot of determination to find these people in your life, but once you find them, listen very carefully to their advice for you. As we've learned from Hilma, this might not be the person that you expected it to be. But when you receive criticism, take it in, think it over, and ask yourself if the person is really seeing your vision and trying to help you improve as a creator.

THE GAP

As with facing down all challenges, the best thing to do is look at revision as an opportunity to learn about yourself as an artist and find out what you're capable of. If your ego is angry that you didn't create something "perfect" the first time, remind it that it has no idea what it might actually be capable of making if it gives up some false idea of perfection and instead engages with the magic of creativity. I promise you that if you push past the discomfort of "not knowing," you will amaze yourself with what you discover every time. Ninety-nine-point-nine-nine percent of the people who give up on their creative life do it because they are unable to push through that discomfort to see what kind of growth might come. Just as we can't judge ourselves for where we are in our own personal growth process, we can't be angry at a piece of art that didn't come to the world fully formed and perfect. Just as a person must, that art has to go through its own process of learning and growth. The more we can look at our work as a magical living being, the more we will understand that this is not so much about being an almighty creator, but as always, about working in harmony with our magical energetic forces.

"I worry about people who have a perfection mindset," I tell Amy, thinking of myself and pretty much every creative person that I know. "That thing of 'If I can't do it really well, I don't want to do it at all. And trying is too much of a risk, because any kind of failure is just going to devastate me.'"

"Even in the social media realm," Amy says, "there's a kind of yearning or direction toward perfectionism, in a way that as an artist just shuts you down from creating altogether."

Amy reminds me of an Ira Glass piece called "The Gap," in which the radio host talks about the fact that most of your early work as a creator is simply not going to live up to your own standards.

"Everybody I know who does interesting creative work," Ira Glass says, "they went through a phase of *years* where they had really good taste and they could tell what they were making wasn't as good as they wanted it to be—they knew it fell short, it didn't have the special thing that [they] wanted it to have. And the thing I would say to you is *everybody goes through that.* And for you to go through it, if you're going through it right now, if you're just getting out of that phase—you gotta know it's totally normal."

Here again is the part of our brain that starts things and can't finish them for fear that they will not live up to our high standards. The pain of not meeting our own expectations becomes too great, and we block ourselves off to even the therapeutic parts of our creative practice, because it feels too vulnerable.

"I mean, I still have that gap," Amy admits. "And I've been doing this for twenty years. But that gap closes over time, the more you create and the more you kind of fail at what you're doing. You get to a point where you can build the skills and build the vision and have the confidence to just put it out."

I ask Amy what she does to help herself when she faces down that gap between the expectation and the reality of something that she's made.

"Do you have a way of talking to yourself around the gap that allows you to move forward?" I ask. "Do you just tell yourself, 'You know what, it's good enough'?"

Amy nods. "What you just said is so key," she agrees. "Saying

'It's good enough.' That was so hard for me to understand when I was younger. It was really hard for me to end projects and to just let them be what they are. To say, 'You know what, mental demons? Just let me have space for a minute, just shut the hell up.' And maybe that just works for ten minutes, but in that ten minutes I'm just going for it. Being free. And the longer you do that, over time you get to be able to be more free and confident. The thing is getting over the fear, which is extremely hard. And knowing that it takes a long time. This is a journey. This is a lifelong process."

This reminds me of talking to Jeffrey about our mindfulness practices, where we try to extend that reaction time after an emotional trigger. If here the trigger is that we add a color to our painting that doesn't quite look the way that we expected it to, then how can we pause before judging? Can we settle into the energy of the moment enough to see the possibility there? Think of the famous TV painter Bob Ross, who insisted that there are no mistakes in making art, only "happy accidents." What is the potential for magic in the unexpected?

Something that also helps me in these "it's good enough" moments is to remind myself to remove as much of my ego as possible from this process. Maybe instead of thinking that I have to write the greatest work of literature anyone has ever seen, I can write a fun, engaging story that will speak to some people. Isn't that thing as worthy of existing as anything else? Again, our capitalist competitive spirit comes in here. We think we are in some kind of competition with everyone on the planet to be declared Top Genius, and it's just not true. There is no Top

Genius, and those who get labeled "Top Genius" by others actually often feel like frauds. It's not your job to decide what your work will or will not mean to other people. It's your job (and privilege) to make a positive creative contribution to the world.

So if you make something that doesn't meet your expectations, ask yourself, "But is it good *enough*?" Maybe take a look around at all the mediocre books, movies, TV shows, and art in the world, and ask yourself why you don't think your creative creation is allowed to exist when all of that does. (Seriously, when I feel stuck creatively, sometimes looking at something that I hate really motivates me. This is a moment when that competitive spirit can help us instead of hurting us. "Okay, I can do better than *that!*")

And here's something that I don't hear creators talk about enough—eventually you may find all your work embarrassing.

I once heard an interview with Toni Morrison, the Nobel Prize–winning novelist, in which she said that when she looks at her published books, all she sees are the mistakes, the things that she would do differently now.

As we grow as creators, our work of the past stays stuck in who we were then. We might be embarrassed that we didn't know back then what we know now, but how could we have known? This is like being embarrassed about old pictures in which we're wearing out-of-style clothes. They were of that moment, they reflected where we were and what we were interested in then, and in twenty years everyone will be wearing mom jeans and slap bracelets again, so don't worry about it!

Any anxiety that you put yourself through in the hopes of

making something "perfect" is wasted energy. Not only because "perfect" doesn't exist, but also because your "perfect" today will not be your "perfect" five years from now. When you know that your work is a separate entity from you, and that your identity as a creator is not determined by anyone else's opinion, you can allow space for this discomfort. Think of Hilma—what if you make work that people are going to love more than one hundred years from now? What would that look like? Sound like? Feel like? Use your witchy sense of time to stretch out the goal here. You are sending your magic to the future.

"When you look back at older work," I ask Amy, "do you ever cringe at it? Or are you able to tell yourself that it was an important step in your creative development?"

"You can look back on it and cringe, and who cares? Right?" Amy says. "You cringe, you look at it, you move on, you make something else, you cringe, right? Getting more okay with it is a process, and we're never going to be perfect. There is no such thing as perfection."

"No one else is keeping score," I say. "Also, no one else is looking at something you did fifteen years ago. They're dealing with their own thing."

"That's another really important point," Amy agrees, "and this might sound harsh, but no one cares as much about your work as you do. No one's judging you as harshly as you're judging yourself. You're sitting there freaking out thinking, 'What did I do? That looks horrible!' And no one else is caring about it like that. Even if it was a little bit awkward, they've moved on. It's cliché, but we are our own worst critics."

Amy points out to me that even the idea of originality is overrated.

"Your internal voice is shutting it down by saying, 'This has been done before, who am I to do this?' But you are making something in a way that no one else has made it, because everyone's unique. Even if the idea has been done before, even if you're copying someone to just start making and playing with an idea. That's how art is made. That's how a spark starts."

The tendency we have to criticize ourselves more harshly than anyone else of course goes back to our ideas about cave person brain protecting itself. If you are doing something vulnerable, there is more likely to be a chance of getting hurt than if you did nothing at all. So your brain goes on alert when you put yourself in that situation, trying to watch out for those saber-toothed tigers that may attack at any moment. Could someone say your art is stupid? That *you* are stupid? Could they say you got something wrong? Could they say it's the worst art they've ever seen and you're a terrible person for making it?

Sure, they definitely could. I am here to tell you firsthand that someone could say all those things, and that almost any creator you know and admire has had those things said to them and survived it, and gone on to make more work that someone else thought was terrible. We know objectively that everyone has completely different opinions on such things, but it really drives it home when you see wildly different reviews for the same piece of work. Not everything speaks to everyone. But it's not supposed to.

There may be no way to tell cave person brain to completely stop worrying about protecting you from these woolly mammoth attacks, but you can reframe for yourself how you feel about these outside opinions. Just as you can look at your natal chart and see that hard-earned lessons are going to be part of the equation no matter what, we can look at those metaphorical woolly mammoth attacks as opportunities to learn about our own resilience, and to redirect our attention away from the external world and center back on our personal practice.

One solution to all this anxiety is to never show your work to anyone. This is what Hilma af Klint did for most of her life after her discouraging critique. The poet Emily Dickinson would sometimes submit her work to publications, but mostly she hid her poems in teapots and books around her house. And it's totally valid if you use creativity in your life to create work that is just for you, and not meant to be shown to anyone else. Your creative practice may not be about creating a product for others to consume. Maybe you create a dance in your bedroom every morning. Maybe you draw flowers in a sketchbook that you carry with you. Maybe you crochet elaborate socks while you watch TV. The important thing is understanding that you have access to creative flow, and it is a tool that is available for you to use to access the magic of the present moment at any time. That can be a tool of self-expression, communication, relaxation, even medicine. Maybe even all those things at once.

SPELLS FOR THE WORLD

So why should we ever bother showing our work to anyone, if we are so worried about protecting that private, personal relationship to it? Because creativity is not just about creation. It can also be about connection.

The writer James Baldwin talked about this in one of my favorite quotes of all time.

"You think your pain and your heartbreak are unprecedented in the history of the world," he wrote, "but then you read. It was books that taught me that the things that tormented me most were the very things that connected me with all the people who were alive, who had ever been alive."

Think about the books, songs, movies, art, and TV shows that you love. Even if they are superficially silly or fluffy, there is still something about them that speaks to you on a deep level. With a TV show it might be about seeing a reflection of your sense of humor. With a song you might simply be connected on a visceral level with the music. Sometimes the connection is even clearer—a book where the author was able to articulate something that you have felt before, but were never able to put into words. Suddenly you find yourself united in understanding with someone you have never met, no longer alone in the experience of that feeling.

What if every work of art that has ever been made is a spell that was cast by someone, and by experiencing it you are completing the spell, allowing it to accomplish its magical task? What spells would you like to cast out into the world?

When I experience work that really speaks to my soul, I feel like I am receiving a letter from someone who just accomplished a jailbreak. They made it out! And here's what they have to report! If we are each survivors of our own lives, then surely we have a lot to teach each other about how we managed to get this far.

This is the truly actualized gift of that creative flow energy. By tapping into the universal energy of creation, we are able to access truths about what it means to be human. Again, this can be super deep or very silly. Laughing and crying are both important, and both bring us into our shared experience of life on this planet.

What's interesting as a creator is that often the more specific your work becomes to your own experience, the more you are able to access these higher truths. Your work will hold the energetic mark of you as a creator, and that is what will draw other people into it. Sometimes you may not even understand exactly what someone else is connecting to in your work, and that's totally fine. It was your job to make it. You don't get to decide what it means to someone else.

The world can be changed for the better through creative thinking. We can see our creative practices as efforts to carry us into a more just and harmonious future. You may even want to make work that engages directly with this process of change.

In Amy's Times Square public art project, people could come and create "wearable protest gear," banners and capes with political slogans on them. I ask her about how she came to make art that is engaging more directly with the political process and community.

"This is another part of who I am," she tells me, "and it has to do with my dad, who was very politically active in Iran, and came to the US for political asylum. So there was always this conversation in my house around politics. When I got to college, I started getting looped into activist organizations, and through the work that I was doing there, I started to become more confident in being able to have a political dialogue. Joining these groups allowed me to feel actualized and have that sense of community where I felt like I was being seen. Then, when I first moved to New York, I kind of shifted away from that and said, 'I'm going to be an artist.'"

Amy tells me that she felt called to merge her artistic practice with her political one as the political landscape in the world started to become more dire.

"At a certain point, I felt like I had to express all the rage and frustration and feeling helpless and disempowered by making work where it provided space, not only for me to process that, but in order to facilitate a political dialogue. And it did create space for conversations with people that I really needed to be having."

"I think some people get caught up in art making around ideas of, 'What does this say about me?'" I say. "'I'm alone in this, and if I show this to the world, this is exposing something that's just about me.' I love the idea of making it about 'us.' This isn't about being the best artist you ever saw. This is about engagement and conversation."

Amy points out to me that it's always about the intention behind the practice that activates the tools we are using.

"A hammer could either be used to put up a painting or to kill somebody," Amy says. "So how are you using it?"

I have had a lot of experience making work as part of a collective, both in the theater company that I worked with for many years and with my band. Tapping into flow through collective creative engagement is a very powerful thing in which an energy is created that is different from our solitary practice. This is similar to working in ceremony by yourself versus working with a group. Sometimes that solitude is necessary, and other times you will feel bolstered by the energy of others. You are able to lift each other up through the vision of the collective.

If the tangible world around us is all about limitations, and if it is our job as people engaging with magic to see the possibilities beyond that tangible world, then creativity is a big way to get us to that other plane of understanding. We are removing those barriers of what currently exists and instead dwelling in the realm of what might be possible.

Things get very complicated for us when we come up against the struggles of trying to manifest our creative visions in the tangible world, but that connection to your creativity can't be threatened. That's all yours. And that is where your personal magic gets to meet up with the force of universal creative energy.

I'm brought back again to Hilma af Klint, who not only showed very little of her work in her lifetime, but also left instructions that none of her work should be shown publicly until twenty years after her death. It took another fifty-five years after even that long for her work to find the audience that it was meant to find. Looking at her work feels very literally like having an intimate conversation with someone across space and time. She was able to give us this direct access to her creative soul by divorcing the work from any outside eye, letting it exist in this time capsule for the future.

I hope that you won't wait quite that long to share your creative inspiration with the world. And know that if you give your creative soul free rein to run and play and ask questions and explore, you will be doing a huge, very magical service, both to yourself and to the world.

Exercises

WRITE A POEM

It doesn't matter if you have never written a poem before, if you hate or love poetry—sit down and write a poem that you will never show anyone. Let yourself release any expectations of what a poem "should" look like and just let the words come. They can be silly or sad. They can rhyme or not. And when you are done, you can throw your poem in the garbage if you want. But check in with yourself and see how it feels to let your creativity flow without judgment or expectation.

MAKE AN INSPIRATION BOARD

What inspires your creativity? Is it certain music, writing, art, or fashion? Get or print out examples of things that fire up your creativity and make a collage putting them all together. Can you see any common threads between these things? What about them inspires you to be creative? Post the collage in a place where it will help to inspire your creativity.

CHAPTER NINE:
What Now?

When I first started watching *The Great British Baking Show*, it took me a while to understand exactly what was happening.

"So, the contestants go home every week in between episodes?" I asked my wife.

"Yes," my wife, an already committed fan, would say.

"And they still have their jobs and live with their families and then they just come and do this on the weekend for, like, fun?"

"Yes."

"And what do they get if they win?"

"A cake stand."

"Not money?"

"No. Just a cake stand."

"Is it a one-of-a-kind trophy cake stand made out of gold?"

"No."

"Is there anything remarkable about this cake stand in any way?"

"They just have a picnic with their families and they get a normal cake stand and everyone has a nice time. Now be quiet and watch the show. It's bread week."

I am not against a reality competition show, especially when it means we get to watch the creative process unfolding first-hand. But I often hit my limit with these shows before I make it to the end of a season (*RuPaul's Drag Race* being the main exception). Usually it's around the time when one of the contestants, who has been sequestered for months from their regular lives and put into a windowless TV studio for twelve hours a day in order to film the show, says something like, "I gave up everything to be here. Losing is not an option!" or "If I win this, it will justify every decision that I have made in my life!" or "I have to win for my children! This is the only way that I can make my family proud!"

To me, most reality shows epitomize the false narrative of capitalist success. The narrative goes like this: There is one winner who will emerge victorious with money, fame, a prestigious career, a proud family, and a sense that they have done everything correctly in their lives, and the rest of the contestants are losers who will be thrown into a pit to be eaten by lions. Or some similar horrible fate of obscurity. The message is that the way to win is through sacrifice, hardship, exhaustion, and Wanting It More.

This false, cutthroat narrative of success would be fine if it stayed on our TV screens, but the problem is that it both reflects and influences a very damaging concept of what success looks like and how you get it. Our capitalist version of success feeds off the concepts of scarcity and self-loathing. We are told that there is only so much success to go around, and that if we do not get it, this means we didn't work hard enough to become an entirely new person who would have been able to get one of those coveted Success Spots.

This system was not designed to lift you up to success, but to keep you believing that you are constantly falling short, and that there is something wrong with you if this one very specific idea of success does not become your life story. It is a system that tries to tell us that every person who experiences success is a self-made high achiever who faced many obstacles and just didn't give up. And the message it sends is that, if you want to become one of those people, you should probably change a lot about yourself in order to look, act, and think the way that those people seem to.

SCHOOL ACHIEVEMENT

For most of us, the first system of achievement that we get thrown into is school, the place where we spend the majority of our waking hours for up to two decades or more. This is where the idea that hard work and achievement equals a very particular kind of success first takes hold. Especially if you go to a school where it is expected that you will go to college, and possibly expected that you will get into a certain kind of college. We can talk all we want about not placing our sense of self on external victories, but it can be really hard to put this into practice. Especially when we're dealing with expectations of achievement in school, where there are very clear measurements of success.

The process of applying to and thinking about colleges requires us to speculate about an uncertain future, maybe for the first time. We are asked to imagine who we *might* be, what we *might* be interested in, and how we *might* feel. This process takes us out of ourselves and the present moment, which is fine for a little while, but the stress comes into play when we don't remember to bring ourselves back.

"We don't teach resiliency," my friend Khaliah Williams, a writer who has worked as a college guidance counselor, tells me when I ask her about how she helps students through this often-demoralizing process, especially at a school where it is expected that the students will apply to and get into highly ranked colleges.

The college application process may be the first time when you are presented with a specific list of requirements for achievement—excellent grades, interesting extracurriculars, excelling in sports, clubs, participating in your community—and feel the pressure to tick off everything on that list in order to secure the specific goal of your dream school.

KHALIAH WILLIAMS is a graduate of Sarah Lawrence College and received her MFA from the Iowa Writers' Workshop. She is a current fellow at the Kimbilio Center for African American Fiction and an instructor and advisory board member of Writers in Baltimore Schools. Khaliah is the former assistant director of college counseling at the Berkeley Carroll School and is currently at work on a novel and collection of short stories.

But just as your favorite competitor on a reality show doesn't always win, we are not always able to secure a goal like this by doing all the "right" things. Think of all the factors at play here that we have no control over—whenever we are meeting up with the world, we are coming into contact with a whole wild map of energies and destinies.

"It can be a pretty harsh initiation into the reality that life's not always fair," I say to Khaliah. I'm sitting in her apartment on Memorial Day, crashing her BBQ to make her talk to me about work.

"Even beyond life's not fair," Khaliah says. "It's thinking, 'I did all the right things.' I have to remind students when things get disappointing," she starts to say. She hesitates for a moment, then says, "It's a controversial thing to say, but it almost doesn't matter where you end up, because you're going to make of that space what you will when you get there."

It may be that the lessons you are supposed to learn are not going to happen in the place you think they will. It may be that you are meant to reexamine what it is you actually want (remember our request to call in feelings rather than specific goals?). Is there something else out there presenting a different kind of opportunity?

"So what do you tell students who are devastated that they didn't get into their top-choice school?" I ask. "That they're going to find their place anyway?"

"I tell them that, but I also let them be sad about it. It's okay to grieve something that you wanted and didn't get. As adults we have to learn to do that too."

"So you recommend that the first thing to do is just sit with that disappointment, because it's there."

"And number two is asking, 'What's next?' The reality for any student is that when they become really attached to a school, it's just about a series of images," she tells me. "You have no idea what life in this place is actually going to be like."

Working hard, getting better at something, and learning about yourself are all important to any idea about success, but in order for each of us to live in alignment with our own life path, we need to closely examine our ideas about what "success" looks like, and ask ourselves why it looks like that.

"Inevitably what happens is the student goes to a college that wasn't their first choice," Khaliah says, "and I get an email that fall telling me how much they love the place where they ended up. This is what I tell kids—there are a few things in this process that you can control. You can maybe control your grades to a certain degree. You can control how much work and thought you put into your essay, how willing you are to be vulnerable. But when you hit submit on that application, it's out of your hands. Someone else is making the decision. And they're making that decision not based on whether or not they like you."

Do we actually believe in the reality competition narrative that there should be one winner, held above all others as the losers are thrown into obscurity and the winner emerges into the daylight victorious? Do we believe that all the "winners" that we see deserve to win? Is that person always the most talented? The hardest worker? The one who "wants it" most?

And if we are being taught this damaging narrative as early as high school, how can we possibly escape it when it comes to thinking about our lives beyond school?

CAREER

Beth Pickens is a consultant for artists and arts organizations, who helps people plan their careers with intention. She is THE person to turn to for career advice, especially if you're going into a competitive field like the arts. The last time I got to see Beth in person, I was sitting on the floor in a tiny feminist store at the magical intersection of First Avenue and First Street in New York City. She was there promoting her book *Your Art Will Save Your Life*, and I was just one of many people huddled together to soak up her words of wisdom. Beth exudes the calm, tough-love authority of a true Capricorn, and as someone often overflowing with watery emotions, I find her practical approach to thinking about careers to be deeply comforting.

"It's just never been true," Beth tells me when I ask her about the idea of people always getting the success they deserve. "Never, ever, ever, ever been true. Sometimes brilliant people get lots of good stuff. And that feels like justice. And sometimes people who make incredible stuff never get anything in their lifetime. And it's really unjust. And having that illusion burst is necessary, but it'll also piss you off."

It is all well and good to be told to accept yourself, nurture your beautiful witchy little heart, live in harmony with the cycles of nature, and find your own unique form of creative expression,

BETH PICKENS is a Los Angeles–based consultant for artists and arts organizations. She is the author of *Make Your Art No Matter What* (Chronicle Books, 2021.) Pickens earned her master's degree in counseling psychology from the University of Missouri. She has a podcast called *Mind Your Practice* and an artist subscription service, Homework Club.

but all that excellent inner work can receive a real beating as you try to figure out what you want to do in your life. And it is important to make sure that you retain your magical power even in the face of the real world's often low-vibe restrictions.

When you're in school, it's likely that all you have to do is sign up for an art class and you are given the opportunity and resources to make art. A good teacher will take you seriously as an artist and help you to grow in a safe and nurturing environment. This changes immediately once you enter the real world. Suddenly you find yourself thrust into that reality TV competition, where only the strongest can survive even the first few episodes, and in the end the choice of the winner feels pretty arbitrary. It is easy to feel cheated and victimized by this dynamic. No matter how supportive your family or teachers or friends might be, in the end very few people find themselves prepared for the kind of rejection that the world is going to throw at them.

"For anybody who's going into any kind of line of work

where rejection is built into the infrastructure, one of the first things to do is transform your relationship to rejection, to make it your friend," Beth tells me. "It's not an enemy."

I have known so many people who created a very specific idea in their minds about how success should look, only to find themselves overwhelmed by the reality of rejection. People who studied acting and tell themselves they will "give it a year" to see if they can find success. People who return to school over and over again because they feel too lost without a reward system with clear markers of success. It's not their fault that they formed these false ideas about success in the first place. It's what we are taught! Because it is very difficult to talk about the truly meandering reality of most people's careers, and we so love our linear narrative: Be born with talent, work hard, achieve success!

This narrative completely negates the different levels of privilege that exist in this world, which tend to overwhelmingly dictate the resources and connections that people often use to even get the opportunity to work hard in a chosen field. And the truth is that even people with immense privilege and access to resources rarely have careers that follow a clear-cut narrative.

"We assume everyone had a linear path," Beth says, "but so much of a career is unplanned happenstance. The plans that I set for myself at eighteen or twenty-two, or twenty-five, none of those came to pass, and thank God, because what was in store for me was so much better than what my limited imagination had at the time. I didn't set out to do any of the things that I've done. They are all unplanned."

"It's hard to explain that," I say to Beth, "even after you've experienced it in your own career, just because it's never a linear story."

"When you're setting off on a path," Beth says, "you can't possibly know what new knowledge or what interesting experience or person is going to come into your life, things that you don't even know about. I was a first-generation college student. I knew very little about higher education when I went to college. So when I picked a major, it was mostly what I knew of. Then when I was almost a senior in college, I found women and gender studies. If I had known about it when I was a freshman, I would have picked that as my major, but I didn't even know it existed yet. We don't know who we're going to get connected to, what's going to send us on some wild new path."

Talking with Beth about this makes me think about one of Bakara's favorite sayings that I think really gets to the heart of the matter: "Don't limit yourself to your own best ideas." If we are keeping our eyes open to the actual potential of this moment, then we can step out of egoistic thinking and into listening to that potentially deeper and more interesting path that life has in store for us. We might even be able to let go of some control, and learn to appreciate that this inability to control is supposed to be part of the journey and not a sign of failure on our part.

Whenever I have reached a low point in my feelings about my own work and career, feeling like my efforts were not paying off, that I was delusional to think I could do something in the first place, and that it was definitely time to give up, there has ALWAYS been something amazing that I could not have predicted around the corner. Always. I don't know how to explain this to you, except to say that it is magic (are you getting tired of that explanation yet?). But let's say it's about listening and getting curious and paying attention PLUS magic.

Think about the things that you wanted and didn't get, and what happened instead. The times when the unplanned actually turned out to be the magical happenstance, even more joyful and exciting because it arose out of the magic of the moment. You can allow yourself to experience the anxiety of things not going the way that you thought they would, while always remembering that there is more to this narrative than you can fully know yet.

Always remember: "This or something better."

REJECTION AS PROTECTION

It is mainly our old friend the ego that is upset by this inability to control. The ego wants to think that it always knows best. It is the ego talking when someone says on a reality show, "If I win, this will justify all the decisions that I have made in order to get here." The ego does not want to be questioned. It does not want to be told that there is new information that it did not have before. And it does not want to be told that the reward that it expected is not on its way. The ego thinks that it made a deal with your life by saying, "We're going to do this, this, and this, and then I want to receive this very specific reward on a very specific timetable."

"As a witch, you know this," Beth says to me, "but sometimes rejection is the goddess of protection. Sometimes you get rejected because you don't want that thing you think you do. It's not good for you."

"Which is so interesting," I say, "because that's where the magic comes in, isn't it?"

The same way that we have to get curious about our astrological charts, our emotions, our bodies, and our brains, we need to get curious about the possibilities of what our lives could look like. We already know from studying our natal charts that we each possess unique combinations of strengths and struggles. Why wouldn't our life paths look just as unique as this starting place?

"I think that becoming an adult is finding out all the ways of being that we just didn't even know existed," Beth says, "certainly for queer people. Certainly for (self-declared) weirdos. It's just finding out, 'Wait, you can live like that. Or you could be a person like that. Or you could have a job like that.'"

Of course, it's very easy to say that the possibilities for your life are going to be more interesting and complicated than you can imagine, but what happens when you feel you are on the right path and you are still being pummeled with rejection? How can you continue to do your work in the face of a world that isn't offering up positive reinforcement in that moment? How are we supposed to make friends with rejection?

"My clients who have who improved their relationship to rejection, and their resilience in the face of it, are the ones who decide to go after a certain number of rejections every year," Beth tells me. "They say, 'I am not going to stop until I get fifty rejections for things.' And then it's just part of the job. It gets built into the infrastructure that I am going to get this much rejection, and that rejection is evidence of my success and of me going after what I want."

This makes me think of my own strategy when I was first trying to get an agent for my writing in my mid-twenties. Once I started reading about other people's experiences and realized how much stubborn devotion it took to get over the initial hurdles, I made it my goal to send out one hundred query letters presenting my first novel to agents. When another rejection email would come into my inbox, it would sting for a while, but then I would simply devote myself to the task of finding someone else to send my work to so that I could get to my one hundred. That was a part of my job. It wasn't until number ninety-three that I found someone who was interested in my work.

(And in the service of full transparency of messy true-life narratives, of course the story is even more complicated than that—my first agent ended up leaving the business with no warning, leaving me back at zero, and my first novel was never published. But I had to go through all that to get to the right moment to meet my current agent, whom I adore and who was obviously always meant for me. And I am now so glad that that first novel was never published.)

If you are attempting to pursue a career in something that is important to you, then it can be very challenging to protect that vulnerable part of yourself that cares deeply about this thing from the sting of rejection.

"The artist self needs a little protection from the business side of things," Beth says. "You're taking your insides and saying,

'Well, you do something with this.' And then when people say no, it's very painful. But I think that one way to lessen the feeling of rejection for artists and creative people is knowing all your favorites have been through a ton of rejection. They have been rejected so many times, probably for the same things you want."

I find that it is really helpful to think of this as using two completely different modes of your brain. This is similar to separating your creative brain and your judgmental editor brain when you're doing creative work, completely banning the judgmental editor brain until the time when you need it, and then letting editor brain go to town. This allows the receptive, inquisitive part of you to work without feeling too vulnerable, which means it feels safe enough to let the more interesting, creative and original ideas in. In the same way, when you are pursuing a difficult goal, let yourself separate the inspiration part of you from the badass business side of you.

For example—let's say you love whales. You have loved whales for as long as you can remember. You love how big they are, the noises they make, how they live. You want to learn as much as you can about whales. This is the beautiful, sincere, creative part of you engaging with something that you care about. But then maybe you want to take your love of whales and make it into a career. You would like to go to school to study whales and then apply for some competitive positions in the field of whale study. Badass business self—activate! This is the moment to let that part of you that can learn to navigate without emotion, understanding that rejection is never personal and taking each rejection as a lesson to find out more about how to navigate this side of making a career. The more you can see this as two different parts of yourself working together, the freer you will be to face the inevitable challenges.

It's also possible that you may discover that you are not interested in having to activate this badass side of you so much, and that a career that requires a lot of from this side of you might not be energetically correct for you. That's totally okay, and that kind of realization may simply help you to shift your goals, rather than give up something you care about altogether. You can still do what you love in the face of rejection, and you are always allowed to define your own ideas about success and what you hope to accomplish.

For example, if your goal is to be an artist with a solo show at the Whitney Museum, but you then realize how much you would have to engage that badass ambitious part of yourself to get there and that just doesn't feel in alignment with how you want to use your energy, so be it! We continue to perpetuate a very damaging narrative that someone who is not going for the very top achievement in their field is somehow selling themselves short. There's that winner narrative again. Winning must be the goal! But the people who tend to "win" are often those who are simply more competitive and determined in their nature.

Take one look at *Hamilton* composer Lin-Manuel Miranda's natal chart and you will understand what drives that person. He has his sun AND moon in Capricorn (and his sun in the tenth house of fame) with Aries rising. Not only does he have a detailed, meticulous business plan for his career that comes from both his heart and his soul, but he also deals with the world with fiery determination. If he had not become an incredibly successful writer and performer, he might have decided to be the dictator of a small country. He is different from me, and probably different from you. And that is okay, and it is correct.

Something that often happens for people who are perfectionists or used to working hard and achieving in school is that they have based a part of their identity on an idea about success to the point where failure becomes terrifying. Does trying something new and not immediately being good at it scare you? Are you worried that you will stop being the Person Who Does Everything Well and be left without an identity? This is an understandable reaction, especially when you have had a school experience that seemed to value achievement over all else. If you received the message that good grades were more important than getting to try something new that you're interested in, then you are going to have to work to break out of that frame of mind.

But that's our old buddy ego saying hello, and the more familiar we become with him, the more we can ask him to step aside when his input is not so helpful. Remember, ego is not always about being "egotistical." It's not necessarily that you're thinking, "Wow, I'm the best!" It might simply be that your ideas about whether or not you are "allowed" to fail at things are coming from this ego sense of self that wants there to be fixed truths about who you are. Because of the ways you may have been rewarded for achievement in your life, an unconscious part of you may have decided that you are only worthy of love, respect, and notice if you are achieving things, so that even a perception of failure puts you at risk to become unlovable.

Now your conscious brain may know that this sounds ridiculous, but the work that we are doing here is digging deeper, challenging our unconscious minds to unlock some of these secret weapons that they seem to be holding against us. We can know that we exist as magical beings in flow with the energy of the moment, always worthy of love and respect, but there is some big, internalized work we need to do here to understand that we have been conditioned to make our value as human beings contingent on how much we can achieve.

RESILIENCE

Most of our ideas about achievement are based on the expectations of the people and the world around us, which means that they are based on what everyone else has done and how we as members of society are expected to behave. That's fine, but it's not where interesting stuff comes from. Interesting stuff comes from the person who lets themselves try something that hasn't been done before, who receives some information through those creative brain receptors and lets themselves follow that path for a bit, even if it seems wild or wacky. Even if it seems very likely to "fail" when put to the test of exposing it to the real world. As soon as you are more worried about failure than your own creativity, you are cutting off that magical high-vibe part of your brain where the good stuff comes from. You have brought yourself crashing back down to the limitations of Earth before you even got started.

I can tell you with complete certainty that my craziest ideas have been my best ideas. The moments when I have sat alone at my laptop typing away and thinking to myself, "I can never show this to anyone," have yielded the writing that I am most proud of, and that has made my writing Mine.

As we talked about in our creativity chapter, whenever you go down a new path into unexplored territory, you make yourself vulnerable. What if you share your ideas with someone and they don't "get it"? What if suddenly, in front of someone else, the idea looks stupid to you? What if you feel embarrassed afterward?

I have two very, very important words for you: "Who cares?" Or, as an alternative, "So what?" Sure, you felt vulnerable, maybe you felt embarrassed. So what? Who cares? You're okay, aren't you? Wasn't it better to work with this new idea than to ignore it? Can't you now go back and look at it and maybe refine it and figure out what about it you would like to change to make it even better?

Saying "so what?" does not always come easily, of course. From your teen years into your twenties, the idea of embarrassing yourself might feel unbearable. This is because you are still forming your identity, and depending on your environment, it might not feel safe to show certain parts of yourself. Even in school, you usually find yourself surrounded by the same group of people for years. Maybe you did something ridiculous in fourth grade that everyone remembers and you've never recovered from being that girl who ate glue.

"So what?" becomes infinitely easier with life experience.

You have to embarrass yourself publicly around twenty to thirty times to realize that it's okay. No one really cares, it probably wasn't nearly as embarrassing as it feels to you, and you survived.

(Another of my favorite sayings of Bakara's is "Did you die, tho?" Sometimes in a reading she'll simply repeat this for a little while.)

Something that helped me a lot with understanding this was performing. For most of my twenties and early thirties I was a member of a theater company that toured shows around the world. Once you have forgotten your lines in front of eight hundred people, you realize that maybe it doesn't all have to be so serious. How about being onstage when the set malfunctions or the power goes out and the show has to stop with the audience sitting there and waiting in the dark for it to get fixed? Or working in a theater where the fire alarm manages to go off during the show at least once a week? How about dealing with hecklers? Or sleeping/snoring audience members? Or another actor falling asleep onstage? How about an audience member whose Life Alert alarm is going off and they don't notice it, and one of your fellow actors finally has to leave the stage in the middle of a scene to go turn it off for them? How humiliating! What an embarrassment!

Did you die, tho?

After each of those incidents, I was fine! We were all fine! Sometimes the show was even more exciting when things went wrong, the audience coming alive as they realized that this was an unexpected moment. Suddenly the illusion of perfection was gone, and we all became humans again, in a room together, experiencing something. But in the moment, for those of us hoping to present a polished piece of work to an audience, things felt harrowing. It's only afterward that we realize—we survived! We're okay! Now we've got a crazy story to tell! And we're probably never going to see any of those people again anyway, so WHO CARES?

This is where the idea of resilience comes in, and our resilience is something that needs to get built up like a muscle. Some people may be more naturally resilient than others in the face of failure, but everyone can learn resilience, and the best way to learn is from experience. If you are learning to ride a bike, you won't know what it's like to fall off and then get back up until it happens. You won't know that you can skin your knees and still try again until you show yourself that you can. And maybe you won't get back up on the bike today—maybe you need a day or two to heal—but the point is to realize that the falling is part of the learning. Part of the challenge is the acceptance of failure.

Early on in my writing career, I was feeling very despondent about my work. I was trying to rewrite my novel based on notes that my editor had given me, and I just felt that I couldn't do it. I had already been working on this book for four years. I was sick of it. I was going to fail, so I couldn't even get started.

I made an uncharacteristically personal post on social media about my despair. It was definitely a cry for help, but I did not anticipate getting much of a response. What happened was eye-opening. The replies to the post were not supportive cheerleaders telling me, "You can do it!" but person after person commiserating about moments in their careers when they wanted to give up. These were people with all different kinds of careers—an architect sent me a private message about a project that took him years of repeated disasters to complete. A musician talked about thinking that every show would probably be his last opportunity to perform. People wrote about complicated victories that felt like failures in the moment, moments when they questioned all their professional choices and truly believed that there was no path toward success. And suddenly I did not feel like a failure for feeling like a failure. I realized that it was completely normal to feel like you were failing sometimes. Especially for people who were trying to make things that had never been made before, who were trying to innovate, push a boundary, or challenge a restriction. The more exciting the things they were doing, the more they had to face these demons of doubt. So I kept going, I rewrote the book, it was published, and then I started the next one.

We don't have to feel bad about experiencing disappointment, frustration, or failure. We simply have to remind ourselves that these things are normal, let ourselves feel the feelings, and continue on anyway. Remember our pastry of suffering from our mindfulness chapter? Try not to add those extra layers on top of the feelings. Let them exist, and eventually they will pass.

NEW DEFINITIONS OF SUCCESS

As a culture, we have not dignified the idea of failure as part of a narrative of success. Sure, there are the stories of incredibly popular children's books that were rejected by thirty publishers, and tech pioneers whose first ten experiments failed, but even these stories reinforce an expectation of eventual astronomical success as the only goal. I often think about this during award shows, when someone gives an especially emotional acceptance speech, instructing the audience to "never give up on your dreams!" To me, this simply reinforces the idea of one very particular kind of success. What about the songwriter with modest record sales and a cult following? What about the avant-garde poet who writes strange, beautiful poems that speak directly from her heart, who never receives any kind of grant or award? Why should these people need external validation for their careers? Why must the dream be to be declared "winner"?

The tricky thing here is to find a way to have goals that motivate you, while letting go of your expectations around exactly how those goals play out. Envisioning goals for yourself involves thinking about and imagining the future, which can be deeply motivating and helpful, especially in moments when the present doesn't feel so great. This goes back to our witchy discussion of manifestation. It's great to have dreams and visions of the future, to have something that we are working for and toward that feels important and exciting. The trick is to both be flexible about how it all plays out, and also to always come back to the reality of the present moment.

You always want to be engaging with your work in the present moment, because, as we know, the present moment is all that exists. The relationship that we have to our work in this moment is probably very similar to the relationship we will have with our work in the future. No level of success will make the process easier. The work remains the same, even when you are given the highest possible outside validation.

This is why people often experience a feeling of depression or letdown after big public achievements. For most people, there is a false expectation that recognition will change them in some positive way. They think that it will make them feel validated, and with that validation will come more confidence, and maybe even an ease to their work that they didn't have before receiving that validation.

"What I find over and over and over again," Beth tells me, "is that the person gets the big award, they get the attention, they get the headline, and they still feel the same. When we look to external validation to make us feel real and authentic, it can't work. It has to be an inside job. So I want people to go after these things, but with a different motivation of why you're doing it. The goal is to have something to work toward without having the illusion that it's going to change how you feel."

We know how to do this. We know how to do the inner work, to sit down and have a conversation with the present moment. We just get tripped up in the face of a big world that we have very little control over. We start to look around and think that what we do is not worthy without this external validation. And that if we can't get some of that external validation for ourselves, as quickly as possible, please, we are failing.

It becomes very easy to idealize the career paths of other people when you see them receiving markers of success. We assume that what they have must have come easily to them, that they got exactly what they wanted, and that now they feel completely fulfilled. We don't see the struggles, the frustrations, and the self-doubt of others. We romanticize the untaken path, assuming that it must be easier than what we are trying to achieve, because everything takes more work than we expect it to, and what we see publicly of other people's accomplishments is simply the tip of the iceberg of what it took for them to get there. Seeing someone's public achievements and thinking you understand their career path is like watching ten seconds of a movie and thinking that you know the plot.

"I think early on for me in my writing career," I tell Beth, thinking about my early dreams of getting a book published, "I was having this panic of, 'If this doesn't happen in the next two years, it's not going to happen.'"

"Doing the hardest work is not writing the book," Beth tells me. "It's letting go of your timeline of when you think it should happen. We have to surrender our timeline while continuing to do the work that's in our power to do, toward what we want."

I tell Beth that I think this pressure that we put on ourselves is partly a result of how we glorify early success as a culture. This is where that competition instinct comes in. When we see someone celebrated for achieving success early on in their careers, our egos start to think that we have lost some kind of race. The limited amount of success available has already been doled out, and now there will be none left for us. Not only is this a completely false concept, but it also assumes that achieving that kind of success early provides some kind of security, which is rarely the case.

"Any artist who's had really early success," Beth says, "they will tell you twenty years later how that harmed them. How that external pressure, that spotlight on them when they're still very young, had big ramifications in their creative life. I've had clients who had really early success financially or in the media, and what that does to them over the long term would definitely make a person think twice about wanting it."

Outward success can also bring a lot of unwelcome things along with it. When my first book was announced, I was still in the process of rewriting it, and it was many months away from even advance copies being made available to reviewers and readers. One day I signed on to a popular book reviewing site to give five stars to a friend's book, only to find that somehow my book, WHICH I WAS STILL WRITING, had received two reviews that gave it two stars. My first two reviews. Two stars. Based solely on the description of the book. For a book that I was still writing. Luckily, the absurdity of this situation was so extreme that I couldn't even bother feeling discouraged. People were going to decide they didn't like my book because they didn't want to like it, and there was literally nothing I could do about it. It wasn't fair, but it didn't really matter.

We have seen moments when frustrated artists lash out at someone who gives them a bad review, and we wonder what this person has to complain about, especially if they have money, success, and a large fan base. What do they care what one person thinks of them? From the outside we only see the stuff that looks very attractive and desirable. We don't get to see the moments of discouragement, the attempts to discredit someone, the flaunted opinions. We tell ourselves that the good parts of the success must be enough to outweigh the bad. Or that the person receiving the success must be some kind of superhuman who is not affected by such things.

But never forget—good old cave person brain is constantly on the lookout for the negative, because it is desperate to protect you. What this means is that it often focuses on the places where you feel vulnerable, to the point of blocking out all the positive narratives that are fighting for you to notice them!

One of the other things going on here is that not everyone is happy for the successful person. Some people may be jealous of you when you experience success, may think that you don't deserve what you are getting, or may simply be bored and have arbitrarily decided that they just don't "like" you (this happens most often with successful women, by the way). But knowing how arbitrary people's opinions are doesn't necessarily make it any easier to weather the storms of potential negativity. You are suddenly in a position of getting a lot of people's energy thrown at you, both good and bad, and most people have to learn the hard way how to protect themselves from that energy and to realize that they are not responsible for it.

CHANGING THE TIMELINE

This is another reason why we need to trust the idea of a longer timeline for success, even if it's not what we were hoping for. The longer you have been doing your work, the less likely you are to be derailed by complicated external reactions to what you are doing. You will have established a strong foundation for yourself that you can continue to return to, that is separate from any kind of outside validation or criticism.

I love what Beth has to say about timelines when it comes specifically to making art: "Artwork has its own timeline, because it has its own spirit. And even though you're making it, it's like you don't have total control over it. You just have to keep showing up for it over and over and over again. And it will become clear what it wants to be. But it's going to take its own time."

If we are working in a creative field, and we want to honor the true connection of our creativity to magic, then we need to leave enough room in the process for magic to make its way in. And magic takes time and space; it's not interested in our ego's desire for instant gratification. This doesn't mean that we shouldn't be disciplined and try to meet our goals, but just to reframe our expectations about a certain milestone in our lives happening in a particular time frame. Even in a so-called "non-creative" field, there is still that element of the helpful unknown. You have to leave space for the ways in which the unexpected can be a huge gift.

Here's where my Ten-Year System comes in. I haven't gotten Kate's Ten-Year System patented yet, but consider this my public declaration of one of my most valuable tools.

It takes ten years to get anything done. Ten years. Not necessarily ten years straight of work (this is different from the "ten thousand hours of practice to become an expert" theory) but ten years from intention to outcome. My first book was published ten years after I became determined to publish a book. My first play was produced ten years after I made it a specific goal to have a play produced. It takes ten years.

What this ten-year outlook has done for me is to widen my perspective on my own life. In school we are used to assignments that need to be accomplished in a week, or even a night. Plays get put up in a month. Just finishing the school year is seen as an accomplishment. When you've been on this planet less than a couple of decades, it can sound insane to hear that something could take more than half of your life to happen. To widen your timeline from working on something for one night to working on something for ten years is a lot to ask. But I promise you that this perspective is life-changing.

There are a few things that are able to happen with my ten-year system. The first is that as time passes and you find yourself to still be enthusiastic about something, you are proving to yourself that this is not a whim. This is something that is important enough to you that you are willing to stick with it for a very long time without much external validation. This also probably means that you actually enjoy the process of working on this thing, which is one of the main indicators of whether or not you are going to be able to continue with it. Because, if you're lucky, the reward for that decade of work will be the opportunity to do more work, so if you don't like doing this work, there isn't much point in simply using it as a means to the end of an abstract idea of success.

Now, when I say that you must enjoy the process of your work, understand that within that "enjoyment" there is an entire spectrum of feelings. I have a big problem with the concept that "if you do what you love, you'll never work a day in your life." In my experience, even work that you love can be a struggle, and that struggle doesn't have to be anything more than a sign that you are trying to do something that is a challenge. Your relationship to your work is like any other relationship: Sometimes it goes smoothly and is joyful, and sometimes the two of you are just not seeing eye to eye. Some days your work feels great, and some days you can't bear to even think about it. Your willingness to push through those moments proves to both yourself and your work that you are willing to see this as a process of growth and discovery, not as a static dynamic.

What this ten years also does is prove to the universe that you are serious. You can take this in both a mystical and practical way. I do believe that your commitment to something creates an energetic relationship between that thing and the universe. You are saying that you are willing to gestate something if the universe can provide the circumstances for the birth. But this is also about the practical side of intention. If you are serious about something, then you are going to be on the lookout for opportunities. You are going to try to meet other people who do this kind of work, and you are inevitably going to learn from them and find yourself in the position to develop your practice.

This development is the other important part of the puzzle. Over those ten years, you are going to get SO MUCH BETTER at what you are doing. The novel that I wrote in my mid-twenties was nowhere near as good as the novel that I wrote in my seventh year of committed fiction writing. And my novel that was published became infinitely better over three years of major revisions, which I fought tooth and nail the entire way. Now when something takes a long time to come to fruition, I try to consider that the time I spend on it is not about waiting for something to happen, but about an essential time of incubation. If success is preparation meeting luck, then wouldn't it be great to have something really reflective of your strongest and most considered work ready to go when luck (magic) comes around?

As is our goal with all our tools in this book, the ten-year system is also meant to empower you. If you care so much about something that you want to keep doing it for this long, then you have taken back your power from the external world. When it comes down to it, having confidence simply means that you do not need external validation to keep going, and that not experiencing external validation does not mean that you have to stop doing something that you care about.

"If it's not happening right now," Beth says, "the only thing you know is it's not happening right now. That's it. There's no other certainty. We have to surrender our timeline, because more is going to be revealed all the time."

The truth is that if you care about something and are working hard in a certain direction, you undoubtedly will receive some validation along the way. When I was getting all those email rejections from agents, sometimes I would get a personalized note saying that they enjoyed my writing and that I should send along the next thing I that wrote. I held on tightly to this encouragement in the face of all the other rejection, and it helped me realize that I was on a good track, even if I hadn't quite gotten to the place that I wanted to be yet.

TALKING TO YOURSELF

"I am a really big fan of calling in ourselves at different ages and times," Beth tells me when I ask her about the ways we can help reinforce our choices for ourselves. "So when a person feels really stuck, I might ask them to imagine themselves in fifteen or twenty years and bring that person to the room to give you some guidance and some answers. Because the person you're trying to impress is not these other people. It's you in twenty-five years. That's who you want to look back at you and say, 'Good job! You did really well!' It's you in the future or even you as a little kid. If you can impress ten-year-old you, if that version of you thinks you have an awesome life, there's no one else that needs to validate you."

Having this kind of conversation with yourself at different ages also makes me think of the role that our guides of any kind can have in helping us make decisions and figure out what path to follow. Even in the moments when we feel the most lost, there is always advice so close by. If tuning in to the advice of your guides or having a conversation with your future self feels too esoteric for you, then have a frank conversation with your present self, living in this moment, on this energetic plane. Ask yourself what you care about, what makes you happy, what you believe in. Everyone, without exception, has answers to these questions. It just takes some work to really dig into the answers and figure out what matters to you.

It is also very important to understand that a career does not always consist of what you do for a living. Especially if you are someone who wants to pursue a creative path, it is very likely that you will not receive income for your creative work for a long time, and you may actually not want to place that kind of pressure on your creative self.

"No matter what you do for money, you're still going to be an artist," Beth says when I ask her about clients she has had who do not make a living from their creative work. "Sometimes you might pursue academic and income-generating lifestyles that are based in your creative skill and your work. Many times you won't, and it's all okay. No matter what you study, no matter what you do for income, you can still be an artist."

I find this concept to be really important even for non-artists. There is such a benefit to having a well-rounded life, to letting yourself explore all kinds of interests. Often, when we are working hard to reach a goal, we can become so single-minded that the goal is all that's left. And once you achieve the goal, then what?

There is also a lot to be said for allowing yourself to explore interests outside the public eye. Although the energetic exchange of the internet can be great for learning more about something or finding people with similar interests, we know that the incubation and exploration period of your interests really benefits from some privacy. You don't have to explain them to anyone. Give them the space and time to figure out what they mean to you. We want to dignify a creative or exploratory practice that happens out of the limelight. This is not something that you are looking to get credit for, or likes for, or outside validation about right now. You are allowed to take the time to have a conversation with yourself and with what matters to you.

Beth tells me that with her artist clients she actually recommends that they always have a project going that isn't about making money, which I really appreciate. I find that I always need to have a few things going at once, just to help my brain shift gears.

"A creative person with a creative practice can have a whole continuum of things that they're working on throughout the year," Beth says. "And maybe some of them are really becoming activated as a way to bring in income, and maybe others serve other purposes. Maybe it serves a community connectivity purpose. And that's not to say it won't make money at some point. But maybe that's not its chief role right now."

We are not here in this lifetime to only make money, to be the "winner," to prove anything to anyone. We have to make money to survive, but this narrative of striving simply for the sake of striving has got to be put to rest.

IMPOSTER SYNDROME

You may also find that there are times in your life when you have no idea what you want to do, and that is totally fine. Sometimes that means that you are in the same energetic space that I fall into when I feel lost about my work. You're in a kind of void space because something is coming, and it needs a lot of room to be made available for its arrival. Maybe you suffer from the problem of having too many interests, and you worry that if you choose one direction, you will lose out on things that are important to you. Or maybe you know exactly what kind of work you want to do, and your current circumstance just doesn't allow for you to pursue that right now. If you want to go into a field that requires a particular degree, suddenly the very real restrictions of financial limitations come into play.

Or maybe it's just not the right moment in your life to be thinking about career. I find it ridiculous that anyone expects college and even high school students to potentially have a clear idea of what they want to do for their careers. Or that they should be able to pick a career for their post-college life and expect nothing about that to change, following a simple linear trajectory of success in one field for their entire lives. The reason I wanted to talk about careers in this book is because I think that so many of the damaging ideas about success are planted in us very early, and they actively separate us from our own personal power, by replacing our internal compass with the external world's ideas about achievement.

The truth is that even if you do have an idea about what interests you, it can still feel like you have no idea what you're doing. This does not mean that you are a failure, that you are losing at some abstract race, or that other people understand how to reach success better than you do. That feeling is called "imposter syndrome," which is when you are absolutely sure that you have no idea what you're doing, and that everyone else does know what they're doing and on top of that can probably tell that you don't know what you're doing.

"When you feel like an imposter in any career," Beth says,

"you're just having the same human experiences as everyone around you. Everyone else feels the same way. Some people might be a little less honest about it."

Finding work that is meaningful for you is not easy for anyone. It's not supposed to be easy, because, as we talked about in our astrology chapter, ease does not bring about evolution. If you are here to learn, evolve, and experience a wide spectrum of what humanness has to offer, that is not going to come from an easy-peasy path through life. Self-doubt is a totally normal reaction to all this, and the only way out of self-doubt is through.

When you come up against these moments of self-doubt, try to imagine them as an energy that is moving through you. We can employ our mindfulness techniques here and watch with interest rather than judgment as this moves through us. We get in trouble when we judge this feeling, because now we are challenging the feeling to a kind of wrestling match. We are mad that it is here at all, so now we want to fight with it, which is a little like challenging a rabid skunk to a duel. You are just going to end up sprayed and covered in your own ability to self-sabotage. Instead, can we allow that self-doubt to wander out of our brains the same way that it wandered in?

You are going to experience self-doubt in life no matter what you do, but you will become paralyzed by it if you think that there is something wrong with you for experiencing it. If you still have your badass business brain in play, guarding the door to protect your creative self, maybe ask them to send self-doubt walking.

"Thanks for coming, we get why you're here, but we are not in need of your input at the moment."

Consider also that even self-doubt can have a helpful side—in order to combat it, you are asking yourself to make a renewed statement of commitment to yourself and your work. You can commit to your process in the present, while working toward goals with a "this or something better" philosophy.

"Two things can happen at the same time that can seem contradictory," Beth tells me. "We can be working toward our dreams and still be having big, beautiful, incredible, abundant lives on the path to those goals. That sounds so much like, 'It's the journey, not the destination,' but it really is the journey."

What that focus on the journey means to me is also that there is no reason not to just start. No matter what, you can only see a section of the path in front of you, so even if you are riddled with doubt and indecision, just take a few steps down that path. You going to start learning so much about yourself and your process, and, as Beth has told us, you never know what is around the corner on that path. So why not go check it out?

Set a goal with your flexible ten-year mindset, or simply ask the universe to present some interesting new information about this meandering path. Pursuing a career is, above all else, about persistence and making friends with the unknown. As with our witchy practices, we are learning not only how to become comfortable with the unknown, but also how to use it as an ally, a place of possibility and wonder.

What you do is not who you are. You are not defined by your achievements. If you base your entire sense of self on your career, then any setbacks are going to threaten your entire sense of self, rather than simply existing as obstacles to overcome. We are not reality show contestants determined to make it to the top of an arbitrary race. We know from our practices that the beauty of our humanity and our lives is that we exist in energetic conversation with the people and places around us. We must allow ourselves to have well-rounded lives, to try new things for fun, to work hard at something and allow ourselves to be disappointed if the outcome is not what we expected, but not to let it completely derail us from doing what we love.

There are always going to be people who will be held up as "winners" in this world—our human competitive instincts will make sure of that—but we know that who is declared "winner" in the end doesn't really matter.

What matters is a fun picnic and a very unremarkable cake stand.

What matters is bread week.

Exercises

PICK A PERSON

Pick a person whose career you admire and find out everything you can about them. Look online, read any biographies, and watch any documentaries you can find about them. This can be someone famous or not, in any field at all. It can even be someone you know—in which case you should ask them directly to tell you about how they got to where they are in their career. Take notes, especially paying attention to the moments when the person experienced a setback. How did they get past that? Did it take them a while? Did someone else help them? What about their story is meaningful to you?

WORK WITH YOUR TOOLS

When you are facing a disappointment or setback, pick one of our tools to help you find alternate perspectives on the opportunities that present themselves to you in this moment. Maybe you didn't get a part that you wanted in the school play. Give yourself some time to do a tarot spread, asking what you need to know about this situation that hasn't been made clear yet. Is there something else you will now have more time to do? Take a look at the upcoming astrology. What planets are in retrograde right now? In what ways are you being especially challenged in this moment, and what wisdom is there for you?

So Mote
It Be

At the end of my conversation with Beth, I'm about to let her go because I have kept her on video chat for hours, when she says, "There's one more mystical thing that I would like to say that you might really like."

This is basically my favorite thing that anyone could ever say to me, so I am all ears.

"Artists are in a conversation that transcends space and time," she says, "because they're all on this lineage of other artists. So you're always speaking to not just your audience, but to artists from two hundred years ago, and artists three hundred years from now. And being in conversation across hundreds of years, across place and time, you get to be a part of this special lineage."

As Beth predicted, I like this idea very much, and it makes me think of the fact that all witches and people who are engaging with the generative energy of the universe are in a generational conversation as well. It's no coincidence that a few of the people I interviewed talked about the idea of calling in past and future selves to engage in conversation—Beth, Aram, and Aja all mentioned it. This zooming out of perspective on our lives can actually give us a deeper insight into the energy of the present. Then Beth says something that I love EVEN MORE.

"My rabbi out here in LA," Beth tells me, "she always talks about how on Shabbat [the Jewish day of rest] you have an extra soul. And every time I hear that, I just think about my clients. I think artists are born with this extra soul that is going with you throughout your life, telling you what to make in order to make sense of the world. They have this extra hovering way of being that's always looking down and understanding and making sense of things. That being is always with them, even when they're ignoring it, even when they're not tuned in. It's just that you're born with this extrasensory thing that's looking around, scanning and making sense of nonsensical things."

Well, that sounds a lot like SPIRIT GUIDES to me!

The thing I love most about the way Beth puts this is that it reinforces this idea that you can tap into a helpful energy to help you process things in a bigger way at any time. To nurture a relationship with the mystery of that is to come to know yourself, because you are just another part of that mystery.

The most important thing for me to communicate to you in this whole book is that we must learn to be in conversation with this current moment, in whatever way works for each of us. Whether the current moment is joyful, challenging, exciting, confusing, or even sad, there is an abundance available to us when we consider this moment as something of value, not merely as a source of potential for the future.

Somehow a message was communicated to way too many of us that the version of us that exists today is not worthy of that enjoyment, that we must come to earn joy. Why would we ever allow ourselves to miss out on the magic of the present in favor of an imagined future? Where do we think the future is going to grow from anyway? The appreciation of this moment is the fertile soil for any dreams and goals we might have. Can we treat it that way? Can we turn the dirt of it over in our hands, lovingly plant our favorite seeds, bring it water, allow the sun to shine down upon it? Can we accept that when it rains, that is an important part of the growth cycle? Can we know that when the wind blows, we are strong enough to withstand it?

You are worthy of the greatest energetic gifts of the universe TODAY. You are qualified to receive joy, learn lessons, express gratitude, follow your curiosity, experience awe TODAY. You are allowed to fully inhabit the story of your own life, to fully immerse yourself in the ongoing conversation of what it means to be human TODAY. TODAY you can experience the joy of connection with another person, with the earth, with an animal companion, with your creativity, with the ground under your feet.

All that really matters is how you spend the energy of your days, and giving the majority of your energy to an imagined future will most likely cause you to have a deep discomfort with uncertainty. Of course we can't predict everything, so if your entire sense of self is resting on that unpredictable future, you are at risk of becoming destabilized at any moment. Any level of uncertainty is going to knock you off course. And there is such deep stability available to you at all times when you ground in your experience of the present moment.

When you must allow a portion of your energy to rest in the future (no one likes making grand plans more than I do), try to allow yourself to imagine your projected future self trusting your current self. Let your future self trust you to plant and fertilize the seeds that they will grow from. Imagine a future where you are thanking your past self for this beautiful gift.

We know that the idea of a very linear narrative of success continues to thrive because it feeds capitalism. What makes me saddest about this society-wide self-sabotage is that the capitalist agenda is exploiting a very beautiful part of humanity—our optimism. And I believe that our optimism is directly linked to our desire for evolution. We want to improve! We want to get better, learn more, experience more! So why wouldn't we want to believe in someone who is telling us that this is all possible (and just sign here!)?

Our goal has to be to shift our human capacity for optimism toward a kind of evolution that can carry us all into this new Age of Aquarius together. We have to work together to decide what kind of progress is really needed. We have to listen to people who have struggles that are different from our own, and ask them how we can help them make progress. We have to accept that this progress may be slow, and it may be difficult, but that we are participants in a very long timeline of history, and we understand that our participation in that timeline is not about individual glory, but about the progress of the collective.

What capitalism does is separate us from that collective, like coyotes separating a deer from its herd in order to make it more vulnerable to attack. If we are taught that we are completely alone, that we must each craft a narrative of success for ourselves without any help, then we are made very vulnerable to being sold on something that is not actually in our best interests. We are completely separated from the truth of the interconnectedness of us all. When we act like we are all alone in the world, we eventually trigger our depression and stress response, because if you are all alone, then everything is on your shoulders, and therefore everything must be your fault.

This is also what prevents people from looking out for each other—if you believe everything that happens to anyone is under their control, then why help them? Why try to understand what they are going through? Why trust them when they tell you about their life experience? We have been taught to believe that if we are not functioning or thriving within this existing system, there must be something wrong with us and we must change ourselves, not that there is something wrong with the system.

I want you to feel permission (I give it to you now) to reject letting any kind of arbitrary standard run your life. Reject any standard that you feel is coming from outside yourself (and which may or may not actually exist), that is keeping you from feeling free in your expression of self. I want you to have confidence in the development of your gifts, to understand that you are the only one who knows best how to use them. How can you empower yourself to do this? How deeply can you trust yourself?

Self-understanding is only part of the equation. The other half is taking that understanding of self and learning how it can function in relationship to the world and to the natural cycles of our human experience. Wanting things, wanting to learn and grow are all great, but we have to allow all this to happen in the context of this bigger reality that we can't control, and aren't meant to control. We have to allow our own desires to live in conversation with the world.

People make the mistake of trying to change their lives through Emperor energy (remember that guy?), through strict rules that must be followed, by treating themselves as formless lumps of clay waiting to be molded into a shape . . . when what would really serve us is to embrace the idea of change through Empress energy, with a kind of foraging around in the forest of ourselves, finding hidden exotic flowers to make into a bouquet. We must be gatherers of our own unique potential.

Can we allow ourselves to be forests waiting to be explored instead of formless lumps of clay waiting for someone else to decide our shape? The human compulsion to exert pure will over ourselves and others had a good run, but I would like to declare it over now. If we let the Emperor enter that mysterious forest, he'll just trample on the wildflowers and throw rocks around trying to build arbitrary walls. We are not treating the forest that way anymore. That way has only brought us grief.

As I'm working on this, the feminist scholar bell hooks has just passed, and our friend Aja posted an interview with her that I found particularly moving. "When we think of Joseph Campbell and the whole idea of the heroic journey, it's rarely a journey that's about love," she states in the interview. "It's about deeds that have to do with conquering, domination. . . . Living as we do in a culture of domination, to truly choose to love is heroic. To work at love. To really let yourself understand the art of loving."

Can our heroic journey reject this idea of domination and hierarchy and instead see love (of self, other, the natural world, the mystical world, the universe) as the highest and more honorable form of engagement? Can we exist not as Emperors waiting to dominate, but Empresses savoring everything the present moment has to offer us?

If we are living in alignment with honoring our inner forest, we are able to be clear with ourselves about the whys of what we want and the lessons that we would like to learn. We look beyond the ego to the source of the actual desire. It is expansive? Is it in touch with our own talents and energetic patterns? Are we able to communicate with this desire freely? Can we call in support around this desire?

Growth is difficult because it is uncertain. If we are in the process of growth, we are unfixed, which can make us feel very vulnerable. We can think back to our caterpillar turning to goo in its cocoon—that time of reconfiguration is when the caterpillar is most vulnerable. But the truth is that we are in a state of change all the time. We will never be fully formed, "finished" humans ready to present a fixed self to the world, completely invulnerable in some plastic-action-figure version of ourselves. Of course life doesn't work this way, and it's not meant to, and the more we can open ourselves up to allowing the discomfort around that vulnerability to move through us, the more easily we will be able to allow for important changes. There is deep wisdom and bravery in that vulnerability.

And remember that your cocoon is always available to you. Transition and growth are not always pretty, but creating a safe space for yourself to process them is always possible. You are your only true witness in this process, and you are the one who is able to understand the real significance of these changes.

We tend to give away a lot of power to other people, imagining that they must know something that we don't. But never assume that someone else is going to be able to understand your journey. On her excellent podcast *Tarot for the Wild Soul*, our friend Lindsay Mack has often said that we shouldn't go to someone who hasn't done their own Fool work and ask them to approve of ours.

We have to allow ourselves to keep our eyes on our own page, to measure our victories and progress on our own terms, not by some arbitrary standard. You can only know by your own intuition where you have truly made progress, what real growth is, where you still need work and need to push yourself or be gentle with yourself (sometimes both). In this way, you get to learn what you are actually capable of. You get to find the true path to growth and resilience.

This is where valuing our privacy comes in—allowing for that cocoon to be crafted for you out of an art and/or magical practice, or even just out of a mental space that you are able to give yourself. Of course find community, but also value the private moments as much as the public. Periods of quiet allow us to integrate what we are learning about ourselves, so that it becomes a part of our understanding of ourselves and the world. A lesson that has been integrated is one that will provide wisdom the next time an issue arises. When the Wheel of Fortune comes back around, you will know better what to do.

We know from all our tools that being alone with yourself is actually not alone at all. However you picture the magic that comes through to you during a tarot reading, through bodywork, while journaling, while making art—this magic is always with you. And it can communicate best with you when you give it time and space to speak to you. Even if you think talk of magic is silly, and you view being alone with your thoughts as simply being alone with your thoughts, why not learn how to do that better? Don't you think you might have some interesting things to tell yourself? You are going to be with yourself for this entire lifetime, and as you change and grow, you will find that you keep meeting new selves that emerge. Can you learn to welcome them in? Can you get curious and excited about being in conversation with them? You can help make your body, mind, heart, and spirit a place where these new selves feel safe to live.

Letting go of old ideas and stories about yourself can be really hard and sad. Maybe you need to let go of an idea about something that you expected to happen, or how you expected to feel. You are allowed to mourn this. And it's okay if it seems to take a very long time for your brain and body (and heart) to shift into being totally comfortable with this new timeline. All our tools are meant to give you a place to acknowledge what is hard, what is good, or even what is confusing.

If you're not ready to let go of something yet, be patient—you can't force yourself to release until you're ready. But I can promise you that if you hold on too tightly to the thing that wants to be released, you are going to get dragged through the mud as it runs away from you. When something wants to go, trust that it is not for you, that something better will take its place. On the other side of heartbreak, there is always love. On the other side of darkness, there is always light. We are allowed to mourn past selves, to miss them, but remember that they are still with us. Just as we carry loved ones we have lost with us, we carry our past selves with us.

It might take a while to figure out how a new version of yourself works. Sometimes your evolution is ahead of you and you need to remeet yourself, giving yourself a lot of credit for the progress that you do make. Know that even as you change your perception of success, of thriving, sometimes the world makes progress more slowly than we as individuals do. That's because humanity is made of up a lot of people like you, but also a lot of people who are not like you—people who maybe do not know how to make these changes for themselves, who are confused and overwhelmed by the call for change. But you're going to lead the charge. And sometimes it will be frustrating to you that the world can't catch up, that many people won't understand your path, but you are not alone in this. You know that the energy of the moment supports your progress.

It only feels right that I end this book with talking to Bakara Wintner, the person who played such a big role in my claiming my full connection to witchy intuition as an adult. I have known her since she was just out of college, years before she became the mystical, business-minded head witch that she is today. She is a bit younger than me, and I think she would agree that we have always had a ton of big sister/little sister love for each other. But when I see her do her collective tarot readings online, she seems decades older in wisdom to me.

"I feel like the older I get, the softer I become," she tells me over video chat. "One of my teachers said to me, 'The best advice that I could ever give you is to let your edges be liquid.' It's just stuck with me. I feel like I do have naturally sharp edges, but life will file them down if by force or by grace, and the best thing to do is kind of just be willing."

I also see myself in Bakara's ambition and determination. Years ago, she quit her nine-to-five job to read tarot full-time, eventually turning it into a business and a store called Everyday Magic and writing her beautiful tarot guide *WTF Is Tarot? . . . & How Do I Do It?* She is someone who dreams big, and has to balance her ambition with the hard-won patience of having to work on the universe's timeline, to work toward goals while releasing control of the outcome.

"I think especially if you're an ambitious person who wants

BAKARA WINTNER is an established tarot reader, author of *WTF is Tarot? . . . and How Do I Do It?*, and owner of Everyday Magic. A believer in the art of cartomancy, she also cocreated the Wayhome Tarot and the oracle deck Visions in the Liminal Space.

to get stuff done," I say to Bakara, "you have an instinct to constantly intervene. Like, if I don't do it, it's not going to happen."

"There's this meme that says, 'Do you ever not honk at someone when the light turns green? And just instead wait one second and they move?'" Bakara tells me. "And I'm like, 'Wow, no, I never do that.' What if I just wait literally one human second, and they will move?"

"We must actually think, 'If I don't honk, they're never going to drive away,'" I offer.

"Ninety percent of the lasting consequences of whatever happens is going to be from my reaction to what is happening," she says. "So in increasing my reaction time, can I just give myself like two more seconds not to do what I would do?"

This makes me think of something that the writer adrienne maree brown said in an interview: "The goal of your life is not to get to a place where you feel calm all the time. It's getting yourself to where you can feel whatever is actually happening in real time and then define how you want to organize yourself around it."

We want to be in that headspace where we can observe the present moment for what it is, letting the truth of it exist, but also not spinning out into a narrative that makes us feel like we need to buckle down into control.

"The human experience is very mystical," Bakara says. "But it doesn't always feel that way. So it's my personal mission to just give myself as many reminders of that as I can, even in the darkest moments."

One of the things I appreciate most about Bakara is her openness in the way that she discusses her mental health. I tell her that I wonder sometimes how to contextualize my own mental health with my sense of magic.

"If it weren't for your depression, would you have your tenderness?" she asks me. "Would you have your ability to bear witness and hold space and write in the beautiful way that you do? I have bipolar disorder. It is incredibly serious if I don't treat it. My mission in my life every single day is to keep myself alive and to make myself happy. And I can't believe that I'm fundamentally whole if I also believe that there's something fundamentally wrong with me. Whoever you are, whatever your brain chemistry is, if anyone makes you feel like there's something wrong with you, that's their own belief that they've been thinking something is wrong with them. Your only job is to take care of yourself and to keep yourself alive and to keep yourself happy and to give yourself a life worth living."

We are so bombarded with messages that there is something wrong with us that we aren't even conscious of them most of the time. But this new age is going to ask us to start at a new baseline—one of self-acceptance—that releases us from spending all our energy on trying to fix that which does not need to be fixed. This is where our tools come in, showing us that we are able to find wisdom and strength in our complicated individual journeys at any time.

"It took me six three-year manic-depressive cycles to understand that I was on a three-year manic-depressive cycle," Bakara tells me. "If you're doing things like checking your chart and working with cards and journaling and making sense of yourself, the more time you put into it, the better off you are. The second those tools can get into your hands, if you're willing to start using them, they will benefit you. Knowing yourself is the most important work you'll ever do."

What can we accomplish when we free ourselves from this energy leak of attempting to fix self, instead learning to help and work with the parts of ourselves that need understanding? How can we help each other when we learn how to help ourselves?

We know that this journey of personal evolution also serves the greater purpose of bringing us back to our common humanity. By better understanding the components of ourselves, we begin to recognize those things in other people. The more we can learn about this, the more we can be like the Hermit card, holding his light up in the darkness so he can see, but also to show others the path that he has fought so hard to learn to navigate.

The Buddhist teacher Ram Dass famously said, "We are all just walking each other home." I like to imagine each of us with our little hermit lamps, illuminating the part of the road that we have explored and can now share with others.

"We need meaning. We are storytellers," Bakara offers. "We live and die by the stories we tell about our own lives. If you're going through something hard, if you can feel narrative, if you understand that there is a light at the end of the tunnel, if you understand that Death isn't the last card, that after Death is Temperance, you start to see your experiences on a continuum, to be able to identify the cycle."

When we feel like this need for growth and evolution is asking too much of us, we have to remind ourselves of the parts that feel unequivocally like a gift—how we feel when we make progress, the victory of learning something new, of being able to do something better than we did it last time, of figuring out a puzzle. That feeling of elation is a signal of evolution. This is how existence feels when it takes a jump forward, when the fish that has grown little legs crawls out of the ocean for the first time. There is a collective joy.

All the conversations that I had in working on this book kept bringing me back to this idea of evolution, of individual and collective growth. I started to wonder why it seems that we are meant to spend our lifetimes engaged in personal evolution, working through old karma, learning how to better navigate the map of ourselves that we have chosen/been given this time around. I think this must be something that we each have to answer for ourselves, through our own individual relationships to Spirit, source, the universe, whatever words you have chosen to use. But I did find an explanation that I really like, which I will share with you here.

It comes from a gnostic text—gnosticism being a philosophy that was developed in the first century among Jewish and early Christian sects, later declared heresy by the church because it proposed that we look at human behavior not through a lens of sin and repentance, but through a belief that illusion should be countered by enlightenment. This may be one of the earliest examples of a low-vibe versus high-vibe philosophy.

(I'm paraphrasing the following a bit to put it in the terms that we use in this book.)

> *Source energy is love, but love itself cannot be perfect unless it has those upon whom it can be lavished and by whom it can be returned. So source energy made itself into matter, in order that through this slow process of evolution we might come into being. And we in turn are to develop until we come to understand it. Then the love will become more perfect, and lavished on those who understand it and return it.*

I love this gnostic concept, because to me it means that our highest forms of ourselves come to exist only through process. Love and magic only truly exist by being given and received. It is a transaction that becomes more itself the more it is used. And so creative energy is not meant to be a static thing—it is something in motion, something that only exists through evolution.

Or maybe bell hooks said it better: "Love is an action, never simply a feeling."

I like to imagine it like this—if there is a museum in a mystical other plane that has such concepts on display, the pedestal for "love" would not have a static object on it, but instead it would show a constantly changing, churning, growing thing. I have a feeling that the thing sitting on that love pedestal might look a lot like you, or like everyone you have ever known, or like the whole entire Earth.

Now *that's* an exhibit that I would like to see.

RECOMMENDED READING LIST

My hope is that this book is just the beginning of what will be a very fruitful lifelong process of learning for you about what tools you like to work with, what methods spark your imagination, and what kind of magic brings you joy. In order to help point you in the right direction, below are some of my favorite books that have helped guide me along my journey. This is in no way a comprehensive list and know that there are also tons of free resources online, along with many great practitioners posting excellent content on social media, and I encourage you to explore all that's out there (always with a critical eye toward the cultural context and credentials of the practitioners, of course.) And don't forget the incredible resource that is the library. If your library doesn't have what you're looking for, talk to a librarian about special ordering books or setting you up to borrow free ebooks. Above all—find what speaks to you! This is your own process of personal, magical evolution! Feed it accordingly!

TAROT

Rachel Pollack's Tarot Wisdom: Spiritual Teachings and Deeper Meanings by Rachel Pollack

WTF is Tarot? . . . & How Do I Do It? by Bakara Wintner

ASTROLOGY

Astrology: The Only Introduction You'll Ever Need by Charles Harvey and Suzi Harvey

Essential Astrology: Everything You Need to Know to Interpret Your Natal Chart by Amy Herring

You Were Born for This: Astrology for Radical Self-Acceptance by Chani Nicholas

WITCHINESS

Basic Witches: How to Summon Success, Banish Drama, and Raise Hell with Your Coven by Jaya Saxena and Jess Zimmerman

Witchery: Embrace the Witch Within by Juliet Diaz

ENERGY

Auras: The Anatomy of the Aura (A Start Here Guide for Beginners) by Eliza Swann

The Empath's Survival Guide: Life Strategies for Sensitive People by Judith Orloff

BODY

The Body Is Not an Apology by Sonya Renee Taylor

The Self-Love Revolution: Radical Body Positivity for Girls of Color by Virgie Tovar

MINDFULNESS

Peace Is Every Step: The Path of Mindfulness in Everyday Life by Thich Nhat Hanh, Arnold Kotler, et al.

MENTAL HEALTH

How to Be You: Stop Trying to Be Someone Else and Start Living Your Life by Jeffrey Marsh

There is Nothing Wrong with You: Going Beyond Self-Hate by Cheri Huber

CREATIVITY

The Artist's Way by Julia Cameron

Make Your Art No Matter What: Moving Beyond Creative Hurdles by Beth Pickens

ACKNOWLEDGMENTS

So much of the motivation for writing this book came from my desire to share the wisdom I've received from people who have inspired me by modeling alternative ways of working with self-care practices. To Lindsay, Jeff, Staci, Aja, Erin, Aram, Jeffrey, Amy, Khaliah, Beth, and Bakara—thank you all so much for your time, your wise words, for being deeply awesome people, and for sharing yourselves so generously with the world.

Endless gratitude to Brianne Johnson, the agent a witchy writer truly dreams of. This book exists ONLY because you believed in it. Nicole Ellul—a dream of an editor—thank you for all of your beautiful guidance on this project. I continue to pinch myself that this book got to find a home with such a kindred spirit.

At HG Literary, thank you to Soumeya Bendimerad Roberts, Ellen Goff, Josh Getzler, and Carrie Hannigan. At Simon & Schuster, so much gratitude to Katrina Groover, Chava Wolin, Sara Berko, Jenica Nasworthy, Kendra Levin, Justin Chanda, Nicole Valdez, and Valerie Shea.

Thank you to Mia Charro for the beautiful cover illustration and to Lizzy Bromley for a cover and book design that truly are beyond my wildest dreams. To write a few hundred pages of wild rantings that you hope will make a difference in someone's life and then to have someone treat it with this kind of care and actually make it BEAUTIFUL is some potent magic.

Mo Lioce, Laura von Holt, Lindsay Hockaday, and Annie McNamara—thank you for always being my IDEAL readers and such deeply supportive friends. And always all the love to The Witch Ones for making music with me.

For the invaluable healing one-on-one work I have been honored to receive from them, thank-yous until the end of time to Aja Daashuur, Heidi Smith, Liz Tortolani, Tracy Primavera, Talia Brooks-Salzman, Lindsay Mack, Michelle Sinnette, and Jeff Hinshaw.

To my wife, Amanda, to Mom and Dad, to all the beings that have been a part of this life, and to the ones still to come, thank you for the beautiful existence.

ABOUT THE AUTHOR

© A. VILLALOBOS

Kate Scelsa is a novelist, playwright, and witch. Her debut young adult novel *Fans of the Impossible Life* was a 2016 Rainbow List top ten pick and has been published in ten languages. She is also the author of the YA novel *Improbable Magic for Cynical Witches*. Her play *Everyone's Fine with Virginia Woolf* has been produced in New York and Dublin and was published by Dramatists Play Service, and you can hear her band The Witch Ones wherever you listen to music. Kate currently lives in upstate New York with her wife in an only slightly haunted house.